When Christ's Body Is Broken

When Christ's Body Is Broken

Anxiety, Identity, and Conflict in Congregations

. . . . .

LEANNA K. FULLER

☙PICKWICK *Publications* · Eugene, Oregon

WHEN CHRIST'S BODY IS BROKEN
Anxiety, Identity, and Conflict in Congregations

Copyright © 2016 Leanna K. Fuller. All rights reserved. Except for brief quotations in critical publications or reviews, no part of this book may be reproduced in any manner without prior written permission from the publisher. Write: Permissions, Wipf and Stock Publishers, 199 W. 8th Ave., Suite 3, Eugene, OR 97401.

Pickwick Publications
An Imprint of Wipf and Stock Publishers
199 W. 8th Ave., Suite 3
Eugene, OR 97401

www.wipfandstock.com

ISBN 13: 978-1-4982-0337-1
HB ISBN 13: 978-1-4982-0339-5

Cataloging-in-Publication data:

Fuller, Leanna

    When Christ's body is broken : anxiety, identity, and conflict in congregations / Leanna K. Fuller.

    xviii + 216 p. ; 23 cm. —Includes bibliographical references and index.

    ISBN 13: 978-1-4982-0337-1
    HB ISBN 13: 978-1-4982-0339-5

    1. Church controversies. 2. Change—Religious aspects—Christianity. 3. Conflict management—Religious aspects—Christianity. I. Title.

BV652.9 .F85 2016

Manufactured in the U.S.A.

All Scripture passages quoted are from the New Revised Standard Version Bible, copyright © 1989, Division of Christian Education of the National Council of the Churches of Christ in the United States of America. Used by permission. All rights reserved.

To Scott and Simon,
my lodestars

Contents

Acknowledgments ix

Introduction xi

1. What's the Problem?
   Understanding Congregational Conflict 1

2. What Do Churches Fight About?
   Case Studies of Congregations in Conflict 28

3. Why Is Difference So Threatening?
   Engaging Psychodynamic Psychology 69

4. Why Do Group Identities Matter?
   Engaging Social Psychology 104

5. Where Is God in All This?
   Engaging Christian Theology 138

6. What Can Conflicted Congregations Do?
   Practices for Faith Communities and Their Leaders 167

   APPENDIX: Reflecting on Lived Experience:
   A Case Study as Pastoral Theological Method 195

   Bibliography 205

   Index 211

Acknowledgments

Writing a book is a strange thing. In one sense, it is very solitary work, requiring countless hours spent reading, writing, and thinking alone. Yet, in another sense, a book is not purely an individual achievement. In fact, I have become convinced that the successful completion of a book often depends just as much on the community that surrounds the writer as it does on the writer herself. Here I offer my thanks for the particular community of colleagues, friends, and family members who have supported me throughout this arduous but fulfilling process.

First, I thank the members of "Grace United Church of Christ" and "First United Methodist Church," whose stories I tell in this book. I am particularly grateful to the members of these congregations who made themselves available for interviews, and whose voices have added incomparable texture and nuance to my writing about these communities' experiences. Telling these stories is simultaneously an enormous privilege and an enormous responsibility, and I hold onto both with deep gratitude.

I am grateful to my mentor, Barbara McClure, who has helped to guide and shape my work in many different ways. In addition to her help with this particular project, Barbara has been generous in sharing with me many important insights related to teaching and to academic life in general. I also thank Bonnie Miller-McLemore, Bill Smith, John Thatamanil, and Mindy McGarrah Sharp, each of whom provided thoughtful feedback on my work and thereby made the project stronger. For her invaluable assistance with preparing this manuscript for publication, I thank Sarah Weinberg.

Writing this book would have been impossible without the support of many other colleagues who have generously offered their wisdom and companionship to me on this journey. Special thanks go to my Vanderbilt classmates: Mindy McGarrah Sharp, Liz Zagatta, Nichole Phillips, Karla Van Zee, Eileen Campbell-Reed, Kate Lassiter, Elizabeth Quirós-Loe, and Naomi Annandale. This book has also benefitted from the insights shared by other grantees at the Louisville Institute in Louisville, Kentucky. Additionally, I am grateful to my fellow faculty members at Pittsburgh Theological Seminary for their encouragement to bring this book into being. I offer special thanks to the members of the PTS writing group—Angela Hancock, Roger Owens, and Heather Vacek—who have celebrated with me each time I managed to bring this book a step closer to completion.

I thank all the members of my family—all the Kelleys and Fullers—who have supported my academic ambitions and have encouraged me at every point in this process. I am also deeply grateful to friends who have become like family, for showing interest in my work and for insisting that I have something important to offer to the world. There are too many such friends to name here, but they know who they are.

Special thanks go to my son, Simon, who came along in the midst of my writing process, and who has always helped me to keep this project in perspective. Each day, Simon invites me to take time to play and laugh, which feels like an enormous gift. Finally, I offer my deepest gratitude to my spouse, Scott Fuller, for his unwavering support through the many transitions and challenges of the last several years. He believed in me at times when I did not quite believe in myself, and that gave me the strength to keep going. Together, he and Simon have been the solid foundation to which I could always return after a long day of writing. They have been my guiding stars, reminding me of what is most important in my life, and inspiring me to continue the hard work of turning ideas in my head into words on a page. To them, and to all who have walked this path with me, I simply say: thank you.

Introduction

A Tale of Two Churches

"Grace United Church of Christ" (Grace UCC)[1] is a medium-sized congregation located in a semi-rural community near the eastern seaboard of the United States. In the summer of 2005, following its denomination's passing of a resolution supporting equal marriage rights for same-sex couples, Grace UCC found itself embroiled in an intense conflict about human sexuality. Some members, deeply disturbed by the UCC's action, insisted that the congregation should leave the denomination and become an independent entity. Others insisted just as strongly that Grace UCC should maintain its ties with the wider church. After a series of very hostile congregational meetings, the conflict ended with a vote; roughly 75 percent of the members voted to remain within the UCC. Those who "lost" immediately left the church, leaving a gaping hole in both the membership rolls and the relational matrix of the congregation.

"First United Methodist Church" (First UMC) is a large congregation located in a well-to-do suburb of a city in the southeastern United States. This congregation's conflict began with the need to consolidate the congregation's Sunday morning worship services from three to two due to decreasing attendance numbers. Some of the congregational leaders suggested eliminating the early traditional service, which had the lowest number of regular worshippers—a proposal that generated great resistance and heightened anxiety within the congregation. As a means to resolve the conflict, the church designed an intentional process for decision

---

1. This is a pseudonym. All names and identifying details of congregations and individuals in this book have been changed to protect their privacy. Each pseudonym will only be noted in quotation marks the first time it is used.

making about the issue. The process involved recruiting members from each worship service to serve on a special committee, which met several times over a period of months to discuss all options. Though it seemed, at times, that the committee would never succeed in accomplishing its work, ultimately the group developed a solution that, while not perfect, was unanimously approved by the committee and enjoyed widespread congregational support.

What This Book Is About

In this book I use extended case studies of the two Protestant churches described above to explore the sources and dynamics of congregational conflict around theological issues. Drawing on specific elements of existing literature in congregational studies, leadership studies, and pastoral theology, I develop an approach to this problem that includes thick descriptions of the lived experiences of congregations in conflict, and that aims toward recommendations for transformed practice. My thesis is that at the heart of congregational conflict lies *anxiety triggered by encounters with difference*. I argue that when persons encounter significant differences between themselves and others, they often feel that their sense of self or identity is threatened. In turn, this experience of threat generates anxiety. Using insights from psychodynamic psychology and social psychology, I show that this anxiety is a normal part of human development, as are the desire for sameness and identification with groups of similar others. However, the anxiety raised by difference can be handled in a variety of ways, some of which can be particularly destructive in their consequences. Such behaviors include splitting and projection, strong needs for sameness, group polarization, and contentious tactics, all of which can lead to divisive conflict and can potentially damage or destroy communities of faith.

With the goal of articulating a more constructive approach to conflict in congregations, I offer a theological reframing of conflict as a natural outcome of the diversity inherent in human life. Further, I argue for diversity as a *desirable* theological norm—one that was intended by God and that should be embraced rather than eliminated. Building on this argument, I explore the notions of vulnerability and hospitality as theological categories that encourage human beings to "sit with" the anxiety stirred by communal life and to seek ways to remain connected across differences rather than simply trying to change them. At the end of the book, with this theological grounding in place, I return to the congregational case studies and reflect further on the similarities and differences between them. This comparison forms the basis for the concrete practices I ultimately suggest for faith communities in conflict.

I approach the subject of congregational conflict by bringing together insights from psychodynamic psychology, social psychology, and theology in a rich, textured conversation about the nature of human being and the place of conflict in human life. While these disciplines all contain important ideas about the limits and potentials of human beings, I argue that the social sciences prove especially helpful in describing the concrete contours of human brokenness. For its part, theology holds out an especially compelling vision of human healing—both individual and communal—that contrasts with the destructive dynamics that so frequently occur within the context of congregational conflict. In this way I offer a pastoral theological perspective on conflict that takes seriously the individual and communal suffering such conflict produces and that includes deep psychological and theological reflection on human existence.

Why This Book Matters

While this book originally grew out of my own personal interest in congregational conflict, it also holds significance for a much wider public and makes an important contribution to the field of pastoral theology. First, from a practical point of view, conflicts around theological issues affect many contemporary congregations. Too often, such conflicts deteriorate into virulent, "us vs. them" disputes that threaten to fragment Christian community. By attending closely and seriously to the real experiences of suffering created by congregational conflict, this book offers key theological insights into how human relationships become disordered and damaged within the context of religious bodies. Typically, pastoral theology has focused on individuals as the primary loci of suffering—whether in terms of personal, intrapsychic pain or in terms of the pain that results from structural injustices like racial oppression, gender inequality, or homophobia.[2] In contrast, this book argues that in addition to these types

---

2. Pastoral theologians who have written on these topics include (but are not limited to) Edward Wimberly, Archie Smith, Homer Ashby, Bonnie Miller-McLemore, Jeanne Stevenson Moessner, Christie Cozad Neuger, and Joretta Marshall.

of suffering, persons experience a unique kind of distress in the midst of intense congregational discord. Not only are interpersonal relationships damaged in such situations but often the entire fabric of the religious community may be torn by conflict that is not handled well. When this happens, the suffering that results is not only personal in nature, but takes on a communal quality to which pastoral theology must attend. The book's title tries to capture this communal quality of suffering and points to the need for the church—Christ's body—to experience healing in the form of new and more effective ways of engaging conflict.

Another way in which this book contributes uniquely to the field of pastoral theology is through its use of social psychology as a conversation partner. While pastoral theology has a long history of utilizing the social sciences as key analytical resources, it has relied most heavily on psychodynamic psychology and has focused on intrapsychic issues. In contrast, in this book I employ social psychology to highlight the group dynamics involved in congregational conflict, as well as the elements of social identity that frequently emerge in situations of theological disagreement. Drawing on the discipline of social psychology in these ways provides important insights that could not be gained with a purely intrapsychic approach and allows me to attend more fully to the communal nature of congregational conflict.

Finally, this book makes an important theoretical contribution to the field of pastoral theology, which, in recent decades, has not placed congregational practice at the center of its reflection.[3] Although in recent years pastoral theology has moved beyond its original focus on individual care to attend to the impact of broader social categories like race, gender, and sexual orientation, it has neglected to offer sustained attention to the practices of congregations themselves as a source for pastoral theological knowledge.[4] My project, which focuses on congregations as both the starting point and intended audience for pastoral theology, addresses this lacuna in the field.

---

3. I should note here that when I use the term *pastoral theology*, I am referring to the Protestant tradition of pastoral theology within the United States. In so doing, I also differentiate the discipline I am discussing from practical theology, which has traditionally given more attention to congregations and their practices than has pastoral theology.

4. I will add nuance and expand upon this claim in chapter 1, where I will review pastoral theological resources in detail for how they attend to or neglect congregational practice.

The Theological Frame

I have briefly described how this book makes a distinctive contribution through its attention to communal suffering, its appropriation of social psychology, and its grounding in congregational practice. Yet, part of what makes this a project in pastoral theology is its use of theology as a primary lens through which to understand congregational conflict. In this book I bring theology, psychodynamic psychology, and social psychology into a productive dialogue in which each discipline critiques and supplements the others. However, I also use theology as the overarching framework for the entire discussion, and I make this choice for two specific reasons.

First, the field of pastoral theology has historically relied heavily on the language and therapeutic models of the behavioral sciences, at times to the neglect of theological themes.[5] Admittedly, the disciplines of psychology and social psychology that I draw upon in this book offer in-depth understandings of how individuals and groups operate and of the ways in which human interactions become disordered and damaged. These disciplines, however, provide only limited accounts of optimal individual and communal functioning. In contrast, Christian theology attends both to human brokenness and healing, typically speaking of the former in general terms like "the human condition," and offering a robust vision of the latter through prescriptive recommendations. Because theology attends explicitly to both human brokenness and healing, it provides a more encompassing view of the human being, which is the subject *par excellence* of pastoral theology.

The second reason for using this theological frame is closely related to the first. As I have said, both psychology and theology make serious attempts to understand the nature of human being, especially human brokenness. However, psychology tends to see human brokenness and its accompanying problems in terms of pathologies that call out for treatment or cure. Christian theology, by contrast, recognizes that brokenness arises, at least in part, from our very nature as created beings who are

---

5. As Bonnie Miller-McLemore notes, "In the 1970s and 1980s, critics drew attention to pastoral theology's psychological captivity and its failure to sustain a theological and moral orientation" ("Also a Pastoral Theologian," 821). Rodney J. Hunter and John Patton have further described this pattern as a tendency—particularly within clinical training programs—to prioritize "examining personal meanings, motives, and relationships rather than communicating religious meanings" ("Therapeutic Tradition's Theological and Ethical Commitments," 35).

finite and imperfect. A theological approach to human being suggests that brokenness is simply part of who we are. It is a condition of living on this planet with other human beings. This does not mean that human beings have no reason to hope for improvements in their relationships with one another, or for some experience of redemption from the conditions of brokenness. On the contrary, Christian theology as articulated through religious traditions insists that hope is indeed possible, and that grace is offered regardless of whether or not it is deserved. Yet, from this theological standpoint, hope and grace become even more meaningful when human beings recognize that brokenness already characterizes their existence in a fundamental way.

Within this theological reflection I intentionally use the term "brokenness" instead of "sin," because I wish to emphasize the "given-ness" of the human condition rather than implying that it has to do primarily with moral transgression. Speaking in this nonmoralistic register emphasizes the basic fragility and limitation inherent in human nature instead of focusing on a fall from an idealized state of sinlessness. Theologically, this will be important when, later in the book, I discuss the possibilities for healing and transformation in the midst of congregational conflict. Casting brokenness in terms of sin for which one must repent might imply that conflict itself is a sin to be avoided at all costs. However, beginning with the theological premise that all human beings exist in a state of brokenness that is part of their creaturely condition makes it possible to see conflict as one of the consequences of living in an imperfect world—a consequence that is not to be eradicated, but rather engaged in ways that emphasize respect and compassion.

How This Book Is Organized

In this book I aim to bring the theological framework I have described above into conversation with the social sciences as a means of addressing congregational conflict. This aim is evident in the flow of the book, which is organized into six chapters. I begin, in chapter 1, by articulating why this project matters: namely, because many congregations today are becoming dysfunctional and divided due to their inability to engage theological conflicts with respect and care. Building on current research data related to congregational life in the United States, I explore the scope of the problem of "serious conflict"[6] within communities of faith. I then make an argument for pastoral theology as a discipline that, because of its attention to context, individual suffering, and practice, is especially well suited to address congregational conflict. I close the chapter by proposing a pastoral theological lens through which to explore congregational conflict. This lens uses *anxiety*—understood as a basic sense of threat to one's identity—as a central organizing principle that carries through the book and helps connect the diverse disciplinary resources I present in the subsequent chapters.

Chapter 2 offers detailed narrative accounts of two churches—Grace UCC and First UMC—which provide the content for analysis throughout the rest of the book. In these case studies I focus on congregational conflict that can be particularly difficult to resolve because it involves significant theological issues. Although each church's conflict developed very differently, these two case studies reveal significant common themes: theological dimensions, identity, polarization and fragmentation, and the pain of conflict and change. These themes illustrate important insights about the complexities of congregational conflict and about the role anxiety often plays in it. I argue that understanding anxiety as a basic sense of threat to one's identity helps explain why and how conflict frequently emerges in communities of faith.

In chapter 3, I explore how two specific concepts from the discipline of psychodynamic psychology—splitting/projection and the alter ego need—contribute to a deeper understanding of congregational conflict. I argue that both of these phenomena begin as normal developmental responses to encounters with difference. However, in situations of heightened anxiety, these responses may become reactive in an attempt to protect the self from perceived threats and may result in destructive behaviors. My interpretation of these concepts helps make sense of the kind of conflicts that threatened both identity and community at Grace UCC and First UMC.

Chapter 4 builds on the insights of chapter 3, while also widening the lens of analysis to include the importance of social patterns. In this chapter I engage the resources of social psychology, which offers a unique way of understanding how people relate to one another: namely, as members of groups. I argue that an adequate analysis of conflict within congregations must also attend to the group identities of those involved.

---

6. Roozen, *American Congregations 2008*, 26.

I draw on three concepts—collective identification, group polarization, and strategic choice—to explain how and why groups form within congregations and why those groups choose specific ways of approaching one another in conflict. I show how these dynamics operated in each of the congregations described in the case studies, clarifying why these conflicts were not just the products of individual disagreements, but complex processes in which group identities became strongly engaged.

In chapter 5, I place theology as an integrative conversation partner in the discussion of congregational conflict. Because of its prescriptive nature, the discipline of theology goes beyond either psychodynamic or social psychology to offer a robust vision of what a healthy community looks like and how Christians should behave toward one another in such a community. I begin with a discussion of the human condition as tragic—that is, as inevitably characterized by encounters with difference and conflict. I then make an explicit theological argument for diversity as a good that God both creates and intends. Building on this notion, I argue for a conception of congregational identity that is both hybrid and plural. I contend that understanding identity in this way could help decrease the sense of threat that the discovery of difference often produces. Finally, acknowledging that strong reactions to difference are simply part of being human, I offer a reframing of conflict through theological categories of vulnerability and hospitality. I argue that such reframing can help individuals in faith communities more fully honor the diversity inherent in the body of Christ.

In chapter 6, I build on the material presented in the preceding chapters to offer practical recommendations for engaging theological conflict within congregations. Drawing on my analysis of their experiences of congregational conflict, I further engage the stories of Grace UCC and First UMC as a way of imagining concrete practices for conflicted congregations and their leaders. I group these practices into the following categories: acknowledging difference and the anxiety it produces; redefining unity and strengthening relationships; and cultivating calm, connected leadership. I conclude the book with this focus on practice in order to point back toward the context out of which all theology arises and in which all theology must ultimately be tested: the lived experience of persons and communities.

1

What's the Problem?
Understanding Congregational Conflict

In the introduction I briefly described Grace United Church of Christ, a congregation that faced a difficult conflict around issues of human sexuality and denominational affiliation. Grace UCC is a congregation that I know well because, at the time of the conflict, I was serving as one of its pastoral leaders. This experience of serving a congregation torn by intense theological conflict raised many questions for me, ranging from the extremely practical ("How can members of a congregation learn to resolve their differences, or at least talk to one another more respectfully when they disagree?") to the psychologically and philosophically abstract ("What makes people want everyone to be the same? What is so threatening about theological difference within a single faith community?"). Over time, these questions became so persistent that they led me to write this book, which seeks not only to understand *why* and *how* theological conflicts are generated and sustained within congregations but also *what resources* pastoral theology can offer to communities who are experiencing such conflicts. By "resources" I mean both general theological frameworks for approaching conflict in communities of faith, as well as specific suggestions for pastoral practice in the midst of congregational discord.

The primary questions that drive this book are as follows:

1. How can we understand the intensity and dynamics of theological conflict within congregations?

2. How can pastoral theology offer an alternative vision of theological disagreement that aims toward *healthy* conflict, rather than toward either extreme of eliminating conflict altogether, or engaging it in destructive ways?

3. What concrete practices could pastoral leaders and congregations use to handle theological conflict more effectively?[1]

I have chosen to address these questions by carefully examining the lived experience of two congregations that struggled with conflict around two very different theological issues. By approaching congregational conflict in this way, I hope to provide a helpful resource for congregations who are challenged by various kinds of theological differences. Furthermore, in this book I focus primarily on experiences of conflict within contemporary mainline Protestant congregations in the United States.[2] This is the social-historical location in which my own experience is grounded, and with which I am most familiar. However, given the ubiquity of conflict within religious bodies of all types, I hope that this book may also be relevant for communities from many different Christian denominations, and perhaps even for other faith traditions.

Yet, in introducing my topic this way, I do not wish to imply that all types of congregational conflict can always be resolved. Indeed, at various times throughout its history Christian communities have endured conflicts over crucial theological matters—matters that ultimately caused its members to break company with one another and to form new groups or traditions. I acknowledge the possibility that, in some cases, members of congregations may decide that the conflicts they are facing rise to this level and that they can no longer continue to be in communion with one

---

1. These questions are modeled on Bonnie Miller-McLemore's typology for how a congregation might address a complex theological issue: (1) descriptive/pastoral (This is how life is these days); (2) normative/prophetic (This is how life should be); and (3) programmatic/proclaiming (Here are some ways to get there). Miller-McLemore, *Also a Mother*, 185.

2. Admittedly, as church historian Elesha J. Coffman notes, "'mainline' is a difficult word to pin down" (Coffman, *"The Christian Century" and the Rise of the Protestant Mainline*, 4). Typically, though, scholars define the Protestant mainline as a collection of denominations, which usually includes "the Episcopal Church, the Presbyterian Church (USA), northern Baptist churches, the Congregational Church (now part of the United Church of Christ), the United Methodist Church, the Evangelical Lutheran Church, and the Disciples of Christ" (ibid.). Since the case studies presented in this book, and much of my own personal and professional experience, are rooted in congregations belonging to one of these denominations, the term "mainline Protestant" seems apt here.

another. Historically speaking, however, broad agreement on theological issues typically comes about only over a long period of time. I suggest that for congregations who are struggling with complex contemporary issues, more time is needed to discern whether far-reaching theological agreement can be achieved. Until that time elapses, congregations must learn how to make room for theological difference in their midst. Otherwise, more communities of faith may face destructive division in their life together.

The Scope of the Problem

The type of intense congregational conflict that took place at Grace UCC is, unfortunately, not unique. A variety of sources within the fields of congregational studies and sociology of religion demonstrate that many congregations within the United States today cite conflict as a perennial part of their common life. For instance, data gathered in 2006 and 2007 as part of the second wave of the National Congregations Study show that of the 1,506 congregations surveyed, 23.1 percent had experienced a conflict within the prior two years for which a special meeting was called.[3] Perhaps more troubling, this same study found that 26.4 percent of the communities surveyed had experienced a conflict within the prior two years that had caused some members to leave the congregation.[4] A similar, though much smaller, study found that 45 percent of the one hundred communities surveyed reported having experienced at least one conflict "significant enough to convene a special meeting or call in outside help" during the five years of the study.[5]

The data reported in the Faith Communities Today (FACT) studies conducted in 2000, 2005, 2008, and 2010 by the Cooperative Congregations Studies Partnership reveal a similar pattern. This study differs from the National Congregations Study in that its sample is much larger—surveying 28,787 communities of faith in all[6]—and it includes a larger

---

3. Chaves and Anderson, "Continuity and Change in American Congregations," 436.

4. Ibid.

5. Brubaker, *Promise and Peril*, 28.

6. This number is an aggregate of all the different congregations surveyed in the FACT study over the entire decade. The 2000 and 2010 studies each surveyed over 10,000 churches, while the 2005 and 2008 studies used much smaller samples—about 1,000 faith communities each. Roozen, *American Congregations 2010*, 2.

percentage of non-Christian communities. However, since Christian congregations make up a significant proportion of the communities surveyed, the FACT study still provides a useful tool for understanding the prevalence of conflict within the types of churches that this book primarily addresses. According to the 2010 FACT data, 65.1 percent of the congregations surveyed had experienced conflict within the prior five years in one of four key areas: worship, finances, leadership, or program priorities. This figure, which represents a clear majority of the surveyed congregations, increased by almost 1 percent from the data gathered in 2000, demonstrating that conflict remains an important issue for most contemporary faith communities in the United States.[7]

This figure, however, refers only to the general presence of "conflict" in churches, which David Roozen, the author of the study, distinguishes from "serious conflict." Roozen defines a serious conflict as "one in which some people left, a leader left or money was withheld."[8] The 2008 FACT study found that this type of serious conflict "is present in a third of congregations overall and reaches a high of 45% for Oldline Protestant congregations."[9] Based on these research findings, Roozen concludes that

> For virtually every measure of congregational vitality contained in the FACT surveys, conflict erodes vitality and the more severe the conflict the greater the effect—whether for spiritual vitality, financial health, numerical growth, or the securing, nurturing and caring for lay leadership.[10]

These findings related to the prevalence of serious conflict correspond closely with the data reported in the National Congregations Study about conflicts resulting in the loss of membership. Taken together, these studies suggest that such serious conflicts, which have detrimental consequences for communities of faith, are present in anywhere from one-quarter to nearly one-half of contemporary congregations in the United States at any given time.

Admittedly, the majority of conflicts reported in these studies do not appear—at least on the surface—to be theological in nature. Yet, congregational researcher David Brubaker notes that of the respondents in his study reporting a single or first conflict in their churches, roughly 25

---

7. Ibid., 9.
8. Roozen, *American Congregations 2008*, 26.
9. Roozen, "Peace, Peace!" 29.
10. Ibid.

percent named homosexuality as the primary problem.[11] Sociologist of religion Penny Edgell Becker discovered a similar trend in her study of twenty-three congregations in the suburban Chicago area: out of sixty-five conflicts reported, ten centered on issues of gender and sexuality.[12] The emergence of gender and sexuality issues as a key category in these studies signals that theology often plays an important role in the development of congregational conflict. Granted, discussions about gender and sexuality in the wider culture do not necessarily engage explicitly theological themes; however, similar discussions within congregations frequently involve appeals to Scripture and other theological resources as a way of wrestling with these highly complex issues. Talking about gender and sexuality within a religious context almost inevitably touches on the nature of human being and God's intentions for the created order, both of which are deeply theological subjects.

In fact, I argue that virtually *all* conflicts within congregations possess a theological dimension. Conflicts about church finances, for example, are not just about money, but about parishioners' theological understanding of the nature of the church and its mission in the world. In other words, how congregations spend their money demonstrates their theological commitments. Similarly, disagreements about worship frequently go beyond differences in preference or personal style and instead touch on people's most deeply held beliefs about who God is and how God relates to human beings. In turn, these theological commitments are deeply connected to practitioners' sense of religious and social identity. If you ask people about their faith affiliation, they are likely to respond with phrases like "I'm a Methodist" or "I'm Lutheran" or "I belong to the United Church of Christ." For many parishioners, these general religious identifiers encompass a host of specific theological ideas and values that they then bring with them into conversations about everyday church matters.

Because these conversations take place within the context of religious bodies in which individuals have made covenant promises to one another, it stands to reason that conflict between congregants will carry significant theological weight. After all, if members of a single congregation have made similar affirmations of faith as part of their membership, what does it mean *theologically* when they discover that they disagree so

---

11. Brubaker, *Promise and Peril*, 29.
12. Becker, "Congregational Models and Conflict," 234.

vehemently on important church issues? How can they reconcile their commitments to one another with the fact that they seem to believe such different things about worship or money or human sexuality? To put it another way: what are the implications for congregants' sense of identity when they realize that their chosen religious identifiers do not guarantee that they will share important theological beliefs and values with their fellow church members?

The statistics cited above are alarming, but not simply because they point to the presence of conflict within faith communities; after all, in any intimate relationship between persons, conflict always plays a role. Yet these figures paint a much more disturbing picture of serious conflict within congregations that is not only widespread but also destructive in its consequences. As these studies have shown, conflict can result in the loss of members, financial support, leadership, and overall vitality within congregations. Indeed, the 2005 FACT study found that the most common result of serious congregational conflict is the loss of community members: of the congregations surveyed that had experienced serious conflict, 69 percent reported that at least some members had left the fellowship as a result.[13] This figure alone provides a striking example of why this kind of congregational conflict is so problematic—namely, because it has the potential to break up the body of Christ into smaller and smaller pieces. In an era when the mainstream Protestant church is already suffering serious declines in membership, it is crucial for congregations to find healthier ways of handling conflict so that continued fragmentation does not remain the only option.

Furthermore, from a theological standpoint, Christians are called to be in covenantal communion with one another. One powerful way in which such communion is ritualized is through the sacrament of the Lord's Supper as it is shared in worship. In that ritual, the bread symbolizes the broken body of Christ, who gave himself in love so that those who came after him could be reconciled to God and to one another. Christ's literal body was broken so that his living, enduring body—the fellowship of all believers—could be brought together in shared service. Christ made this sacrifice so that forgiveness and reconciliation between individuals could become possible; yet, in contemporary times, it seems that members of Christ's church have difficulty finding ways to embody the grace modeled by Jesus.

---

13. Roozen, *American Congregations 2005*, 20.

Of course, at times Jesus also embodied divisiveness and judgment—such as when he rebuked the moneychangers in the temple,[14] or when he declared, "I have not come to bring peace, but a sword."[15] Some would argue that these aspects of Jesus' ministry show that he was more concerned with proclaiming "right" theology than with bringing people together. I contend, however, that standing firm on principle and confronting injustice—as Jesus did—do not necessarily entail cutting oneself off from those who disagree. In other words, seeking unity and wholeness for a religious community does not have to mean adopting an "anything goes" mentality.[16] Although Scripture tells us that Jesus corrected the Pharisees and shirked many of the religious conventions of his day, he also admonished his followers to love their enemies and to seek reconciliation with one another before offering gifts to God.[17] Even on the cross, as he was dying, Jesus extended himself in a conciliatory gesture, saying "Father, forgive them; for they do not know what they are doing."[18] In my view, then, the account of Jesus' life that we find in Scripture paints a picture of a righteous leader who had integrity and held fast to his convictions, but who ultimately did not allow his theological "rightness" to hinder his relationships with others. In contrast to this model provided by Jesus, many congregations today are generating brokenness and division in their midst through their inability to handle conflict in peaceful and productive ways. This problem tears at the very fabric of Christian communities, and threatens to create an environment where disagreement on theological issues almost immediately becomes grounds for the dissolution of fellowship and covenantal relationship. Such an environment proves contrary to the spirit of unity and mutual love that the body of Christ is called to emulate.

These reflections on the importance of church unity are undoubtedly shaped by my own theological commitments. As I write this book, I find myself deeply concerned about the division and fragmentation I have personally witnessed in congregations and that is occurring in

---

14. This episode, often called the "cleansing of the temple," may be found in Mark 11, Matt 21, and Luke 19.

15. Matt 10:34 (NRSV).

16. I will explore the theological tension between the commitment to inclusivity and the search for truth much more fully in chapter 5.

17. Both of these admonitions are found in the Sermon on the Mount—in Matt 5:44 and Matt 5:23, respectively.

18. Luke 23:34 (NRSV).

Christian communities across this country. These developments trouble me greatly because, as a person raised and ordained in the Baptist tradition, and now serving in the United Church of Christ, I have great respect for both freedom of conscience *and* commitment to community. Although it is now quite conservative theologically, the Southern Baptist Church was founded on the principle of the priesthood of all believers, which means that each Christian has the ability to relate to God, and can read and interpret the Scriptures himself or herself. Along with this emphasis on individual relationships with God, Baptists have historically affirmed each believer's freedom to follow his or her own conscience in matters of spiritual importance.[19] Even now, the website of the Southern Baptist Convention states that each member of a Baptist congregation "is responsible and accountable to Christ as Lord."[20] This suggests that from its earliest days to contemporary times, the Baptist church has recognized the possibility that its members might not agree with one another on all issues, and has affirmed the importance of being able to follow one's own conscience.

Although very different theologically from the Southern Baptist Church, the United Church of Christ (UCC)—the denomination that now holds my ordination credentials—displays similar commitments in terms of the spiritual freedom of each individual believer. According to the UCC website, "We seek a balance between freedom of conscience and accountability to the apostolic faith. The UCC therefore receives the historic creeds and confessions of our ancestors as *testimonies, but not tests* of the faith."[21] In this sense, the UCC also recognizes the potential for theological disagreement between its members. However, this does not mean that the UCC has no concern for the unity of its congregations. In fact, the key motto of the denomination is taken from John 17:21, "That they may all be one." The UCC thus seeks to strike a balance between freedom of conscience, on the one hand, and covenant commitment to fellow believers, on the other. As I reflect on the shape that congregational conflict has taken in mainstream Protestant churches in

---

19. For a summary of Baptists' historic commitments to liberty of conscience, see the following internet article: Deweese, "Doing Freedom Baptist Style," http://www.baptisthistory.org/pamphlets/freedom.htm.

20. Southern Baptist Convention, "Basic Beliefs," http://www.sbc.net/aboutus/basicbeliefs.asp.

21. United Church of Christ, "Testimonies, Not Tests of the Faith, http://www.ucc.org/beliefs/, emphasis added.

recent years, I fear that many congregations are focusing on one side of this dialectic to the exclusion of the other. In churches where freedom of conscience is emphasized too strongly, the result can be intense conflict and fragmentation when people find they cannot agree on all theological issues. Conversely, when church unity is interpreted as uniformity, individuals find themselves forced to choose between being true to their own spiritual consciences and being inauthentic for the sake of "peace" in the church body.

In light of these dangers, what can be done? What resources are available for those who wish to think more deeply about the problem of congregational conflict and to discover ways of helping communities of faith deal more effectively with theological disagreements in their midst? And why is congregational conflict a problem that pastoral theology should address? After all, many definitions of pastoral theology describe it as a scholarly discipline that focuses specifically on practices of *pastoral care* rather than on other pastoral practices like leadership or administration. Some might wonder whether other fields—such as congregational studies or leadership studies—might more appropriately address this topic.

Here, it is helpful to distinguish between *practical theology* and *pastoral theology*. While closely related, important differences exist between these two disciplines, and each term has held varied meanings at different points in history. Even so, the current distinction between the two terms may be succinctly stated as follows: "Whereas practical theology is integrative, concerned with broader issues of ministry, discipleship, and formation, pastoral theology is person- and pathos-centered and focused on the activity of care."[22] In other words, practical theology is a broader, more encompassing term that includes a wide range of activities, methods, curricular areas, and academic disciplines.[23] Pastoral theology thus represents "one among many valued subdisciplines within practical theology"—a subdiscipline that is also unique in its appropriation of psychology as a key analytical tool for interpreting lived experience.[24] Pastoral theology's appeal to psychology as an important resource, and its simultaneous focus on individual persons, suffering, and practices of care

22. Miller-McLemore, "Introduction," 6.

23. Miller-McLemore describes these categories as emblematic of "four distinct enterprises with different audiences and objectives" contained within practical theology. Ibid., 5.

24. Ibid., 6.

lead me to situate my own work squarely within its borders. However, before elaborating on my own pastoral theological approach, I briefly describe the fields of congregational studies and leadership studies to discover what their unique contributions might be for examining the topic of congregational conflict. Ultimately, though, I return to the field of pastoral theology, further illustrating how its approach differs from these other practical theological disciplines.

Congregational Studies and Leadership Studies: Contributions and Limitations

The discipline known as congregational studies is quite new on the academic scene. Over the last three decades, this field has emerged out of the work of scholars who seek to understand more fully the dynamics of congregational life. Practical theologian and congregational researcher James R. Nieman defines congregational studies as

> the disciplined process for examining a congregation holistically that uses multiple research methods. In place of random intuitions and impressions is an orderly exploration of what actually happens in a group, both the obvious and the hidden, in a way that accurately reflects the interaction of component features while also noticing overall patterns and structures.[25]

Even in naming these core commitments of congregational studies, however, Nieman admits that it remains a developing discipline with "no simple defining feature."[26] Indeed, because the field is so new, it is just now beginning to take a definite shape, with only nascent consensus on what resources belong within its borders.

Nonetheless, part of what makes congregational studies unique is its emphasis on the "thick description" of situations, particularly those faced by specific congregations.[27] In other words, rather than speaking of "the church" in generic terms, writers in this field use close examination and analysis of particular congregations as ways of understanding what is happening on the ground in very specific places and times. While many resources in congregational studies attempt thick descriptions of

---

25. Nieman, "Congregational Studies," 133.

26. Ibid.

27. The phrase "thick description" is credited to anthropologist Clifford Geertz in his text *The Interpretation of Cultures*, and has been embraced by qualitative researchers and practical theologians alike.

an entire congregation and its culture,[28] others seek to examine particular issues—such as community relations[29] or pastoral leadership[30]—as they arise within their congregational contexts. Even within this discipline, however, there is a dearth of resources dealing specifically with *conflict in congregations*.[31] Those texts that do address conflict tend to advance an understanding of congregations through their emphasis on the thick description of lived communal experience. Such descriptive approaches are important and, as the next section will show, they provide a much needed balance to many of the popular resources currently available to pastoral practitioners. Yet, because these texts often do not take the next step toward recommendations for transformed practice, or do so in only a partial way, their usefulness for a pastoral theological approach to congregational conflict remains limited.

Resources in congregational studies also tend to sketch the contours of congregations as corporate realities, which may miss the individual forms of human flourishing and suffering taking place in their midst. Granted, such resources emphasize the inclusion of individual voices through qualitative methods of interviewing and participant-observation; yet, in the end, these texts wish to paint a picture of congregations as unique entities rather than simply collections of individuals. This is a valid point, and represents one of the key contributions of congregational studies as a field. In focusing primarily on the broader shape of congregations, however, these analyses may lose sight of the unique individual plights that take place within the communal context.

Although I employ methods frequently used in congregational studies—such as the inclusion of case material and interviews with church members—this is not a project in congregational studies *per se*. Unlike congregational studies, which emphasizes the "overall patterns and structures"[32] of church life, this book seeks to balance a view of con-

---

28. A key example of this more general approach is James F. Hopewell's *Congregation*. In this text, Hopewell uses ethnographic data from two specific congregations to theorize a broad theological approach to congregations that emphasizes the importance of narrative.

29. See Ammerman, *Pillars of Faith*.

30. See Carroll, *God's Potters*.

31. Some notable exceptions to this statement include Ammerman et al., *Studying Congregations*—specifically, Carl Dudley's chapter entitled "Process: Dynamics of Congregational Life"; Becker, *Congregations in Conflict*; and Stockton, *Decent and in Order*.

32. Nieman, "Congregational Studies," 133.

gregations as corporate realities with a simultaneous focus on the unique persons who comprise them. To achieve this goal, I provide detailed descriptions of two faith communities, while also highlighting the voices of specific parishioners in an attempt to reveal the shape of individual suffering in the midst of congregational conflict. This approach allows me to focus on how individuals are shaped *by* and *in* their context, and not only on the context itself.

More well established than congregational studies, the field of leadership studies focuses broadly on leadership within organizational contexts and in human life. This discipline has its primary roots in the fields of sociology, psychology, philosophy, and management, many of which are resources upon which congregational studies also draw. Unlike congregational studies, however, leadership studies literature tends to focus less on description and more on specific recommendations for improved pastoral practice.[33] This proves especially true for resources that are aimed primarily toward practitioners rather than scholars. In fact, such texts often jump directly to recommendations for practice without describing any particular community of faith in detail. This can sometimes cause the suggested strategies to seem too generic or broad because they are not connected to an in-depth exploration of any particular congregation.

One special subcategory of leadership studies literature bears mention here. This subcategory includes practically oriented church leadership texts that use *family systems theory* as the primary analytical lens for understanding congregational dynamics.[34] I mention this literature here because these texts typically address congregational conflict in a more specific way than many other resources in church leadership studies. As a result, these are some of the most well-known texts for leaders struggling with conflict in their communities. The primary contributions of these resources lie in their concrete descriptions of what happens in organizations infected by high levels of *anxiety*, defined as a "sense of threat" experienced both by individuals and by the systems of which they are a part.[35]

---

33. Examples of such resources include Leas, *Moving Your Church through Conflict*; Sawyer, *Hope in Conflict*; and Brubaker, *Promise and Peril*.

34. This category includes texts such as Friedman, *Generation to Generation*; Steinke, *Healthy Congregations*; and Richardson, *Creating a Healthier Church*.

35. Richardson, *Creating a Healthier Church*, 42. Throughout this book I will draw on the notion of anxiety presented in leadership texts like Richardson's as a helpful tool for analyzing conflict in congregations.

According to family systems theory (FST), the antidote to such high levels of anxiety is *differentiation*, which is the process by which individuals learn to define their selves more clearly within the context of relationships. Yet, FST also recognizes that for most people, the pull toward sameness is much stronger than the pull toward individuality, which makes differentiation the key developmental challenge to which all persons must respond. In the process of differentiating, individuals develop the ability to respond calmly in the midst of anxious systems, and to take full responsibility for their own thoughts, feelings, and actions. Put simply, then, differentiation involves the ability to "maintain a position and still stay in touch."[36] The concept of differentiation forms a core concept for church leadership texts, which emphasize its importance for leaders who are attempting to manage conflict in religious organizations.

Interestingly, the fields of congregational and leadership studies overlap in a variety of ways. Both disciplines provide important insights into the problem of congregational conflict, although they approach this problem quite differently. Qualitative and quantitative approaches in congregational studies provide rich descriptions of the communities being examined, and identify patterns of conflict that may point to common underlying causes which church leaders may then address. Leadership studies literature uses theoretical frameworks such as family systems theory to analyze conflict and to make suggestions for improved pastoral practice. These differences highlight two vital elements for understanding theological conflict within communities of faith: thick description and recommendations for pastoral practice. Yet congregational studies and leadership studies tend to focus on one or the other of these elements, rather than bringing both together in their search for a fuller understanding of faith communities.

Contributions of Pastoral Theology: Context, Suffering, and Transformed Practice

Pastoral theology is uniquely suited to address the problem of theological conflict within congregations because of its pairing of thick description with a turn to improved pastoral practice. Certain resources in congregational studies and in leadership studies approach each of these elements in helpful ways, but a pastoral theological approach has the potential to

---

36. Friedman, *Generation to Generation*, 230.

integrate both, while simultaneously engaging important theoretical concepts. Additionally, congregational and leadership studies literature does not typically offer keen attention to individual experience or sustained theological reflection on human being, both of which have become hallmarks of contemporary pastoral theology. For these reasons, I have chosen to situate my own work on congregational conflict firmly within the field of pastoral theology. In this book, I seek not only to understand what happens when theological conflict erupts in a religious community or why people behave as they do under those circumstances. Instead, I intend to go beyond description and explanation, and also offer pastoral theological understandings that can guide more effective pastoral interventions. As a pastoral theological project, then, my work includes close attention to human suffering, theological reflection grounded in lived experience, and a rootedness in care and concern for all of God's people.

Pastoral Theology as Contextual Theology

The discipline of pastoral theology understands the context of lived experience as not only the subject for sociological or organizational analysis, but as the very ground for the generation of new theological ideas. In an article on Protestant pastoral theology in the *Dictionary of Pastoral Care and Counseling* (1990), J. Russell Burck and Rodney J. Hunter argue that, in addition to a specific focus on practices of care, contemporary definitions of pastoral theology describe a form of theological reflection in which pastoral experience serves as a context for the critical development of basic theological understanding: "Here pastoral theology is not a theology *of* or *about* pastoral care but a type of contextual theology, a way of doing theology *pastorally*."[37] By defining pastoral theology this way, Burck and Hunter point toward the importance of *lived experience* as a resource, which also helps to differentiate pastoral theology from other theological disciplines. Indeed, although pastoral theology presupposes other areas of theology (dogmatic, systematic, biblical, and historical), it is unique in its use of pastoral experience as both a source and a norm for theological reflection.

In a similar vein, Stephen Pattison and James Woodward define pastoral theology as "the place where the relationship between belief, tradition, and practice meets contemporary experiences, questions and

---

37. Burck and Hunter, "Pastoral Theology, Protestant," 867, emphasis in original.

actions, and conducts a dialogue that is mutually enriching, intellectually critical, and practically transforming."[38] Again, this definition points to the key role of experience, which establishes a two-way interaction between theology and pastoral practice within pastoral theology—i.e., practice both informs the generation of new theological ideas, and also provides the context in which theological ideas are tested for their adequacy.[39] While resources in congregational studies are often useful in describing the lived experience of congregations, they typically do not take the next step into the kind of sustained theological reflection that would lead to the development of new theological ideas. Without this step, congregational studies literature tends to remain at the level of identifying patterns of behavior within communities of faith, rather than reflecting on what those patterns *mean* theologically. In this sense, a pastoral theological methodology proves more effective in examining the issue of congregational conflict in the service of theological insight and transformative practices.

Pastoral Theology as Reflection on Individual Human Needs and Suffering

Just as congregational and leadership studies provide rich descriptions of congregations' lived experience, they also often offer insight into the particular shape of human needs and suffering within the context of faith communities. For instance, the FACT studies cited earlier in this chapter tell us that for most congregations experiencing serious conflict, fragmentation through the loss of membership remains a real risk. However, these resources do not typically utilize the reality of human suffering as a basis for continued reflection on human nature; they do not address what this suffering may mean theologically or pastorally. Furthermore, the congregational and leadership studies literature tends to take a macro view of congregations in an effort to identify the social and organizational dynamics that are at play. As a result, attention to the individual human person may be overlooked in such resources.

The discipline of pastoral theology, in contrast, takes human suffering as it is experienced by individuals as a key starting point for theological reflection. Pastoral theologian Bonnie Miller-McLemore claims

---

38. Pattison and Woodward, "An Introduction to Pastoral and Practical Theology," 7.
39. Jennings, "Pastoral Theological Methodology," 863.

that pastoral theology attends to those situations where "human suffering evokes or calls for a religious response and sometimes at the point where a religious response is given and/or experienced."[40] In more recent writing on this subject, Miller-McLemore argues that pastoral theologians have "inadvertently created a distinct set of alternative loci" to those usually found within systematic theology.[41] Some might say these loci are "simply subcategories within the traditional doctrine of theological anthropology,"[42] but Miller-McLemore disagrees:

> Pastoral theologians study human behavior in the midst of Christian faith and the divine. But even as categories of the traditional doctrine of theological anthropology, foci such as suffering, lament, anger, violence, and care break convention. They embody graphic encounter with life rather than the standard categories abstracted from it, such as body, soul, and mind or sin and salvation. We might call these *loci of human angst and flourishing*.[43]

In these descriptions of pastoral theology, Miller-McLemore points to an understanding of the discipline that takes human need, loss, and suffering seriously, not only as foci for practices of pastoral care, but as critical junctures of experience that may challenge traditional theological ideas, and out of which new theological ideas may be generated. More specifically, throughout its history pastoral theology has utilized particular methods of analysis—including the use of psychology, individual case material, and sustained theological reflection—that not only describe what human suffering looks like but also provide key insights into human nature itself. Thus, one of the key characteristics of pastoral theology as a discipline is its ability to hold in tension the unique experience of specific persons, on the one hand, with deep reflection on human existence, on the other. Instead of overlooking the particular shape of individual experiences, pastoral theology has the capacity to honor and learn from such experiences while placing them in larger psychological, cultural, and theological contexts.

---

40. Miller-McLemore, "The Subject and Practice of Pastoral Theology," 179.
41. Miller-McLemore, "Also a Pastoral Theologian," 823.
42. Ibid.
43. Ibid., 823, emphasis in original.

Pastoral Theology as Aiming Toward Transformed Practice

As discussed earlier, congregational studies literature often does not attempt to make recommendations for improved pastoral practice, except in limited ways. Leadership studies literature, in contrast, focuses heavily on concrete recommendations for pastoral practitioners. However, because these recommendations are usually not grounded in deep theological reflection, they can seem like simplistic "how to" lists that are not fully integrated with important theoretical resources. Pastoral theology, on the other hand, uses scholarly resources within the social sciences and theology as categories for analyzing situations of lived experience, and then uses these categories as the ground for imagining improved pastoral practices. Indeed, pastoral theologians have long insisted that the discipline cannot be content with simply describing and reflecting on experiences of human need, but must also make the next step toward envisioning more effective ways of attending to such need.

For example, feminist writers have, for years, been pointing to transformed practice as a standard for pastoral theology. In her 1996 text *Transforming Practice*, Elaine Graham asserts that liberating praxis serves as a guiding norm for her vision of pastoral theology in a postmodern age.[44] Similarly, in *Liberating Faith Practices* (1998), editors Denise Ackermann and Riet Bons-Storm claim that the essays in their volume begin with practice, engage in practical theological reflection, and then lead back into emancipatory praxis.[45] In this same volume, Pamela Couture echoes the editors' claim by insisting that pastoral theology cannot afford to utilize so many resources if it does not, in the end, become a vehicle for justice and love.[46] And, in *Feminist and Womanist Pastoral Theology* (1999), Bonnie Miller-McLemore argues that a feminist approach to pastoral theology includes *pastoral intent* in addition to its revised correlational method, its use of psychological and cultural resources, its feminist positioning, and its appeal to power analysis.[47] In this way, Miller-McLemore suggests that pastoral theology's critical analysis of situations of human suffering must ultimately lead to improved pastoral practices. All of these writers thus point to the element that I see as the

---

44. See Graham, *Transforming Practice*.

45. Ackerman and Bons-Storm, "Introduction," 5.

46. Couture, "Feminist, Wesleyan, Practical Theology and the Practice of Pastoral Care," 42.

47. Miller-McLemore, "Feminist Theory in Pastoral Theology," 89.

core of progress in pastoral theology: more effective pastoral practices that attend adequately to human suffering and that seek human flourishing and liberation for all. At its heart, then, pastoral theology is a normative discipline that describes both the way things are and the way things should be. Likewise, this book aims to describe not only what congregational conflict actually looks like but also a vision of how Christian communities might understand and engage conflict in more life-giving ways.

Limitations of Pastoral Theology

I have argued that because of its keen attention to context, suffering, and transformed practice, the discipline of pastoral theology stands well equipped to address the problem of theological conflict within congregations. However, in making this claim I am not suggesting that pastoral theology does not have limitations. In fact, in what follows I argue that pastoral theology as a field has, in large part, neglected congregations both as sites of individual and communal suffering, and as a key context in which pastoral theological knowledge is generated. I will contend that, in light of this tendency, pastoral theology must now be more intentional about engaging the lived experience of congregations as a basis for sustained theological reflection.

This is not to say, however, that that pastoral theology has *never* been attentive to congregations or to the wider cultural context of pastoral care. Indeed, in *Pastoral Care and Social Conflict* (1995), co-editor Pamela D. Couture notes that the pastoral care movement in the United States was born at the turn of the twentieth century—a time of great social upheaval when people were wrestling with the realities of international conflict, needs for social reform, and the rise of the human sciences.[48] As a result, this nascent field struggled to find ways to attend both to social issues and to individual problems. Couture explains that,

> As pastoral care and counseling became a mature movement . . . the people in care and counseling whose identities were deeply formed by liberation movements struggled to keep one side of their efforts in social reform and one side in the need of the movement to legitimate itself according to the demands of technological society. These demands created within the movement a bifurcation of pastoral theology from social ethics, increasing specialization of pastoral counselors, a focus on individuals and

48. Couture, "Introduction," 12.

families almost to the exclusion of groups and communities, and a loss of connections with local congregations.[49]

The "bifurcation" that Couture describes emerged with particular clarity in the struggles that took place within pastoral theology during the 1950s and early 1960s regarding the appropriate role of congregations in pastoral care and counseling. Key pastoral theologians like Seward Hiltner and Wayne Oates insisted that the church remain the institutional ground in which all pastoral care and counseling ministries are rooted.[50] Meanwhile, other emerging figures in the field, such as Howard Clinebell and Carroll Wise, lobbied for the professionalization of pastoral counseling as a ministry related to, but not contained within, the church. Ultimately, this latter group won out with the establishment of the American Association of Pastoral Counseling in 1963, with Clinebell serving as its first president. From that point forward, as the field of pastoral theology developed, its emphasis on the individual counseling relationship grew ever stronger, with most pastoral theological texts focusing heavily on psychological frameworks and individual care. As a result, attention to the practices of congregations faded into the background.

This turn in the trajectory of pastoral theology's development, and its consequent lack of attention to congregations, became emblematic of modern pastoral theology's tendency to distance itself from institutionalized religion and to focus instead on individual psychotherapeutic modalities. Pastoral theologian Rodney Hunter reflected on this tendency in a 1998 article entitled "Religious Caregiving and Pedagogy in a Postmodern Context: Recovering Ecclesia." In that article, Hunter writes, "Pastoral care literature . . . often proceeds as if hurting individuals and families and our ministries for and with them were occurring in a public sphere unrelated to the ends, meanings, and structures of the church; our caring practices seem intended mainly to achieve psychological aims disconnected from the specific spiritual and moral meanings of institutional religion.[51] Hunter further explains that pastoral theology (particularly in its clinical form) "has always been wary of institutional claims and agendas that it fears will be imposed coercively on people," and that for

---

49. Ibid., 12–13.

50. For an elaboration of the specific concerns Hiltner and Oates had about professional pastoral counseling, see Hiltner, "The American Association of Pastoral Counselors"; and Oates, "Association of Pastoral Counselors."

51. Hunter, "Religious Caregiving," 19.

this reason, it is not "institutionally oriented."[52] In other words, pastoral theology's critical stance toward the church was born of a desire to protect individuals from an institution that had, historically, proved capable of perpetrating egregious forms of injustice and oppression. In this sense, pastoral theology's focus on the care of individual persons was a much needed corrective to the reigning pastoral models of the day.

As I have already established, however, the current religious and cultural contexts in which contemporary pastoral theology finds itself are rife with conflicts that are tearing communities of faith apart and creating intense individual and communal suffering in the process. The realities of this situation call out for a renewed corrective to pastoral theology—one that more closely attends to the lived experiences of individuals within their ecclesial contexts. It is true that within the last two decades, pastoral theology has moved beyond its original focus on individual care to attend to larger social dynamics like race, gender, and sexual orientation. However, it has often failed to offer sustained attention to the practices of congregations *themselves* as a source for pastoral theological knowledge.

Hunter further addresses the importance of religious institutions and membership in the body of Christ, claiming that

> religious institutions are important for the welfare of society and individuals. They socialize and enculturate people into particular worlds of experience, meaning, and value, thus generating an organizing sense of philosophic and moral orientation which is vital not only to society but to individual health and wellbeing. . . . And from a theological perspective, in the mainstream of Christian tradition, faith is intimately connected with committed membership in sacred community; to believe *is* to belong, to be a member of the body of Christ as branches participate in the vine.[53]

According to Hunter's argument, then, religious communities are not simply a given with which pastoral theology must reluctantly contend, but rather a key element in the health and spiritual formation of individuals, which are central themes for pastoral theological reflection. For this reason, pastoral theology must refocus its energies on the institutional forms of faith communities and the ways in which they contribute to or detract from human health and healing. Indeed, as Hunter puts it, "the

---

52. Ibid., 18.
53. Ibid., 17, emphasis in original.

creation of strong, durable religious communities and individuals within those communities should be two of the basic aims of practical theology in general and pastoral theology in particular."54

Hunter's claims highlight the tendency of modern pastoral theology to focus on the care of individuals and families, often to the neglect of faith communities and the particular ways in which they shape the care of their members. Yet, it should be noted that in recent years, pastoral theology has tried to correct this trend and to recapture the importance of congregational life that early pastoral theologians like Seward Hiltner and Wayne Oates emphasized. In fact, in the early 1990s, the field of pastoral theology attempted to move away from its previous focus on psychology and individual pastoral relationships through the development of what has become known as the "communal contextual" paradigm. This phrase, first coined by John Patton in his 1993 text *Pastoral Care in Context*, refers to a new way of conceiving the work of pastoral care and counseling—not primarily as a clinical intervention by a psychologically trained pastor, but as a ministry of the entire faith community that attends closely to "the importance of cultural and political contexts shaping persons' lives."55 The communal contextual paradigm also includes a renewed recognition of the importance of ecclesial communities as places where individuals are nurtured in the life of faith and that provide the "normative themes" that shape the care offered in those communities.56 For example, much of pastoral theologian Don Browning's work places practices of congregations themselves at the center of theological reflection, as I will explore in more detail in chapter 2.57

In the 2004 supplement to the *Dictionary of Pastoral Care and Counseling* (DPCC) entitled *Redefining the Paradigms*, editor Nancy J. Ramsay

54. Ibid., 16.

55. Ramsay, "A Time of Ferment and Redefinition," 11.

56. Ibid.

57. Perhaps the clearest example of this trend in Browning's work is *A Fundamental Practical Theology*, which begins with extended descriptions of three different congregations. These descriptions form the foundation for Browning's analysis of particular aspects of each congregation's communal practices. In this sense, *A Fundamental Practical Theology* continues the important work Browning began in *The Moral Context of Pastoral Care* and *Religious Ethics and Pastoral Care*, in which he had argued that pastoral theology and care had become increasingly separated from their moral and theological roots. As a remedy for this separation, Browning argued in *Religious Ethics* for a new model of "practical moral thinking" within communities of faith (15)—a model he then revised and expanded in *A Fundamental Practical Theology*.

argues that along with the "intercultural" paradigm, the communal contextual paradigm represents one of the most important developments in the field of pastoral theology since the original publication of the DPCC in 1990. According to Ramsay, these paradigms are now "eclipsing" the more traditional clinical pastoral paradigm that predominated in the DPCC and are guiding pastoral theology to a renewed focus on "ecclesial contexts that sustain and strengthen community practices of care."[58] This claim seems to be borne out by the fact that many pastoral theological texts published since the mid-1990s utilize the communal contextual paradigm as a guiding metaphor and critique pastoral theology's historic tendency to rely too heavily on psychological resources and individual models of care.[59]

Even with the increasing recognition of the communal contextual paradigm, however, the question remains as to whether pastoral theology as a discipline has fully embraced its implications[60]—particularly its emphasis on ecclesial communities as a key element in the creation of new theological ideas. Indeed, it has now been nearly two decades since Rodney Hunter wrote the article referenced above, yet the academic discipline of pastoral theology still has not produced many resources that address the concerns he so convincingly named. This trend may be changing, however, since a few recent texts have attempted to bring congregational experience back to the center of pastoral theological reflection.

For instance, Mary Clark Moschella's *Ethnography as a Pastoral Practice* (2008) offers a concrete methodology for discovering the lived practices and wisdom of a congregation. In this text, Moschella asserts that "when conducted and shared as a form of pastoral practice, ethnography can enable religious leaders to hear the theological wisdom of the people, wisdom that is spoken right in the midst of the nitty-gritty mundane realities of group life."[61] In making this claim, Moschella in-

---

58. Ramsay, "A Time of Ferment and Redefinition," 1.

59. Notable resources that intentionally engage the communal contextual paradigm include Moessner, ed., *Through the Eyes of Women*, especially the essays "The Living Human Web: Pastoral Theology at the Turn of the Century" by Bonnie J. Miller-McLemore and "Weaving the Web: Pastoral Care in an Individualistic Society" by Pamela Couture); Ali, *Survival and Liberation*; and Kornfeld, *Cultivating Wholeness*.

60. In her text *Moving beyond Individualism in Pastoral Care and Counseling*, pastoral theologian Barbara J. McClure argues that in the field of pastoral counseling specifically, most practitioners still subscribe to an individual model of care that tends to neglect the social, cultural, and ecclesial contexts of their clients.

61. Moschella, *Ethnography as a Pastoral Practice*, 4.

directly argues for the importance of congregations in the generation of theological ideas—ideas that come not only from the academic pastoral theologian but also from the lived experiences of individuals within faith communities. Moschella envisions ethnography not only as a tool for describing and explaining the unique worlds of congregations but also as a way for "religious leaders to harness the power of social research to transform a group's common life and its purposeful work in the world."[62] In this sense, Moschella demonstrates the commitment to transformed practice that I have named as a hallmark of the pastoral theological discipline. Moschella's use of congregational experience as a basis for sustained theological reflection, with the intent of improving practices of care, thus embodies the type of pastoral theological approach for which I argue in this book.

Susan Dunlap's *Caring Cultures*, published in 2009, represents another pastoral theological text that attempts to place congregational experience at the center of theological reflection. Utilizing many of the ethnographic methods proposed by Moschella, Dunlap conducted extended research studies of three different congregations in Durham, North Carolina—one Euro-American mainstream Protestant, one African-American Pentecostal Holiness, and one Hispanic subcongregation of a large Roman Catholic parish. Dunlap's study seeks to understand how each of these congregations cares for community members experiencing illness; the author then uses the data gleaned from her research to identify each congregation's "belief-practices," which she defines as "units of assumptions and behaviors that characterize these churches."[63] Following a thick description of these belief-practices, Dunlap interprets and critiques them as a means to construct, in the final chapter of the text, her own practical theology of caring for persons experiencing illness. In this way, Dunlap looks to the real, lived experience of congregations as a starting point for theological reflection, and then uses that reflection as the ground from which to imagine a normative vision of faith communities.

Despite the encouraging new trend in pastoral theology represented by writers like Moschella and Dunlap, resources addressing the specific issue of congregational *conflict* remain quite limited within the field. In 1995, two essays related to congregational conflict—one by Joretta

---

62. Ibid., xi.
63. Dunlap, *Caring Cultures*, 185.

Marshall and the other by Carl Schneider[64]—appeared in the edited volume *Pastoral Care and Social Conflict*.[65] Both of these essays address issues of stress and conflict in congregations within the parameters of the communal contextual paradigm, focusing on the lived practices of communities of faith. These essays seem to have been on the cutting edge of pastoral theology at the time they were written because they clearly embody the emerging paradigm and because they point to an area of interest that was ripe for further pastoral theological exploration.

Yet for many years after these essays appeared, there seems to have been little in-depth exploration of congregational conflict as a pastoral theological topic. Quite recently, however, two texts have addressed the subject. The first, *How to Lead in Church Conflict* (2012) by K. Brynolf Lyon and Dan P. Moseley, clearly represents a pastoral theological approach to conflict in its use of psychological theory as a conversation partner, and in its attention to transformed practices within the context of congregational life. This text also bears some similarity to my approach in emphasizing both the importance of group dynamics and the crucial role of leadership within church conflict. While it contains profound wisdom about transforming homiletical and liturgical practices as responses to congregational conflict, the text is limited by dislocating these recommendations from embodiment in particular congregational contexts. Lyon and Moseley's text begins with three different case studies related to conflict that appear to be fictional congregations, and thus are not grounded in the lived experience of any *particular* community of faith. As such, they are not able to offer the kind of thick description of congregations for which Moschella advocates and which Dunlap embodies in her work.

Deborah van Deusen Hunsinger and Theresa F. Latini's *Transforming Church Conflict* (2013) also explores the issue of conflict in congregations from a pastoral theological perspective. Instead of beginning with descriptions of conflict and using them as a base from which to engage other resources, Hunsinger and Latini make clear that their purpose in this text is to introduce readers to a particular approach to handling conflict: Nonviolent Communication, or NVC. In the introduction, the authors write, "We have become convinced that *nonviolent* or *compassionate communication* is the best single resource available for learning

---

64. Marshall, "Pastoral Care with Congregations in Social Stress"; Schneider, "If One of Your Number Has a Dispute with Another."

65. Couture and Hunter, eds., *Pastoral Care and Social Conflict*.

the complex interpersonal and pastoral leadership skills needed by today's church. This is the motivation for writing this book: to describe the knowledge and skills that offer such promise and to place them into theological context so that they can function as a practical guide for revitalizing the church."[66] Although this text offers examples of how Nonviolent Communication might work in a congregation, it does not use field research to provide actual case studies for analysis. In this sense, it also lacks the kind of thick description of situations that other pastoral theological resources have recently moved toward adopting.

To summarize: in recent years, pastoral theologians like Moschella and Dunlap have begun to utilize the lived experience of congregations as grounds for theological reflection, and scholars like Lyon & Moseley and Hunsinger & Latini have returned to the issue of congregational conflict as a matter of pastoral theological importance. It seems, however, that no one has yet brought these pieces of method and content together in a pastoral theological text. This book, which focuses on congregations as both the starting point and intended audience for pastoral theology, helps address this lacuna in the field.

A Pastoral Theological Approach to Conflict in Congregations

In this chapter I have described the strengths and limitations of congregational studies, leadership studies, and pastoral theology for addressing the problem of congregational conflict. I have argued that each of these disciplines offers tools that illuminate particular aspects of this problem. In the remainder of this chapter, I present a way of combining the most useful aspects of these disciplines to create a new pastoral theological approach to congregational conflict. This approach offers a more complex understanding of the role of *anxiety* in conflict, and how such anxiety is connected to individuals' and communities' sense of *identity*. In this way, I am able to use the theme of anxiety to unite the three major disciplinary frameworks I will use in this book: psychodynamic psychology, social psychology, and theology.[67] More specifically, I argue that within

---

66. Hunsinger and Latini, *Transforming Church Conflict*, xv, emphasis in original.

67. Although these disciplines do not all refer explicitly to anxiety, I will argue that anxiety nonetheless represents a key social force through which these theories can be interpreted.

the context of faith communities, *encounters with difference* frequently produce perceived threats to identity, both individual and social. These perceived threats raise levels of anxiety, and can cause conflict to develop or to become more intense. Likewise, increased levels of anxiety can cause individuals to become more rigid in their expressions of identity, which also contributes to the development of conflict. Conversely, conflict itself can also cause increased levels of anxiety, creating a perpetual cycle marked by intractable, destructive patterns.

Within such a theoretical framework, one might assume that the goal for congregations should be the elimination of conflict. However, such a goal is patently unrealistic and, I will later argue, theologically undesirable. Instead, I wish to reframe the goal as reducing (not eliminating) levels of chronic anxiety in congregations so that they can learn how to engage in healthy conflict. I will argue that conflict itself is neither negative nor positive; it simply represents the differing aims and desires of human beings. How conflict is engaged, however, may take on extremely positive or negative aspects. Conflict may, as in the case of Grace UCC, become extremely destructive and lead to the fragmentation of an entire church community. Or it may, as in the case of First UMC, become an opportunity for church members to communicate more effectively, resulting in an increased sense of cohesion and fellowship.

To make my argument, I take particular aspects of the disciplines I have discussed in this chapter and carry them forward as elements of a lens through which to view the issue of congregational conflict. From leadership resources drawing on family systems theory, I use the concept of anxiety as an overarching framework in which to understand the ways in which conflict emerges and develops within congregations. Family systems theory's description of anxiety as a generalized sense of threat contributes to this investigation because it helps to explain what is really at stake for individuals and groups in the midst of conflict: namely, their sense of self or identity. Later in the book, I use resources from psychodynamic psychology and social psychology to describe some of the specific forms reactions to this threat may take. I also use anxiety as a springboard from which to reflect theologically about why difference feels so threatening, and how faith communities might develop practices to approach difference more hospitably. In this way, the notion of anxiety as a key social force that affects both individuals and communities serves as a common thread, connecting various means of understanding what happens (and what should happen) when congregations discover significant diversity in their midst.

From congregational studies, I take the importance of thick description and integrate it into my work through the inclusion of two detailed case studies of congregations that dealt with conflicts around specific theological issues. These case studies reveal the particular shape of conflict within individual communities of faith and move away from generic discussions of "church conflict" to a more focused analysis on the ways in which conflict develops in specific places and at specific times. From general leadership studies literature, I also take the importance of recommendations for improved practice. As a pastoral theologian, I take seriously the challenge to create new thinking that ultimately leads to transformed practice and to the reduction of suffering. Texts in the field of leadership studies offer a helpful reminder that even as we delve into the depths of theory and theology, we must always keep the practical relevance of our theorizing in mind—even if we do not fully develop both parts of this endeavor at the same time. Because of my deep concern for the ways in which my thoughts in this book might play out in practice, I return to the realm of practice in chapter 6 and offer some concrete recommendations for communities of faith that are facing protracted conflicts.

Finally, throughout this book I use a pastoral theological approach to unite these individual elements and to create a new and more complex way of understanding congregational conflict that supports transforming practices. The discipline of pastoral theology is well-suited to bring these disparate pieces together because of its keen attention to context, individual needs and suffering, and practice. Through its historic commitment to deep, theological reflection on the nature of human being in the midst of suffering, pastoral theology provides the interpretive tools that a problem like congregational conflict demands. In this book I apply these interpretive tools to specific instances of conflict in congregations—namely, case studies describing the experience of two particular faith communities.[68] It is to the telling of these congregations' stories that I turn in chapter 2.

---

68. For a description of case study as pastoral theological method, or for a list of the interview questions I used to generate the case studies presented in this book, please see the Appendix.

2

What Do Churches Fight About?
Case Studies of Congregations in Conflict

Introduction to the Cases

In his now classic 1991 text, *A Fundamental Practical Theology: Descriptive and Strategic Proposals*, practical theologian Don Browning writes, "For some years I had thought that writers in pastoral care (or poimenics) needed to spend more time studying what pastors and congregations actually do in addition to making proposals about what they ought to do."[1] Building on this conviction, Browning grounds his text in extended descriptions of three different congregations in different denominations and geographical settings, and uses them as a basis from which to analyze particular aspects of their congregational practice. Browning takes this approach to illustrate the practical wisdom contained within communities of faith; as a result, his work serves as a helpful model for what I hope to do in this book for two reasons. First, in *A Fundamental Practical Theology*, Browning brings communities of faith to the center of theological reflection. As I noted in chapter 1, one of the key critiques of pastoral theology over the past few decades has been its tendency to focus only on individual care, thereby overlooking the importance of the care-giving

---

1. Browning, *A Fundamental Practical Theology*, 27.

systems within congregations and their potential to generate fertile theological material in the form of practical wisdom.[2] In utilizing extended case studies of congregational practices, Browning makes a significant step toward recognizing the community of faith as a crucial context for the production of new theological ideas.

More broadly, in his analysis of congregational *practices*, Browning helps to refocus attention on lived experience and its key role as a starting place for pastoral theology. In so doing, Browning demonstrates that *all* theology begins with practice. He argues,

> We never really move from theory to practice even when it seems we do. Theory is always embedded in practice. When theory seems to stand alone it is only because we have abstracted it from its practical context. We have become mentally blind to the practical activities that both precede and follow it.[3]

Although the centrality of the practical context has long been a hallmark of pastoral theology, Browning's attention to the experience and practices of a congregation lends freshness and breadth to what has always been one of our discipline's greatest strengths—namely, its attention to human life through thick description[4] and its investigation of lived religious experience within the wider study of religion.[5] In this way, Browning exemplifies an approach to pastoral theology that I find crucial to my own work: beginning with practice, moving to theories and resources that one can place into critical conversation with practice, and finally implementing the insights of reflection into renewed approaches to practice.

To this end, I now present my own case studies as the foundation from which I will analyze two congregations' practices of conflict resolution.[6] Like Browning, I have chosen faith communities from different denominations located in separate geographical areas; I have also selected churches that struggled with conflicts around diverse types of theological

---

2. See, for example, Hunter, "Religious Caregiving"; McClure, *Moving beyond Individualism*.

3. Browning, *A Fundamental Practical Theology*, 9.

4. As I noted in chapter 1, the phrase "thick description" is credited to anthropologist Clifford Geertz in his text *The Interpretation of Cultures*, and has been embraced by qualitative researchers and practical theologians alike.

5. See Miller-McLemore, "The Subject and Practice of Pastoral Theology."

6. For a description of case study as pastoral theological method, or for a list of the interview questions I used to generate the case studies presented in this book, please see the Appendix.

issues. The first congregation, Grace United Church of Christ (Grace UCC), endured a fiercely divisive dispute centered on issues of same-sex marriage, homosexuality, and, ultimately, denominational affiliation. The second, First United Methodist Church (First UMC), faced a conflict regarding changes to its worship structure. These two locations, Grace UCC and First UMC, confronted issues that are quite distinct theologically, and the ensuing conflicts differed greatly in terms of their intensity and their long-term effects on the respective congregations. Recalling the definition of "serious conflict" introduced in chapter 1—i.e., conflict in which some church members left, a leader left, or money was withheld—we could say that Grace UCC suffered a serious conflict, whereas First UMC's conflict proved much milder (though no less important).

Despite these key differences, I contend that examining these two cases side by side allows common themes to emerge—themes that point the way toward a deeper understanding of the sources and dynamics of theological conflict within congregations. As I wrote and reflected on the case studies, I noticed that many of these themes center on notions of selfhood or identity, and that they all relate in important ways to the concept of *anxiety*. This made me wonder whether anxiety might be an important (if not *the* most important) "underground source" from which conflict springs. Given the prevalence of themes of selfhood and identity in the case studies, I suggest that conflict erupts and/or becomes more intense when individuals and groups experience *anxiety produced by encounters with difference*. However, before I can delve more deeply into exploring the themes that link these case studies, I must first tell the stories of these two communities of faith, and of the conflicts that became part of their life together.

Grace United Church of Christ

The congregation I am calling Grace United Church of Christ (Grace UCC)[7] is a church I served as a pastoral leader for several years. The congregation is located in the town of "Fairview,"[8] near the eastern seaboard of the United States. Fairview is a semirural community, made

---

7. The United Church of Christ denomination was formed in 1957 through the joining of the Evangelical and Reformed Church with the Congregational Christian Churches. Grace UCC originally belonged to the Congregational Christian side of the tradition.

8. This is a pseudonym; the name of the town in which Grace UCC is located has been changed to protect the congregation's privacy.

up of active downtown and commercial districts, as well as large areas devoted to farming and other agricultural pursuits. At the time that the conflict erupted at Grace UCC in 2005, the town had a population of roughly 79,000 people, and the most recent census information available estimates that approximately 40 percent of Fairview's population is African-American.[9] The particular area of Fairview in which Grace UCC is located is called "Wood Hollow"; Wood Hollow has a quaint, village feel and features a very small cluster of businesses including a gas station, hair salon, restaurant, and the local post office. In fact, Fairview residents who live within the borders of Wood Hollow proper cannot receive mail directly at their homes, but must go to the post office to retrieve it. As a result, the village post office has become an important social hub at which many residents—including many members of Grace UCC—see one another and catch up on local news. In Wood Hollow, one has the sense that everyone knows one another, even though the village is situated within a much larger town.

Grace UCC is located just up the road from the heart of Wood Hollow. It is a white, clapboard structure, similar to many other rural churches built in the same era. Though the building is much larger now than at the time of its initial construction in 1872, the sanctuary features the original stained glass memorial windows that were added in 1893—an aspect of the physical plant of which members are very proud.[10] Indeed, one Grace UCC member once boasted to me that these windows are "the prettiest in all of Fairview." The sanctuary of Grace UCC has pews arranged in a large half-circle facing the altar, over which sits a large, stained-glass depiction of a scene from the life of Jesus. Other stained-glass windows line the entire right side and back wall of the sanctuary, while the left side is open to the fellowship hall in order to accommodate overflow crowds.

The stained glass windows comprise only one aspect of Grace UCC's historic feel. Directly behind the church building is a large cemetery, in which members of the church and other members of the community are buried. Many of the gravestones in the cemetery date back to the turn of

---

9. Due to the need to preserve this congregation's confidentiality, I cannot provide a precise source for this information here. However, it is well known that Fairview—like so many other locations in the United States—has had a long history of racial tensions, which continue to divide the community.

10. The windows are called "memorial" windows because each one features the names of long-dead Grace UCC members, in whose memory the windows were originally donated.

the century or even earlier, as the cemetery was established in 1882. In fact, many times during my years at Grace UCC I encountered people who had shown up at the church wishing to examine headstones, cemetery records, or the stained glass windows as part of their genealogical research.

At the time that I began serving Grace UCC in 2002, the congregation was comprised mainly of working class or professional individuals, rather than farmers or agricultural workers. However, a significant number of people within the congregation still owned large portions of land, some of which they paid others to farm for them. Many of the families at Grace UCC had lived on the same land for generations, which gave the church a very close-knit feel. In fact, many members said that they liked how Grace UCC made them feel like part of a "family"; indeed, a great many people in our congregation were actually related to one another through blood or marriage. Yet, even with the deep family interconnections at Grace UCC, the community around the church was changing rapidly. In 2010, it was estimated that the population of Fairview had grown by 32.8 percent since the 2000 census.[11] More and more families were moving into Fairview, and often these families had little or no connection to the land or to the traditional Fairview of years past.

By this time, Grace UCC had made steps toward recognizing the ways in which their community was changing. When they hired their pastor, "Bill Turner,"[12] in the early 1990s, they deliberately sought someone who they thought could help their church to grow. Rev. Turner turned out to be quite successful in this regard; for the first ten years of his tenure at Grace UCC, the church had grown significantly in membership. Many of the new members were young families with children, which boosted the church's youth and Christian education programs, and revitalized the congregation as a whole. Due to this influx of new members, Grace UCC hired me as a full-time associate in 2002. Although by 2003 the number of church members had reached a plateau, Grace UCC still seemed to be a healthy, thriving church, active in its surrounding community and poised for further growth into the future.

Indeed, everything seemed to be going quite well for Grace UCC. That changed in the summer of 2005, when the General Synod of the

---

11. Due to the need to preserve this congregation's confidentiality, I cannot provide a precise source for this information here.

12. Unless otherwise noted, all names of congregation leaders and members have been changed to protect their privacy.

United Church of Christ (Grace UCC's parent denomination) passed a resolution supporting equal marriage rights for same-sex couples. While the members of Grace UCC had previously seemed quite uninterested in the national decisions of the UCC, this resolution caught their attention and, for many of them, sparked outrage and disgust. However, Rev. Turner and I were not fully aware of these strong feelings until the night of the summer quarterly business meeting, when a large group of angry parishioners voiced their displeasure with the passage of the equal marriage resolution. This group was composed primarily of members of one particular Sunday school class which, I later learned, had spent the three weeks prior to this meeting expressing their disapproval of the resolution and discussing strategies for airing their grievances to the wider congregation. By the time these parishioners arrived at the meeting, they had already built up a great deal of emotional investment in this issue and were determined to do something about it.

Although the discussion in the meeting proved heated, it seemed at first that the dissatisfied individuals might agree to voice their displeasure through a letter to the president of the denomination. However, as the debate continued, participants became increasingly volatile in their emotional expression and more aggressive in their demands. As the rhetoric of the meeting rose in intensity, one group of parishioners became more and more critical of the UCC. At the height of this emotionally charged discussion, one very vocal member—"Peter Vance"—made a motion that the congregation should sever all ties with the denomination. Peter, and others who shared his perspective, said they had never realized that the UCC stood for such liberal theological and political values, and that they could not in good conscience remain part of such an institution. Rev. Turner requested that Peter amend his motion to allow two months for the congregation to discuss the issues more fully before taking a vote. Peter agreed, and the vote was set for late September. At the end of the meeting, Rev. Turner and I voiced support for our parishioners' right to express their views, but also reminded the group that due to our denominational commitments, we could no longer serve the congregation if it chose to disassociate from the UCC.

During the two-month period between this meeting and the actual vote, the division between the two opposing "sides" of this issue grew wider. On one side—which I will call the "protesting group"[13]—were Pe-

---

13. I recognize that this may not be a completely accurate term, since the members of this group would not necessarily have described themselves this way. In this case,

ter Vance and most of the members of his Sunday school class, as well as other members of the congregation who felt that the UCC was too liberal to continue associating with it. On the other side—the "defending group"—were Rev. Turner, me, and a significant number of other parishioners, who felt that leaving the UCC would prove highly detrimental to the congregation. In the weeks prior to the vote, both groups engaged in a variety of strategies aimed at making sure that their own viewpoint would garner the most votes: calling inactive members and encouraging them to vote a particular way, engaging in letter-writing campaigns aimed at the entire congregation, and publicly calling into question the values and intentions of opposing group members. All of these tactics were designed to further each group's cause, and to ensure victory on the day of the vote.

In the midst of this contentious atmosphere, Rev. Turner and I tried to provide opportunities for conversation about the issue of homosexuality. Unfortunately, this vision for peaceful, productive conversation between church members was never realized, but instead mirrored the conflict that was already taking place behind the scenes. In fact, the "dialogue" that we worked so hard to create often dissolved into angry exchanges in which people accused each other of being "un-Christian" or of ignoring scriptural mandates. Indeed, from the time this conflict first emerged at the summer business meeting, members on both sides of the issue appealed to religious tradition and Scripture as a means of justifying their own positions. For instance, on more than one occasion individuals quoted Lev 18:22 as proof that the General Synod's support for same-sex marriage, and the denomination's support for LGBT rights in general, goes against scriptural mandates.[14]

In contrast, those who wished to remain in the UCC, and particularly those who personally agreed with the General Synod resolution, emphasized how their approach to Scripture differed from those who wished to disassociate. I recall very clearly a congregational meeting that Rev. Turner and I organized after worship one Sunday for the purpose of fostering conversation about the issues at stake. "Noelle Faulkner," an

---

however, this seems like a helpful way of distinguishing between the group that wished to change the current state of affairs in the church (the "protesting group"), and those who wished to keep the existing organizational structures in place (the "defending group").

14. Lev 18:22 reads, "You shall not lie with a male as with a woman; it is an abomination" (NRSV).

avid supporter of the denomination—at least in part *because* of its stance on LGBT rights issues—stood up and stated that when she reads the Bible, she places more importance on some parts than others, and even chooses to disregard some parts as no longer culturally relevant. As soon as Noelle spoke these words, people around the room uttered audible gasps. Clearly, some members of the congregation were shocked by the idea that anyone would admit emphasizing some parts of the Bible while ignoring others.

Rev. Turner and I had hoped that these meetings would provide an opportunity for our church members to listen to and learn from one another. In effect, though, the meetings we held seemed to do little more than uncover deep theological disagreements that were already present within the congregation without pointing the way toward bringing differing viewpoints together. In fact, over time, Rev. Turner and I actually became a focus of the conflict itself. For example, some of the parishioners who wished to leave the UCC turned their anger directly onto us, perhaps because we represented the denomination in bodily form. Early in the conflict, these parishioners roundly criticized me in particular, because I had served as a delegate to the General Synod and had not (in their view) accurately represented the church's feelings about same-sex marriage through my vote.[15] Others in this group openly questioned why Rev. Turner did not preach against homosexuality from the pulpit. Additionally, at one of the after-church discussion meetings, a woman stood up and asked Rev. Turner and me to state publicly whether or not we believed homosexuality was a sin. When we declined to do as she asked, she became angry and declared that she and her family would not stay in a church where the pastors would not publicly condemn homosexuality.

Those who believed that remaining in the UCC was the right course of action (even if they did not agree with same-sex marriage) became quite defensive of Rev. Turner and me, and felt deeply offended by what they perceived as the other group's disrespect for the congregation's pastoral leadership. "Charles," who was serving in a position of leadership at the time of the conflict, recalled that some of those advocating disassociation from the denomination "did say some real ugly things about our pastor. . . . And I think that's wrong." "Tom," a longtime member of the congregation, remembered events in a similar way: "I felt that the pastor

---

15. I should note that I never disclosed how I voted, since in the UCC delegates are directed to vote their conscience; still, many church members assumed that I had voted in support of the resolution.

was publicly attacked by some in not-a-kind way. It was demanded that he say how he felt about certain things and that, and that is not . . . I mean, they were trying to back him into a corner and make him say things that could then be held against him. I didn't think that tactic was fair." Several of the other people I interviewed from Grace UCC echoed Charles and Tom's sentiments and stated that part of the reason they felt so strongly about staying in the denomination was because they wished to keep the church's pastoral leadership in place. For them, getting out of the UCC simply was not an option if it meant that Rev. Turner and I would have to leave.

These complex and growing tensions ultimately produced an extremely polarized situation: by the time of the vote, many individuals with opposing perspectives had stopped speaking to one another. Then, when the results were announced, those who perceived themselves as "the losers" immediately transferred their membership to other churches. In the end, the congregation chose to stay in the United Church of Christ, but at the cost of some sixty members who believed that an essential tenet of their faith had been ignored. For a church that, at the time, claimed an active membership of about 250 persons, this exodus of nearly 25 percent of its core participants proved a crushing blow—especially since most of the people who left had been members at Grace UCC for many years and were deeply rooted in the community. Many of those who remained at Grace UCC felt torn between their conviction that the congregation had made the right decision and their intense grief about the damage done to their relationships with friends, neighbors, and even family members because of this conflict.

This division and relational rupture also went beyond the bounds of the congregation and extended into the wider community life of Fairview. As would be expected, those who chose to leave Grace UCC following the vote remained active in a variety of community causes, as did those who chose to stay. This meant that people who had formerly shared close relationships as fellow church members were encountering each other in the community, often with little sense of how to relate to one another following the conflict. Although several of the Grace UCC members I interviewed stated that their interactions with former members in the community were always cordial, others shared that people who had been their close friends at Grace UCC would barely speak to them when they saw them at community events. As a result, leadership and participation in some of these community causes suffered because former Grace UCC members on opposite sides of the conflict were reluctant to work together any more. To this day, many of these friendships and community relationships remain broken.

From a technical standpoint, the conflict at Grace UCC was about denominational affiliation; the question on the ballot was whether or not the church should remain in the United Church of Christ. Yet, as this case study shows, several different concerns were actually at issue within the conflict at Grace UCC. First, what might be called the "presenting issue," was the topic of same-sex marriage raised by the General Synod's resolution. This was the issue about which the members of the protesting group were so upset, and that they initially came to the summer business meeting determined to address. Closely related to the specific issue of same-sex marriage was the general notion of homosexuality. I make this distinction because, while the conflict at Grace UCC originally erupted in response to a resolution supporting same-sex marriage rights, the discourse within the congregation quickly broadened to include arguments about homosexuality more generally.

Interestingly, very few people at Grace UCC (including those who wished to stay in the denomination) actually supported the particular Synod resolution of 2005 or same-sex marriage in general. In fact, in public discussions at Grace UCC, many members of the defending group stated openly that they disagreed with same-sex marriage as a legal and social policy. Yet the focus at the original business meeting shifted almost immediately away from same-sex marriage and toward homosexuality more broadly. As it did, the accompanying emotions in the room seemed to grow stronger, especially on the part of those who disagreed so vehemently with the Synod resolution. Many of these individuals felt that the UCC represented values so liberal that they simply could not embrace them. This contributed to yet another issue within the conflict at Grace UCC: namely, tensions surrounding the pastoral leaders. For those who wished to leave the denomination, the loyalty that Rev. Turner and I shared toward the UCC seemed to mark us as "liberals" who stood for the very same values that troubled them so deeply.

As I have mentioned, many of those who advocated for staying in the UCC also disapproved of same-sex marriage and/or had conflicted feelings about homosexuality in general. Yet, the parishioners in this defending group firmly believed that to disassociate from the UCC over this issue would prove destructive for the congregation in the long run. For these congregants, the loss of pastoral leadership and of the overall supporting structure of the denomination seemed too costly to risk, even if they personally believed same-sex marriage or homosexuality was wrong. It seemed that many in this group arrived at their position primarily out of loyalty to Rev. Turner and me, and to the congregation as a whole, and not so much out of devotion to the United Church of Christ itself. So, while the congregation ultimately elected to remain part of the UCC, it did so in the midst of a complex web of tensions surrounding not only same-sex marriage but broader issues of human sexuality, scriptural interpretation, pastoral leadership, and denominational identity.

First United Methodist Church

As I began to think about my research for this book, I became increasingly convinced that telling only the story of Grace UCC would be inadequate to address the topic of conflict in congregations. I have argued that there is great value in examining the lived experiences of faith communities in all their concreteness; yet, Grace UCC represents only one particular church and its approach to conflict. Furthermore, my personal involvement at Grace UCC means that I necessarily bring a biased perspective to the events that occurred there, though I have attempted to represent the church and its members as fairly as possible. I concluded that in order to add some nuance to my study, I would need to include the story of at least one other congregation that had experienced conflict in its life together and would be willing to share its experience with me.

Identifying such a congregation proved challenging, since many churches that have experienced intense conflict are reluctant to talk about it, especially with an outsider. During the time that I was looking for a second research site, I happened to meet a local clergy person who provides consultations to churches in conflict and helps to train their leaders in conflict management techniques. This person put me in touch with the pastors at First UMC, with whom he had recently consulted. First UMC's pastors—"Bob Fisher" and "Carol Stewart"—agreed to meet with me and gave their permission for me to do research at First UMC. Revs. Fisher and Stewart then contacted members of the worship committee and explained that I would be conducting interviews for my research and encouraged them to participate. Prior to my first meeting with Revs. Fisher and Stewart, I had never visited First UMC nor was I acquainted with anyone there. In this sense, I was a true outsider and had to learn everything about First UMC from its written documents and from interviewing its pastors and members.

The first time I turned onto the shady street that leads to First United Methodist Church, I immediately noticed the large spire that rises above the trees in the surrounding neighborhood. The spire is grandly traditional, pointing skyward as a reminder of the awe-inspiring, transcendent God worshipped within the 500-seat sanctuary below. Indeed, several of the parishioners I interviewed described First UMC's sanctuary as "high church," given the size and layout of the space. The sanctuary is long and narrow, with multicolored stained glass windows that stretch all the way up to the high vaulted ceiling. The flooring throughout the sanctuary is ceramic tile in green and earth tones, except for an area at the front that features dark green carpeting. Twenty-five double rows of pews, all facing forward, flank the center aisle, which leads to the chancel. Separated from the pews by a kneeling rail, the chancel is a raised platform that supports the main pulpit on the right side, and the lectern on the left. Due to the height of the chancel, both the pulpit and the lectern seem to loom over the sanctuary. In addition to being raised, the chancel is also deep; behind the pulpit and lectern are two choir lofts as well as a grand piano and pipe organ. At the very back of the chancel, in a recessed alcove, sits the table on which the communion elements would typically be consecrated. The table is round, and a large cross hangs from the top of the alcove over it. Given its position at the back of the chancel, it seems likely that worshippers in the back rows would have difficulty even seeing the table on a communion Sunday.

Across the courtyard from the main sanctuary sits a much more humble structure. From the outside, you might not even know that the modest building houses a worship space. Inside is a 240-seat chapel, markedly different from the main sanctuary in almost every way. Where the sanctuary is grand and spacious, the chapel has a much more intimate feel. The communion table is nearly on the same level as the pews, and very little distance separates the chancel from the worshippers. Instead of a raised pulpit or lectern, the chapel features a very small podium, placed not on the chancel, but on the floor just beyond the front pews. On one side of the chancel is a large display of candles; on the other, an electronic keyboard, microphones, and a drum set. Above the candles is a large screen, with a high-tech projector mounted to the ceiling in front of it. Two decorative banners depicting the communion loaf and cup, respectively, hang from the front wall above the musical instruments. The chapel boasts the same beautiful stained glass windows as the sanctuary, but here they are smaller and more understated.

These depictions of the physical worship spaces at First United Methodist Church are crucial to understanding the nature of the conflict that occurred there in 2009, because they vividly illustrate the varying theological understandings of worship held by congregation members. The conflict between these perspectives began in earnest when, in 2008, the church's administrative board issued a directive to reduce the number of Sunday morning worship services from three to two. On the surface, such a change might appear relatively minor within the wider context of a congregation's life. However, my research revealed that individuals' feelings about their particular services were deeply-rooted, and were tied closely to their understanding of how God relates to human beings in worship.

In talking with the pastors at First UMC, I learned that the seeds of this conflict had been planted many years before. First UMC was organized in 1950 in an area called "Forestdale,"[16] located in a medium-sized city in the Southeastern region of the United States. According to the booklet that First UMC produced for its "jubilee" year in 2000, the founding of this congregation occurred when "God put it into the hearts of some thirteen families" to start a Methodist church in Forestdale, which, at that time, was beginning to grow rapidly in population.[17] By 1953, First UMC had nearly 200 members; amazingly, just ten years later, it had over 1,100. Because of the exponential growth it experienced in its early years, First UMC had to hold multiple worship services to accommodate its members. During the 1960s and 1970s, First UMC continued to expand in size—both in terms of membership and physical space. By 1977, the congregation had 2,150 members, a budget of $355,000, and had added educational facilities and an administrative wing to its physical plant.[18] At that time, First UMC continued to hold two Sunday morning services in the sanctuary to accommodate its members—one at 8:30 and one at 11:00.

---

16. This is a pseudonym. The name of the neighborhood in which First UMC is situated has been changed to protect the congregation's privacy.

17. Due to the need to protect the congregation's confidentiality, I cannot provide more precise source information here.

18. All of the numerical data in this paragraph come from the booklet cited above, which was published by First UMC in celebration of its fiftieth anniversary.

Beginning in the early 1980s, the membership of First UMC began to decline gradually. By 1991, the church had just under 1,400 members—quite a drop from its peak in the late 1970s. Numerically speaking, there was no longer such a pressing need for multiple services on Sunday morning; however, because both services had been going on for so long, they seemed an integral part of First UMC's structure. Both Sunday morning services could be called "traditional" in style, and both met in the sanctuary.[19] The 8:30 service was typically a bit more informal in that it involved a smaller group of worshippers, featured a choir that rehearsed less often than the 11:00 ensemble, and included more leadership from the youth (as ushers, musicians, etc.). The 8:30 service also included communion every week, whereas at the 11:00 service, communion was served only once a month.

These two worship services coexisted for decades, with the pastor preaching at both each week. In 1997, however, a major shift occurred when active parishioner "Roy Sanderson," with the support of the senior pastor, introduced a new opportunity for contemporary worship at First UMC. Musicians were brought in from outside the congregation to provide leadership for the new service, which was held at 8:45 in the small chapel each Sunday morning. The new service took off and began attracting many people who had never previously been associated with First UMC. Attendance at this service grew to over one hundred people per Sunday, and remained at that level for several years. Over time, however, the contemporary service began to falter a bit. The outside musicians, who had previously given such strong leadership to the service, left in favor of other opportunities. This produced a temporary vacuum in leadership for the service, and attendance began to drop.

Simultaneously, attendance had been shrinking at the 8:30 and 11:00 services as well. Pastor Bob Fisher described this turn of events as a result of "generational recycling": the generation that had helped found First UMC was aging and dying, but it was not being replaced quickly enough with newer, younger members. As a result, both the 8:30 and 11:00 services were beginning to feel sparse, particularly since they were both being held in First UMC's large sanctuary. By 2009, the 8:30 service had a maximum attendance of ninety people, and the 11:00 had a maximum attendance of roughly 250 people. Furthermore, because there were now three morning services, whoever was preaching on a given Sunday had

---

19. By this time, the chapel was used only for special services, such as small weddings.

to attend all three, which meant literally running from the 8:30 service in the sanctuary to the 8:45 service in the chapel in time for the sermon.[20]

When Rev. Fisher came to First UMC in 2005, there had been some discussion about reducing the number of worship services, but there had also been powerful resistance to making such changes. By 2009, however, attendance at all three services had shrunk enough that the congregation's administrative board felt it was time to revisit the issue. Members of the board were especially concerned about two things: first, the considerable strain on the preaching pastor, and second, the perception that the 11:00 service felt "empty" because the large sanctuary was usually half-full, at best. The board felt that having the sanctuary look and feel empty could potentially make a negative impression on any visitors that might attend the service. Based on these concerns, the administrative board charged the church's worship committee with devising a plan to reduce the number of morning services from three to two, with one being traditional and one being contemporary. Rev. Fisher told me that some individuals within the congregation had long considered the contemporary service an "irritant"; however, by 2009 the service had been in place for twelve years and included some key members of First UMC. As a result, the board felt it was important to keep a contemporary service as one of the two worship opportunities on Sunday morning.

From the twelve interviews I conducted with parishioners at First UMC, I learned that when the administrative board's directive was announced, people within the congregation immediately became anxious about losing "their" service. This was especially true for the 8:30 traditional worshippers, since the most obvious solution to the problem would simply be to get rid of the 8:30 service and merge it with the 11:00 service. Rev. Fisher was aware of this anxiety, and believed that to simply eliminate one service and merge it with another would create a great deal of resistance and hostility. Rev. Fisher felt strongly that in order to avoid a highly contentious conflict, the church needed to put an intentional decision-making process into place. By "intentional process," Rev. Fisher meant a carefully designed course of action that would have clearly defined goals and that would ensure that stakeholders from all three worship

---

20. This had not always been the case; at certain points in First UMC's history, another member of the pastoral staff (usually an associate pastor) would preach at the contemporary service. This arrangement caused conflicts of its own, however. By 2006, the church had returned to the practice of having the same person preach at all three services.

services could contribute to the development of the ultimate solution. As a means to this end, Rev. Fisher worked with "Judith Murray," the chair of the worship committee, to convene a special group to address this problem. He and Judith invited between six and eight individuals from each worship service to participate in this committee, and asked members to commit to being present for four separate meetings. However, it was also made known throughout the congregation that anyone who wished to attend the special committee's meetings was welcome to do so, even if they could not come to all four sessions.

The sessions themselves were held between January and March of 2009, and each one opened with a structured devotional time that included Scripture reading, prayer, and reflection. Rev. Fisher and Judith Murray intentionally included these spiritual elements in the meetings in an effort to head off some of the hostility and resentment they expected committee members to bring with them. Evidently, these fears were well-founded. According to some of the parishioners I interviewed, at the very first committee meeting, everyone sat with people from their own service. One interviewee said he could feel the tension in the air because, as he put it, people were "loaded"—they were ready to "line up and fight" for their service. Those who attended the 8:30 service expected their service to be eliminated entirely, while some of those who attended the 11:00 were concerned that there would be an attempt to "blend" their service and make it more contemporary. For their part, the 8:45 contemporary worshippers also worried that significant changes might be made to a service that had become extremely meaningful to them.

In addition to the intentional inclusion of devotional time at each meeting, the sessions were designed according to a specific plan, which was described to me in detail both by Rev. Fisher and by others who I interviewed. At the first meeting, committee members spent time getting to know one another and also worked in small groups made up of people who attended the same service (i.e., 8:30 worshippers met together, 8:45 worshippers met together, etc.). Subsequent meetings also included small group work, but these groups were made up of members from different services. The small groups were charged with coming up with potential plans for fulfilling the administrative board's directive to reduce the number of worship services from three to two. These plans were described and discussed at the third meeting, but no decision was made at that time. In fact, by the end of the third meeting, more than a few committee members were beginning to feel hopeless that a consensus could ever be reached.

The fourth meeting began with a devotional time that included members serving communion to one another. The committee then reviewed together the various plans that the small groups had generated over the previous weeks, all of which included having the traditional service remain at 11:00. Yet, according to the meeting minutes from that night, "Early traditional worshipers wanted to continue worshiping at an early time and *were not at all comfortable* with leaving the late service at 11:00."[21] "Not at all comfortable" seems to be a mild way of describing the feelings in the room that night. In fact, First UMC's pastors shared with me that during this last meeting, there was a point at which it seemed that all three groups might "dig in their heels." The 8:30 worshippers, in particular, became "belligerent" because they felt that they were the only ones being asked to change. At this point, it seemed that the group might be at a stalemate. However, at that moment, Roy Sanderson made what many of the interviewees described as an "out of the box" proposal. He suggested that Sunday school should be moved from 9:30 back to 9:00; traditional sanctuary worship moved from 11:00 to 10:30; and the contemporary service be held at 5:00 on Sunday afternoon, with covenant groups and other spiritual growth opportunities offered afterward.

Although the administrative board's directive had clearly stated that there should be two services held on Sunday morning, the committee members ultimately agreed that Roy's proposal offered the best solution for what had, just moments before, seemed an intractable problem. Some committee members did express concern about what effect this proposal might have on Sunday school, but in the end, the committee unanimously voted to accept Roy's plan and to present it to the administrative board for consideration. In talking with committee members about how this unorthodox solution came about, most indicated that they believed it was a result of the Holy Spirit's work among the group. In fact, interviewees described the solution as "a God thing," "God intervening," and even "miraculous." Similarly, in his charge conference report to the congregation the following fall, Rev. Fisher described the events this way: "The Spirit moved and the proposal was made to move the Praise Service to Sunday evening. This gesture of sacrifice transformed three groups with each inclined to defend its right to its own service into as [sic] shared

---

21. Emphasis added.

spirit of mutual love and concern. The result was an 'out of the box' option that seemed right to everyone."

At least two of the people I interviewed did not see this development in quite the same light. Instead of understanding the solution as direct intervention from the Holy Spirit, these individuals thought that the decision to move the contemporary service to the evening was more likely due to the fact that no other solution seemed viable, or to the fact that Roy Sanderson decided to make a more dramatic compromise in an effort to avoid further conflict within the committee. Still, it is difficult to underestimate the importance that interviewees attributed to the chain of events during the last meeting; even those who disagreed with the "God thing" language admitted that the solution was reached much more peacefully than they would have thought possible.

Ironically, the creative solution that received such acclamation within the committee did not work out in the end. The new worship schedule was implemented in June of 2009, but by August, it was clear that the 5:00 time for the contemporary service was not viable. Attendance at the contemporary service had dropped dramatically, and even those who were still coming felt that they had to choose between coming to worship in the evening or going to Sunday school in the morning. For them, it simply did not seem feasible to come to church twice in the same day. By the end of the summer, the decision was made to move the contemporary service back to Sunday morning, although because of the new schedule, it had to begin at 8:15 so as not to overlap with Sunday school. This posed a new problem for the contemporary service, since even when it had been held at 8:45, participants often had trouble getting there on time. Due to this early time slot, attendance at the contemporary service continued to be lower than in the past, but began to grow slowly from the slump it had experienced when it was in the evening. Eventually, the time of the contemporary service was changed to 8:30 to try to allow a bit more time for worshippers to arrive.

Given the failure of the attempt to move the contemporary service to an evening time slot, one might be tempted to assume that the whole decision-making process at First UMC was a waste of time. After all, the church now has essentially the same schedule it had before: a traditional late morning worship service in the sanctuary and an earlier contemporary service in the chapel. From the outside, it would appear that the church could have obtained the same results simply by eliminating the 8:30 traditional service from the beginning. Yet, in my interviews with members of First UMC, there was widespread consensus that even though Roy Sanderson's idea ultimately failed, it had to be tried in order for the committee members (particularly those from the 8:30 service) to feel that everyone involved had made some sacrifices. In other words, if the committee had simply decided to eliminate the 8:30 service without exploring any other creative solutions, 8:30 worshippers would have felt extremely disenfranchised and might even have left the church in protest.[22] Instead, by the time the contemporary worship service was moved back to a morning slot, the 8:30 worshippers had become integrated into the new 10:30 traditional service—which, by all accounts, is now going extremely well and drawing more attendance than it has in years—and were not bothered by the fact that the contemporary worshippers ended up with the coveted early morning spot.

In addition, given the fact that both 8:30 and 8:45 worshippers were accustomed to having communion every week, a very brief service of communion and prayer was added to the Sunday morning worship schedule at 8:45. This service helped provide an opportunity for early worshippers to have communion every week, but at a time that would not interfere with the Sunday school classes that are so important within the life of First UMC. Looking back on all that has happened within the last few years, most of the people I interviewed admitted that the solution generated by the worship committee has included some significant losses: 8:30 worshippers still keenly miss certain aspects of their previous service, and attendance at the contemporary service has never quite recovered. Yet, they almost all agree that the current worship schedule is what is "best for the church" as a whole, and they continue to stand behind the committee's decision.

Common Themes

Clearly, Grace UCC and First UMC are two very different congregations that faced very different problems. Not only did these two churches wrestle with distinct issues but also the intensity and outcome of their respective conflicts varied widely. Grace UCC endured a severely divisive conflict over the extremely volatile topic of same-sex marriage and lost a

---

22. In fact, a few members of First UMC's 8:30 service did end up leaving the church because they were unhappy with the committee's decision, but by all accounts the number of people who left was much smaller than what the committee feared might happen if they had simply eliminated the 8:30 service from the beginning.

significant portion of its membership as a result. First UMC, on the other hand, dealt with important changes to its worship structure and lost a few members, but overall it weathered the situation well and arrived at a solution that garnered widespread support within the congregation. Additionally, the process that these two churches used to confront the disagreements in their midst differed dramatically. Because the prospect of denominational separation was raised so suddenly at Grace UCC, the pastors and lay leadership there were put in a position of reacting rather than carefully planning an approach to the conflict brewing within the congregation. First UMC, by contrast, had been indirectly dealing with the worship issue for a number of years and was thus able—through the initiative of its pastors and other congregational leaders—to design an intentional, structured process by which the conflict might be handled carefully and calmly. Given these significant differences, the value of examining these case studies side by side might not be immediately clear.

I argue, however, that exploring these case studies together yields important insights about congregational conflict. First, the very differences between these two congregations raise questions that bear further investigation. For instance: why did the conflict at Grace UCC become so intense, while that at First UMC did not? What factors allowed First UMC to find a relatively peaceful solution to its problem? Were those factors absent at Grace UCC, or, if they were present, why didn't they have the same effect? What can we learn about conflict from a church like Grace UCC that has suffered a violent rift, and what can we learn from one that has managed to deal effectively with a potentially divisive problem? Seeking answers to these questions—born out of the differences between the two congregations—may lead to new insights about congregational conflict, and especially about what steps pastoral leaders might take to deal with it more effectively.

At the same time, considering these cases together also reveals important areas of similarity between them. Exploring these points of connection opens a pathway for analysis of some of the common features of congregational conflict, and provides a foundation from which to reflect on these events using psychodynamic, social psychological, and theological tools—a task to which I will turn in later chapters. In the remainder of this chapter, I describe what I see as the most significant similarities between the two case studies, how these similarities are connected, and what they may reveal about the nature of theological conflict within communities of faith.

Anxiety

The first important similarity between Grace UCC and First UMC involves the notion of *anxiety*. As this book has taken shape, I have become increasingly convinced of the fundamental role that anxiety plays in interpersonal and communal conflict. Through the lens of family systems theory, I have come to recognize some of the ways that such anxiety was operating in the conflicts that took place at both congregations. In each faith community, anxiety seems to have been most acute and recognizable when the initial "presenting issue" emerged. At Grace UCC, for instance, this anxiety took the form of an almost palpable feeling of tension that permeated the summer business meeting. Such a feeling of tension is common in communities experiencing an increase in anxiety: "With a gradual or sudden elevation of anxiety in your congregation, a different tone or mood develops. . . . The minute you arrive at church, you know something is different. The usual lighthearted banter and general chatter has given way to serious silence."[23] This description proves quite apt for what occurred at Grace UCC that night: the moment the senior pastor and I entered the room, we could feel the anxiety in the air and knew that something significant was going to happen. The tension continued to rise throughout the meeting, and culminated in the explosive interactions that accompanied the discussion about leaving the denomination.

At First UMC, anxiety was also present, but it appeared in a more gradual and understated way. Because the congregation had been discussing making worship changes for some time, the initial charge from the administrative board did not set off the kind of volatile conflict that took place at Grace UCC. However, the pastors of First UMC told me that the administrative board's directive immediately caused many members—particularly those from the 8:30 service—to become "anxious" about the prospect of losing their worship opportunity. Additionally, several of the interviewees stated that at the first meeting of the worship committee, a feeling of "tension" permeated the air, and that individuals sat with others from their own service as if they were ready to "line up and fight." Clearly, then, First UMC's need to make a firm decision about changing their worship structure caused anxiety to rise throughout the congregation—anxiety that the worship committee members then brought with them into their deliberations.

---

23. Steinke, *Congregational Leadership in Anxious Times*, 5.

As I am using it here, the term *anxiety* refers to a general "sense of threat" that causes persons to feel unsafe in the world.[24] This understanding of anxiety naturally leads one to wonder: what, specifically, made the parishioners at Grace UCC and First UMC feel threatened or unsafe? In other words, why did these conflicts over sexuality and worship have such a powerful effect on those involved? I will answer this question more fully later in the book, but for now I suggest that perceived threats to *identity* likely played a key role in the development of anxiety within these two congregations. That is to say: threats to one's identity or sense of self typically create anxiety—anxiety that is difficult to relieve and that frequently results in unhealthy behaviors. When read with this idea in mind, the disparate case studies presented in this chapter begin to appear more connected, since parishioners in each congregation struggled to cope with challenges to beliefs and institutions that had become closely tied to their own sense of identity.

In addition to the general notion of anxiety, which I have identified as a common feature of the conflicts at Grace UCC and First UMC, the interview data from these congregations also reveal a number of other similarities. I have summarized these similarities through the following themes, all of which, in different ways, illustrate the complex nature of conflict: (1) the theological dimensions of conflict; (2) identity; (3) polarization and fragmentation; and (4) the pain of conflict and change. In the sections that follow, I describe each of these themes, and I illustrate them by including the voices of specific interviewees. These themes not only represent similarities between Grace UCC and First UMC but, as I will show at the end of the chapter, they also all relate to the dynamics of anxiety in important and interlocking ways.

Understanding the Complexities of Conflict

As I explained in chapter 1, this book focuses on congregational conflicts that include an important theological dimension. In making this my focus, however, I am not suggesting that theological disagreement was the only cause of the shape these conflicts ultimately took. Common wisdom tells us that conflict is a multivalent reality that almost always contains many layers—layers that are formed by a complex interplay of events and relationships. Naturally, the more individuals involved in a conflict, the

---

24. Richardson, *Creating a Healthier Church*, 41–42.

more complicated it becomes to tease apart just what is happening and exactly what the issues are. At both Grace UCC and First UMC, there was widespread acknowledgment that although theological issues played a key role, many other factors were at work as well—some of which had originated years before.

In the case of Grace UCC, many of the people I interviewed believed that the conflict over same-sex marriage actually had its roots in long-standing tension between certain members of the church and the congregation's pastoral leadership. "Leah," who had been a member of Grace UCC for over twenty years at the time of the conflict, said, "I think there was an underlying motive. I think there were some people who were not pleased with our pastor. And I think that became an issue, kind of a hidden agenda in it." "George," a relatively new member of Grace UCC, agreed with Leah's assessment, but felt that the underlying tension revolved not only around specific pastors, but around the church leadership in general. He told me, "Over the five years [since the conflict] I have come to believe that the fight was much more a 'systemic control of the congregation fight' between people who felt entitled to run the church and the changing leadership of the church."

Of course, this is not to suggest that those parishioners who wished to leave the UCC were only pretending to be opposed to same-sex marriage just so they could disagree with the pastors. Indeed, the emotional intensity with which these congregants expressed their opposition to the General Synod resolution easily persuaded me and many others present that their position reflected deeply held beliefs. Yet, as the preceding quotations show, many in the congregation felt that these parishioners' staunch opposition to same-sex marriage was only part of the story. Admittedly, it was a very important part, but certainly not the only factor behind the divisiveness that ultimately came to characterize the conflict at Grace UCC.

At First UMC, the tension surrounding the upcoming worship changes also seemed to intertwine with both past and ongoing struggles related to the leadership of the church. Carol Stewart, the associate pastor at First UMC who had been serving that congregation for twelve years at the time of my interview with her, noted that when Rev. Fisher and a previous associate pastor arrived in 2005, there was already a strong theological conflict going on within the congregation. This conflict had itself been fueled by conflict between the previous pastor and one of his associates. The new associate was drawn into the conflict because she was preaching at the contemporary service, and her theology tended to be more conservative than Rev. Fisher's, but quite similar to that of the contemporary worshippers. As a result, some of those attending the contemporary service questioned Rev. Fisher's theology. Ultimately, the new associate left after only a year at First UMC, due at least in part to the growing tension in the congregation. It was at that point that Rev. Fisher decided that First UMC should start having more consistency in its preaching, so he began preaching at all three services. When the administrative board announced that the number of services would be reduced in order to help the pastors manage the Sunday schedule, some in the congregation wondered whether Rev. Fisher was actually behind this decision as an indirect way of eliminating the contemporary service.

It is also noteworthy that at the time the worship discussions began in 2009, First UMC was in the midst of looking for a new minister of music. The previous music minister had been asked to leave because the church felt that they needed someone with a different set of skills to help revitalize the late-morning traditional service. As is always the case with staff changes, some in the congregation were quite loyal to the previous music director and harbored resentment over his dismissal. Furthermore, in a conversation with First UMC's pastors, I learned that the administrative board chair—who had overseen the entire process relating to worship changes—ultimately resigned his post in protest of Rev. Fisher, with whom he had some fundamental theological disagreements. Interestingly, just a few months later, in March of 2010, the youth director of seventeen years also resigned due to friction with the pastoral staff. Given these factual pieces of First UMC's story, it seems likely that although the primary issue in 2009 was the reorganization of the congregation's worship structure, issues surrounding staff relationships and pastoral leadership were part of the story as well. In essence, these various other conflicts formed a complex backdrop of tensions that were already swirling throughout the congregation when the worship change issue came to the fore.

Theological Dimensions of Conflict

Perhaps the most striking similarity that emerged between the situations at Grace UCC and First UMC is the fact that both of these conflicts took on theological significance for those involved in them. In other words, it felt as though something was at stake theologically for the individuals who participated in these conflicts. In chapter 1, I argued that it is possible to discover a theological component to almost any conflict within a congregation because such conflicts take place within a religious context. As a result, they necessarily raise the following question for parishioners: how can we believe such different things about worship or the nature of the church or human sexuality (or any other issue) and still be members of the same religious body? As I conducted my research for this book, I found that my assumptions about the theological dimension to conflict were largely borne out in the interviews that I conducted with parishioners from both congregations.

In the case of Grace UCC, the theological dimension seems quite obvious; after all, from the beginning, the conflict there took the form of biblical and theological language as people argued over interpretations of Scripture and over what a "Christian" approach to homosexuality should be. Particularly for those who wished to separate from the UCC, it seemed that conforming to a specific way of understanding biblical teachings about homosexuality was paramount. For instance, "Phyllis," a woman who had been a member at Grace UCC for twenty years but then left following the conflict, said to me, "It's just when it says in the Bible that it's an abomination for man to lay with a man, you know, to me that's not right." To clarify the reason that she decided to leave Grace UCC, Phyllis added, "I did not leave the church because of the people; I left because of the issue."

Others who elected to stay at Grace UCC had just the opposite viewpoint; for them, *staying* in the UCC carried a great deal of theological significance. "Christine," who was in the youth group at the time of the conflict, said,

> I personally at the end of the day don't want to be a person who shut other people out. And I don't think that's the purpose of a church so I would have fundamentally had a lot of problems if we had left [the denomination] because I think I would have been lost and it would have made me question my faith a whole lot. . . . I think that's what I had to lose, was my footing.

Similarly, Tom, an older man who had held a variety of leadership roles at Grace UCC, stated that "the more I've learned about the larger denomination, the more I find that it corresponds to how I've felt for a long time about social issues as well as religious beliefs and it just speaks to me like no other denomination does about my faith." Thus, for these and other individuals at Grace UCC, the conflict initially generated by the 2005 equal marriage resolution took on powerful theological significance as it touched on deeply held beliefs about the Bible, sin, and the nature of the church.

Admittedly, the theological component of the conflict at First UMC is a bit more difficult to discern; after all, the disagreement in this congregation seems to have centered primarily on logistical matters and preferences in worship style. However, since worship constitutes one of the central ways that human beings collectively relate to God, I wondered whether there might not be more theological significance under the surface than was readily apparent to an outside observer. To explore the theological dimension of the conflict at First UMC, I included questions in my interviews relating to how individuals understood worship and what they felt they might lose from their worship service if changes were made.

Interestingly, some interviewees answered these questions by reflecting on the worship space itself, and what that communicated to them about God's presence in worship. "Nancy," a middle-aged woman who had been attending the contemporary worship service at First UMC for several years, said,

> One of the appeals of having worship in the chapel was the intimacy of the room. . . . The windows in that time of morning and the light coming through and the fact that it just—the room would just take on a glow. And the warmth was just—you felt it. And you just couldn't feel that same atmosphere in a huge, big sanctuary with tile floors and high ceilings and people scattered all over the room.

Judith, the chair of the worship committee, was very comfortable with the 11:00 traditional service, which she had always attended, but the process of chairing the worship committee helped her understand the theological importance of the worship space for the contemporary worshippers: "[The chapel] is an intimate space; they [the 8:45 worshippers] like that small community/small church feeling. Our sanctuary is very lofty. There were things about it that those people appreciate. But apparently, that smallness of the chapel is what helps them see God on a Sunday morning, that connection with others. That's where the veil becomes very thin for them, that connecting with community. And that is where they are able to encounter God."

Of course, the theological importance of the contemporary service was not limited to the role of the worship space; interviewees also shared what they found meaningful in the music and general atmosphere of the contemporary service. "Bart," a middle-aged man who is deeply committed to the contemporary service, explained, "I love this worship style because I can connect to God better. . . . I love to sing, but you put a hymnal in front of me, it's like you've got to be a professional . . . to me, singing is part of worship. And if I've got to think about the song, there's a barrier between me and God. And so that's why I love contemporary so much is because there's no barrier there." "Esther" agreed:

> To me worship is like an opportunity . . . to kind of move the obstacles in your life out of the way so that you can connect with God in that setting while there's people standing around you. . . . And I don't find that in the traditional service. I get cluttered by the number of verses in the hymnal and by looking down at the hymnal when I'm a "look-up-er." And I think the difference to me in contemporary is when you go in, it's not [that] you're best friends with Jesus, but you're much more relational. . . . And I prefer being one-on-one more than separate.

This notion of a more relational feeling in the contemporary service was also echoed by Nancy, who expanded upon the importance of relationality and community for her in worship:

> I felt like it [the contemporary service] really was filling my spiritual need of the way that I communicate with God, in that I feel it's a very personal thing. . . . One thing that continued to be really important was that that service seemed to—we became friends. It became a community. It became—it was informal enough that we could stop and pray for each other. People could be spontaneous if they had something on their heart that they needed to share during the morning service, which certainly couldn't have been done in a traditional service. And it just—it allowed for some freedom. It was the first time I had really ever felt free in a church, free to be me, who I am and what I needed to share.

These quotations demonstrate that many individuals who attended the 8:45 contemporary service see an intimate connection between the style and space of worship and their ability to feel connected with God. In theological terms, we would call this God's *immanence* through an indwelling presence, which appears to be what these interviewees were seeking. For them, such immanence seemed more elusive within the context of traditional worship in the large sanctuary; indeed, some described their experience in traditional worship as "awestruck," "high church," or "separate," which, for them, prevented the kind of spiritual experience they hoped for in worship. In addition to a sense of God's immanence, contemporary worshippers seem to have longed for the intimate connections of community that often seemed absent to them in a larger worship setting. Several interviewees told me that the actual physical space between bodies in the large sanctuary made them feel disconnected, thus rendering the worship experience less meaningful.

The 8:30 worshippers seemed to share this desire for close contact between participants in their service, as well as the quieter atmosphere that comes with a smaller group. "Dorothy," who has attended the early service for decades, talked about how the smaller setting allowed worshippers to get to know one another and keep up with each other: "We knew where everyone sat. If someone wasn't there, we knew they weren't there." "Colin," who in his twenty-five years at First UMC had never attended anything but the 8:30 traditional service, said, "I like the 8:30 service, because the sanctuary is quiet. I liked the idea there were fewer people in there.... [The 11:00 service] was always full of people. You go in there before the service, there's all this chatter, this loud noise in there. To me, it never felt like a worship service." One might imagine that this is just a personal preference on Colin's part, and not something of theological import. However, Colin went on to explain that on the first Sunday that First UMC instituted the new worship schedule, he tried to attend the 10:30 worship service in place of his beloved 8:30 service, which had been eliminated. Colin described his experience this way: "And I go in there [the sanctuary] and, like I say, it was just packed full of people and just—I didn't enjoy it that much. I remember the next Sunday, certain people in Sunday school were talking about how they could just feel God's presence, how we all came together. And I sat in there going, 'Well, I wish I had felt him.'" Clearly, for Colin and for others accustomed to the 8:30 worship time, the peaceful, quieter atmosphere of the early service provided a clearer pathway toward connecting with the presence of God.

Likewise, worshippers from the 11:00 service imbued elements of their worship with theological significance. "Ann," who was relatively new to First UMC, said she prefers the 11:00 service because of the liturgy and the fact that there is a full choir; for her, the more formal atmosphere of this service meshes well with her desire for a "non-chatty" worship experience. When I asked Ann to elaborate on what she meant by "non-chatty," she said, "I think it's good to be friendly in the vestibule . . . and to make sure you welcome all the visitors and look to make sure that if they're in your row that you introduce them to the clergy afterwards, all those kinds of things. But I kind of—probably prefer . . . the time when there's silence so you can actually focus on the Lord and not be distracted." For Ann, then, it would seem that the very close-knit feel and personal sharing so cherished by the contemporary worship-goers could actually get in the way of her experience of God's presence in worship. As Ann makes clear, she very much values friendliness and personal interaction within the community of faith, but does not see those elements as particularly appropriate in a worship setting.

Like Ann, Judith expressed a strong affinity for the liturgy used at the 11:00 service. Judith explained her understanding of worship this way: "I need people around me worshiping because watching them worship is part of how I see God. . . . So I would say liturgy is hugely important to me, the words that connect me back with the saints." Judith went on to expand upon her love of traditional liturgy and hymnody:

> And then the liturgy, the words are more important to me. . . . I mean, I'm glad to have a sermon illuminate Scripture. But I don't want the sermon to be the focal point of the service. There's plenty of other elements in the service where the veil becomes very thin and you see God. . . . I'm kind of a person of the metaphor. So those hymns come to me in times when I'm just living my ordinary life because I've sung them so much or I've spoken a creed so much that those words pop into my head at times when I need for them to. So I'm kind of a person of order and I need that.

Interestingly, the sense of community connection that 8:30 and 8:45 worshippers said they missed in the 11:00 service was important to Judith too, but she said she *found* such a sense in the traditional worship setting:

> It's easier for me in a group where you're packed in and you can pat someone on the shoulder in front of you instead of they're three rows up and I might get to speak to them after the service. . . . I like the fact that if you're in a group closely together, then to me it says that what we're doing is important because we've all come together to do it. And I think it's easier to nurture when

you've got people around you than when you're sitting there alone. And I think worship is corporate. It's not your time alone with God; it's your time with God with others.

As these quotations show, First UMC members' reflections on what they find meaningful about particular worship services reveal deep theological dimensions to what otherwise might seem a superficial issue. Thus, the decision First UMC faced was not only a logistical one but also one that surfaced real tension between parishioners' different understandings of who God is, the nature of God's relationship to human beings, and the purpose of worship. For this reason, I maintain that although Grace UCC's conflict proved much more intense and volatile than First UMC's, both congregations had to cope with contending views about issues of theological significance.

Identity

The theological dimensions of these congregational conflicts were also inextricably linked with parishioners' sense of identity. These links often surfaced in the form of identifying with a specific group or position as the conflicts unfolded. Some members of Grace UCC, for instance, had strong ties to the denomination itself, which profoundly influenced their belief that the congregation should stay within the UCC. Charles said simply, "The history of the denomination means a lot to me. I grew up [in it]; it was the only church I ever knew." Similarly, Noelle, who became a member of the UCC later in life, stated that, "The more we've learned about the denomination, the more we felt at home, where our values coincided with the prevailing norms at the church. . . . So, you know, I'm committed to the church because I like its values, its national values. . . . And you know [leaving the UCC] would really be like leaving home." Noelle's use of the words "values" and "home" signals that, for her, the UCC represents more than just a denomination she chose from among others. Instead, it is an institution to which she feels intimately connected and which reflects her own deeply held personal commitments.

Others at Grace UCC felt less committed to the denomination itself, but more to keeping the congregation intact or preserving some of what they perceived to be its core values. "Jack," a lifetime member of Grace UCC, explained, "I've got no ties to the Conference, but I've got ties to Grace UCC." For this reason, Jack said, he wanted to do all he could to keep the congregation healthy and strong, and to him it seemed the best way to do that was to remain in the denomination. Christine supported staying in the denomination because it seemed like the option that most coincided with her personal beliefs: "I think that it's not up to us to determine who can be a part of our church and who can't.... I think the moment that when we stop welcoming people, we stop leading a faithful life." In fact, for Christine, these beliefs form a central part of who she understands herself to be—namely, an inclusive, welcoming person: "at the end of the day [I] *don't want to be a person* who shut other people out."[25]

At First UMC, people seemed to identify less strongly with their particular position on the worship issue than did Grace UCC members with their views on leaving the UCC. Yet, individuals' preference for their specific worship service frequently included very personal and theological elements, which they often described in identity-based terms. For instance, in talking about their preferred worship style, interviewees would frequently say "I am" rather than "I like" or "I prefer." Colin, who had worshipped at the 8:30 traditional service for twenty-five years, said, "I'm an early-morning person. Always have been." "Marion," a traditional 11:00 worshipper, described herself as a "real music [person]" who had participated in the choir for many years, which is why she preferred the 11:00 service and its traditional music. Similarly, in describing her affinity for the liturgy and hymns at the 11:00 service, Judith noted that "I'm a person of order" and "I'm a person of the metaphor." And Nancy, who found deep spiritual nourishment at the contemporary service, said that that particular style of worship allows her to be "free to be me, who I am." This tendency to talk in such personal terms belies an understanding of worship that connects deeply with individuals' sense of who they are. Parishioners' choice of one particular worship service over another often points beyond simple stylistic preferences to more profound theological convictions about how human beings relate to the divine. Thus, commitment to a specific kind of worship experience also appears to be intertwined with notions of "who I am in relationship to God" or "who I am as a spiritual person."

In addition to individual identifications with particular theological understandings of worship, many parishioners at First UMC experienced their service as a place where they took on a unique identity as a *member of a group*. As Nancy put it, "we became friends. It [the worship service]

25. Emphasis added.

became a community." Judith expressed a similar sentiment: "I think worship is corporate. It's not your time alone with God; it's your time with God with others." In this sense, each worship service at First UMC became a key category through which congregants interpreted important aspects of their religious identity. Gathering regularly with others who shared their understandings of worship helped form parishioners' understanding of themselves as church members and as Christians, and thereby cemented the link between their theological commitments and their sense of identity.

Polarization and Fragmentation

Another key theme that emerged in both the conflicts at Grace UCC and First UMC was the tendency to split into factions according to the positions individuals held about the issues at hand. At Grace UCC, this tendency proved quite dramatic: the congregation, made up of seemingly harmonious relations only days before the conflict erupted, suddenly polarized into two clearly defined sides. Jack, a lifetime member of Grace UCC, put it this way: "I don't know anyone that was on [one] side of the fence or the other that crossed over after the lines had been drawn." Others in the congregation seemed to agree with Jack's assessment. A teenager at the time of the conflict, "Sean" remembered the events this way: "And almost instantly the church was just split into like two factions, one that was ready to go because they didn't agree." Charles, who was serving in a position of leadership when the conflict began, observed that parishioners had quickly "divided into 'you' and 'they,' which is never good in a church situation." Indeed, this sense of impending fragmentation appears to have been extremely troubling for most everyone involved. As she looked back on the conflict and reflected on her feelings about it, "Lily," a longtime member of Grace UCC, said, "I guess to me it was just the thought that everybody that I felt was family was getting ready to split. It was kind of intimidating, scary."

As it turned out, the split at Grace UCC was not only a division between members but also an actual exodus of one entire group from the congregation. Early in the conflict, the group that had originally raised objections to the General Synod's resolution made it clear that if their position did not prevail in the vote, they would no longer remain members of Grace UCC. Tom, who shared deep personal friendships with some in this group, said, "those who wanted to separate made it very clear that if they lost the vote, they were leaving." Several of the other people I interviewed also remembered this aspect of the conflict quite clearly, and saw it as a factor that only exacerbated the sharp disagreement already present within the congregation. Jack put it this way: "I'm a little perturbed at, you know, 'okay, I'm not getting my way, I'm leaving.' You know, you don't always get your way, and I'm not saying conflict is good, but I'm saying it gives you a chance to come together with ideas and try to derive something from it." Similarly, Sean said, "I know churches will have disagreements in beliefs, but I really think it's not worth splitting a church in two for anything."

Congregational leader Charles had a slightly different view; he believed that some of those who initially advocated for leaving the UCC would have liked to stay at Grace UCC, but found it too difficult to do so from a relational perspective: "I think many of these people had painted themselves in a corner to where they said if you don't—if we don't leave, I'm going to leave. . . . I think in order to save face they just felt they had to leave." In any case, whether interviewees saw Grace UCC's fragmentation as a result of rigidity or simply the inability to reconcile relationships, all seemed to agree that the conflict in their congregation resulted in a rapid split into two opposing camps, with very little possibility of resolving the disagreement in a way acceptable to both sides.

The situation at First UMC was quite different, in that the various groups involved in the worship discussions did not become as hostile toward one another as they ultimately did at Grace UCC. Also, by virtue of the decision that had to be made at First UMC, the congregation naturally divided itself based on which worship service individuals attended, rather than according to a "pro" or "con" position on a particular issue. In this sense, the contending groups at First UMC were an artifact of the congregation's preexisting worship structure; that is, the groups were already formed when the conflict got started, whereas at Grace UCC, the groups seemed to form in response to the issue at hand. Yet, because the groups at First UMC were based on worship attendance, these individuals had already self-selected to be in those groups; in other words, just as Grace UCC members chose one side or the other in their conflict, members of First UMC essentially had done the same thing—they had simply chosen their position earlier, when they decided which worship style most closely matched their personal theology. For this reason, individuals' identification with their particular groups often proved quite strong, which ultimately contributed to the fragmentation that began to occur within First UMC in the face of impending worship changes.

Indeed, early on in my research at First UMC, Rev. Fisher shared with me that some traditional worshippers were quite suspicious of those who attended the contemporary service. To them, it seemed as though the contemporary worshippers were taking part in something strange, something that they did not understand and the value of which they had difficulty appreciating. In fact, according to Roy Sanderson, the founder of the contemporary service, some members of First UMC saw this service as "cheap worship" that held no spiritual depth. Roy also told me that contemporary worshippers were frequently stereotyped as Johnny-come-latelies who did not contribute much money to the church and who did not make a regular pledge of time and talents.

Yet, as the case study showed, the division among First UMC members was not limited only to their preferred style of worship, but also involved which particular worship service individuals habitually attended. At the first committee meeting, people sat with members from their own worship service, and there was palpable tension in the room as individuals braced themselves to fight for "their" service. Nancy, a committed contemporary worshipper, described the situation as follows: "I was involved in the [worship] committee meetings where people came and expressed their views and it seemed like the two [early] morning services were going to have to sort of battle it out. Who was going to win over who was going to get the morning slot? And that became really uncomfortable for everybody, I think." Thus, while 8:30 and 11:00 worshippers may have shared an affinity for a more traditional worship style, early service participants felt strongly about maintaining their own, more informal worship opportunity.

These 8:30 participants were clearly upset when, by the last committee meeting, they began to realize that the worship service they had attended and cherished for so long would probably not survive. Dorothy, who had attended the 8:30 service for more than forty years, described her feelings this way: "And of course, going into it, those of us who had been at 8:30 for so long . . . felt like we're having to give up the most, that this was comfortable to us." Roy agreed with Dorothy's take on the situation; according to him, at the point in the meeting where everyone acknowledged that the 8:30 service would likely be eliminated, "You could see some really, really, really good people being really, really frustrated and hurt. I could see it in the room going around. We're fixin' to—this thing's fixin' to blow. Because 8:30 folks felt like, 'You just crammed it down my throat. Why didn't we just do this four weeks ago?'" Thus, the challenge that First UMC faced in making substantial worship changes resulted in division along two different lines: one line divided traditional from contemporary worshippers; another divided 8:30 worshippers from those whose services were perceived to be "safe" from major alterations (8:45 and 11:00). In such an atmosphere, it was easy for tension and even distrust to develop, particularly when one group (8:30) felt as though no one else would be making any significant sacrifices.

The Pain of Conflict and Change

In reviewing the data I collected at Grace UCC and First UMC, a theme that kept recurring was the pain that interviewees experienced due to the conflicts and tensions within their congregations. This aspect came out especially vividly in the interviews I conducted at Grace UCC. Almost every single person I spoke with talked about how painful this conflict had been, and continues to be, for the faith community. Christine, who was a teenager at the time of the conflict, told me that "It was really difficult. . . . I know that some of those people, my family was close with before, don't really talk to them anymore and that's kind of hard." Similarly, Tom, who had been part of Grace UCC for many years, said, "For me, at stake was the loss of some very good church workers and close friends. And that has happened and my wife and I still feel that loss. People that we felt were good friends, anyway, have been very distant. . . . We still don't see them very much." Noelle, who had only been a member of Grace UCC for a short time before the conflict erupted, stated, "I still see the effects of that conflict in the congregation. . . . We're very careful about talking about the issue [of homosexuality] . . . for fear of stirring it up. . . . So I feel the conflict, the rending of the common fabric, or the fear of that is still great and still lingers in the congregation." Finally, Jack, a lifetime member of Grace UCC, simply said, "I just felt like it [the conflict] was going to tear the church apart and in essence it did."

Because the conflict was less intense at First UMC, this theme of pain took on a different form—more akin to pain resulting from the necessity of making any change, rather than pain from the decision-making process itself. In describing the process First UMC used to make its worship changes, Judith Murray, the chair of the committee, said, "We wanted it to be a process of many weeks of actually sitting and trying to discern what was right for the church. And we knew there was going to be pain." Esther, a vocal proponent of the contemporary service, described her feelings this way: "I was—yeah, I think I could say angry, frustrated—frustrated definitely, angry sometimes, that my opportunity for worship got moved and that the church was willing to give that up—not just for me, but for the other people who cherish that . . . that really bothered me." Nancy described her memory of the resulting worship changes in terms more akin to grief than anger: "And actually, I mean, it was just sad. I mean, the last few services of that 8:45 service when we knew we were going to nighttime, it was just sad because we just didn't like it, it was sad and we were giving up friendships and things that we'd established and it was kind of like having to leave town, move to a new city or something."

Clearly, the pain that people at First UMC experienced when they contemplated making changes to their preferred worship services was quite real. In fact, at times, members of different worship services felt that they were being asked to bear more than their share of the pain. Yet, at the same time, many of the people I interviewed from First UMC agreed that in the end, the solution that the church came up with meant that everyone would have to make sacrifices, and consequently, everyone would have to experience at least some pain. "Simon," a middle-aged man who had attended the contemporary service since its beginning, observed, "I guess the feeling was you wanted to make all three groups accept a little of the pain that would be involved in consolidating services." Esther, who had originally expressed frustration and anger about the contemporary service being moved to the evening, reflected on the events at First UMC this way: "Somehow it worked out and everybody came out with the feeling that this was the answer. Everybody was going to hurt in some way. It was going to cost a little bit in some way. But that was the answer." Nancy agreed with Esther's perspective, stating, "I felt like that what we had done had unified the church and that everybody had compromised a little bit and everybody had won a little bit and everybody had given up a little bit. So there wasn't one group that was being picked on. Everybody had to make some kind of concession for the times to change." Even Dorothy, who had attended the 8:30 service for more than four decades and worried about her group having to bear a disproportionate share of the pain from the proposed changes, said, "So in one respect I feel like everybody gave up something for what would be the better good. And I think overall we've adjusted."

The Role of Anxiety in Conflict

The common themes that emerged from the interview data are interesting in their own right, because they illustrate important similarities between two congregational conflicts that, on the surface, seem to have been quite different. Placed in conversation with the more general theme of anxiety, however, these themes take on even greater significance. In fact, as I will show below, each of these elements points the way toward a deeper understanding of how the *anxiety produced by encounters with difference* contributes to the development and intensification of conflict in congregations.

As I am using it here, the term *anxiety* refers to a basic sense of threat that may be either acute (in response to a specific danger) or chronic (generalized and diffuse). According to family systems theory, high levels of chronic anxiety within an organization tend to create more intensely emotional responses to acute anxiety-producing events. In other words, in any organization, major changes or problems will create a rise in acute anxiety. In a chronically anxious organization, however, these changes or problems will unbalance the system more dramatically than in an organization with less chronic anxiety. Family systems theory uses the term *reactivity* to refer to the "emotional expression of people's sense of threat."[26] Thus, while members of a healthy congregation can usually handle significant problems with relatively little difficulty, those same problems will often cause members of a chronically anxious congregation to experience more powerful emotional responses. In turn, such responses give rise to more intensely reactive behaviors—such as aggression, extreme compliance, or disengagement—all of which allow individuals to avoid dealing directly with their feelings of threat.[27] Given this framework for understanding how anxiety operates, one can now see how the themes I described above connect with the concept of anxiety as a key social force in congregations.

First, in describing the themes contributing to the complexities of the conflicts, I noted the many different layers of history, events, and relationships that formed the backdrop to the conflicts at Grace UCC and First UMC. Both congregations, for instance, shared long histories of previous conflicts among different pastoral leaders, and between pastoral

---

26. Richardson, *Creating a Healthier Church*, 91.
27. Ibid., 93.

leaders and their parishioners. Such elements seem to have caused levels of chronic anxiety in both communities to rise over time. As a result, when conflicts over the specific issues of denominational affiliation and worship structure arose, they triggered acute anxiety responses and threatened to create a severe imbalance in these congregational systems. In other words, because the history of both congregations already included complex webs of tensions, both communities were operating with elevated levels of chronic anxiety that made it more difficult to respond calmly.

As I have noted, the acute anxiety-triggering events in these case studies took the form of disagreements over important decisions that each congregation had to make. I argue that the core of this anxiety revolved around *encounters with difference* that individuals in these communities experienced in relationship to one another. These encounters with difference are illustrated through the themes of theology and identity discussed above. Indeed, as I stated in chapter 1, disagreements around theological issues within a single faith community raise a compelling but disturbing question for many church members: how can we be members of the same congregation and believe such different things? At Grace UCC, parishioners were suddenly confronted by the fact that they all belonged to the same church, but held vastly different theological views, both on the specific issue of homosexuality as well as on broader notions of scriptural interpretation and denominational affiliation. In the same way, the need to make structural changes forced the members of First UMC to face just how differently they understood the relationship between God and human beings as it is expressed in worship.

These theological commitments, in turn, contributed to individuals' affiliation with particular groups within the congregation. At Grace UCC, parishioners identified with either the group that wished to disassociate from the denomination or the group that wished to remain within it. Important elements of these individuals' sense of *identity*—including their commitment (or lack thereof) to the denomination and their allegiance to particular beliefs and values—had a strong impact on which group they chose. Likewise, at First UMC, parishioners had already expressed important aspects of their theology and their identity through their selection of a primary worship experience. When the administrative board required a fundamental change in the congregation's worship structure, these identity groups were brought into conflict with one another. Thus, in the events that unfolded at both congregations, church members were forced to confront significant theological differences in their midst—differences that raised levels of anxiety and that caused the development or entrenchment of particular subgroups within the faith community. The friction that then developed among these subgroups produced even more anxiety, which ultimately contributed to reactive behaviors and to the threat of fragmentation.

As the case studies revealed, the conflict at Grace UCC was far more reactive in nature than that at First UMC. In fact, all of the behaviors that Peter Steinke lists as characteristic of congregations with high levels of chronic anxiety—secrecy, accusations, deceit, triangulation,[28] and complaining—were on display at Grace UCC at some point during the conflict.[29] It is not surprising, then, that this congregation experienced such a rapid polarization of its members into two opposing groups—a development that, in itself, suggests the presence of reactivity.[30] In contrast, at First UMC, the conflict was much less intense. However, the interview data showed that this congregation also experienced the threat of fragmentation, since the conflict began with individual parishioners identifying strongly with their own worship groups. These groups had the potential to become rigid in their positions, which could have made the conflict at First UMC quite intractable. I suggest that in both cases, elevated levels of chronic anxiety, combined with the acute anxiety-producing trigger of encountering significant difference within the congregation, made the situation ripe for polarization and fragmentation. Yet, because each congregation coped with anxiety so differently, the outcome in each case proved markedly different as well.

Finally, although the respective conflicts at Grace UCC and First UMC developed in very different ways, interviewees in both places spoke frequently of the pain that accompanied the disagreements in

---

28. Within family systems theory, *triangulation* is a technical term referring to a phenomenon that often occurs when anxiety rises between two individuals or groups. Instead of addressing the anxiety directly, the anxiety is passed on to a third party. As Steinke notes, "A person feels relief from tension when anxiety is shifted to a third party, yet the anxiety in the original relationship is unchanged. It has been merely relocated" (Steinke, *Healthy Congregations*, 62). A classic example of triangulation is when person A talks to person B about her problems with person C, rather than talking to person C directly.

29. Ibid., 56–62.

30. See, for example, Richardson's discussion of "power struggle" as one of the most common patterns of reactivity within congregations (*Creating a Healthier Church*, 94–95).

their congregations. On closer inspection, though, the pain described by parishioners at Grace UCC appears to have been more intense, and primarily caused by ruptured relationships. At First UMC, the pain that interviewees described was more akin to the discomfort that accompanies any significant change, and seems to have been mitigated by the maintenance of important relationships throughout the faith community. The difference between these descriptions of pain, I suggest, lies in the varied ways these congregations handled the anxiety produced by the discovery of important differences in their midst. At Grace UCC, the acute anxiety created by the initial conflict unbalanced the entire system; consequently, church members began engaging in unhealthy behaviors in an attempt to cope with their emotional distress. These behaviors caused severe damage to parishioners' relationships with one another, and resulted in the literal fragmentation of the church body. At First UMC, the anxiety triggered by the need to make worship changes also threatened to unbalance the system, but in the end the congregation was able to handle the situation calmly without resorting to destructive or divisive behaviors. Consequently, the congregation did not experience the same kind of severe discord that plagued Grace UCC.

The major themes that emerged from the case studies at Grace UCC and First UMC are thus tied together by the central concept of anxiety. The complexity of the conflicts at both congregations signaled elevated levels of chronic anxiety and set the stage for severe system imbalance triggered by an acute event. Such an event came along when parishioners in both places discovered significant theological differences in their midst—differences that compelled them to identify with subgroups in the congregation and move toward the possibility of polarization and fragmentation. The development and entrenchment of identity groups, and the subsequent splitting of the congregations into smaller pieces, raised anxiety levels even further and threatened to make both conflicts impossible to resolve. At Grace UCC, anxiety translated into harmful behaviors, which produced severely broken relationships and a subsequent loss of membership. At First UMC, leaders and parishioners managed to minimize such behaviors and find a mutually agreeable solution to the problem at hand. As a result, members at First UMC ultimately felt that everyone bore their share of the pain that comes with important changes in communal life.

Conclusion

In this chapter I have told the stories of conflicts that emerged in two specific congregations: Grace UCC and First UMC. These conflicts took very different trajectories and, as a result, each congregation bore very different consequences. Yet, in certain ways, the conflicts in these two communities of faith also displayed strikingly similar themes—including theological dimensions, identity, polarization/fragmentation, and the pain of conflict and change. As I have shown, the combination of these themes illustrates the complexity of conflict, as well as the role of anxiety in the development of the congregations' struggles. Despite these insights, however, important questions remain: why, exactly, do feelings of threat to the self or identity arise in the first place? Why do these feelings produce such destructive behaviors in some situations of conflict and not in others? Are such experiences of anxiety necessarily a sign of pathology, or are they part of normal human behavior? To begin to answer these questions, I turn to a scholarly discipline that focuses explicitly on the understanding of the human person: psychodynamic psychology. In chapter 3, I will engage the resources of this discipline to see how they might further illuminate the etiology and dynamics of conflicts like the ones that surfaced at Grace UCC and First UMC.

3

Why Is Difference So Threatening?
Engaging Psychodynamic Psychology

At the end of chapter 2, I argued that *anxiety* is the central theme tying the cases of Grace UCC and First UMC together. To make this claim, I showed how anxiety interlocks with the four other major themes that emerged from the case studies, all of which demonstrate the complex nature of conflict—namely, the theological dimensions of conflict, identity, polarization/fragmentation, and the pain of conflict and change. The concept of anxiety helps explain why and how the disagreements at Grace UCC and First UMC developed as they did. Because anxiety played such an important role in both of these conflicts, I will carry it forward as an organizing principle in the remaining chapters of this book, which further analyze the case studies from psychodynamic, social psychological, and theological perspectives.

As I embark upon this analysis, I continue to rely on the definition of anxiety as a basic "sense of threat" to one's person or selfhood.[1] I acknowledge that the other scholarly disciplines I engage in subsequent chapters do not necessarily use the term *anxiety* in their descriptions of human functioning. Nevertheless, I argue that anxiety as a sense of threat to the self can be broadly applied in a wide range of discussions about human life and functioning. This foundational definition of anxiety forms

---

1. Richardson, *Creating a Healthier Church*, 42.

a central thread connecting the other disciplines I am using, bringing them together to illuminate the problem of congregational conflict. In this chapter, I tie this theme of anxiety even more closely to the notion of identity by arguing that when individuals experience threats to their sense of self, they become anxious. As a result, persons often engage in ineffective or destructive behaviors in an attempt to soothe the anxiety they are feeling.

I begin my analysis of the case studies by engaging a discipline that specializes in exploring human personhood: psychodynamic psychology. The term *psychodynamic psychology* refers to psychological theories that understand the human person in terms of conscious and unconscious forces, which guide individuals toward particular goals in their growth. Sigmund Freud, widely recognized as the father of modern psychology, was one of the first to theorize such unconscious forces, or "drives," as key factors in the development of the human personality. Freud understood the human psyche in terms of ongoing conflict between three basic structures of the mind—the id, ego, and superego.[2] According to Freud, intense sexual and aggressive drives emanate from the id and seek release within the closed system of the mind; that is, if energy builds up in any part of the system, it must necessarily seek relief, or "discharge," somewhere.

Freud thus understood the central task of psychological development as the ego's successful negotiation of the competing demands of the id, superego, and external reality. Under ideal conditions, the ego is able to meet these demands by finding appropriate means for the release of the id's energies without conflicting too severely with the harsh strictures of the superego or the expectations of the external world. However, when the ego feels weak in the face of these demands and is unable to satisfy them appropriately, it uses *repression* as its key defense mechanism. Repression relieves the ego's anxiety by removing troubling thoughts or affects from consciousness. Yet, even when the ego represses the impulses generated by the id, they continue to seek reentry, like someone pounding on a locked door. When repressed thoughts and affects continue to place strain on the ego, the person develops symptoms, and neurosis results. For Freud, neurosis represents the central problem human beings face, and it is the primary ailment psychoanalysis is designed to heal. As is clear from this very brief sketch of Freud's theory, Freud presents a model

2. Though Freud's theory of the mind shifted over time, he eventually committed to this theory, a "structural model."

of mental life that is almost completely intrapsychic in its focus. Indeed, Freud's understanding of human development as dominated by constant negotiation between psychic structures proves highly individualistic, and leaves very little room for the self to attend to the impact and influence of interpersonal relationships or wider social contexts.

For some of the psychological theorists who built on Freud's work, this highly intrapsychic model based primarily on the drive to attain pleasure or satisfy aggression seemed out of touch with the way that human beings actually mature. Although many of these thinkers agreed that sexuality and aggression are important aspects of human behavior, they wondered whether Freud's structural theory missed a key aspect of human development—namely, the drive toward *relationships*. This interest in the role of relationships in personality development became the capstone of two specific schools of thought within psychodynamic psychology: object relations theory (ORT) and Heinz Kohut's self psychology. Although these schools of thought vary in important ways, they also share two important characteristics: both are grounded firmly in the psychoanalytic (Freudian) tradition, and both understand the drive toward establishing relationships—rather than the drive to release sexual or aggressive energy—as the central factor in human health and transformation.[3]

To state it simply: object relations theory and self psychology focus on the role of primary relationships in human development rather than on the discharge of physiological drives. Because this book deals with the fundamentally relational and communal issue of conflict in congregations, object relations theory and self psychology prove a more natural fit for my analysis here than does classic Freudian theory. In what follows, I utilize ideas from these two schools of thought to explore the psychological aspects of congregational conflict. In so doing, I also use the concept of anxiety as a lens through which to examine human functioning from a psychodynamic perspective. More specifically, I draw upon particular concepts from object relations theory and self psychology—namely, splitting and projection and the alter ego need—to argue that anxiety is a natural human response to *difference*, which may be perceived as complexity or ambiguity in the self, in important others, or in groups. Such difference often causes individuals to experience threats to their sense of identity, which also generates higher levels of anxiety. If it is not

---

3. See St. Clair, *Object Relations and Self Psychology*.

managed well, this anxiety produces highly defensive and/or destructive reactions such as splitting and projection or rigid needs for sameness. In discussing these kinds of reactions, I also illustrate the ways in which they manifested themselves in each of the congregations described in the case studies.

While resources from ORT and Kohut's theory illuminate both case studies in certain ways, they do not apply equally well to both situations. As I noted in chapter 2, the conflict at Grace UCC proved much more emotionally volatile and divisive than did that at First UMC. For this reason, the defensive mechanisms of splitting and projection seem to have been much more pronounced at Grace UCC. In other words, because Grace UCC members' sense of self and the sense of the congregation's group identity felt more threatened, their anxiety was much more intense, and the defensive processes of splitting and projection surfaced much more strongly. In contrast, at First UMC, the congregants' overriding sense of identity was rooted more firmly in the church as a whole rather than in the subgroups represented by various worship services. In fact, many of the people I interviewed at First UMC said that although they very much wanted to keep their particular worship service intact, in the end they really wanted "what was best" for the congregation. This is not to say, however, that the parishioners at First UMC did not display strong desires for sameness. In the latter part of this chapter, I will argue that the pull toward sameness is helpfully clarified by Kohut's concept of the alter ego need, which was also operative in both of the case studies under examination here.

Splitting and Projection

History of Terms

In *Splitting and Projective Identification*, psychoanalyst James S. Grotstein notes that the concept of splitting first appeared in the field of psychoanalysis in the nineteenth century. Many psychiatrists of that era referred to it as "double consciousness," while in their 1895 text *Studies in Hysteria,* Joseph Breuer and Sigmund Freud describe a similar phenomenon that they call "splitting of consciousness."[4] In both cases, the kind of splitting described is a deeply pathological response, often in reaction

---

4. Grotstein, *Splitting and Projective Identification*, 3.

to trauma, which splits off an unwanted idea or memory and makes it inaccessible to the conscious mind. In his early work Freud referred often to "splitting of consciousness," but he gradually moved away from this terminology, choosing instead to emphasize the defense of repression as it functioned within his structural theory of the mind.[5] In other words, instead of focusing on the actual splitting of intrapsychic phenomena, Freud concentrated on the second part of the process: namely, the removal and suppression of unwanted elements from conscious memory through repression. Freud returned to the study of splitting much later in his career; however, the concept was more widely explored in the work of object relations theorists. For this reason, I engage the concepts of defensive splitting and projection primarily through the lens of object relations theory, while acknowledging that these terms have their genesis in much earlier psychoanalytic thought.

Basic ORT Terminology

Object relations theory (ORT) refers to a psychological school of thought that grew out of the psychoanalytic tradition originally established by Sigmund Freud. Primarily associated with theorists like Melanie Klein, Ronald Fairbairn, and D.W. Winnicott, ORT departs from classical Freudian notions of child development as a process of harnessing sexual and aggressive drives. Instead, ORT views human development in terms of "individuation," a process that "proceeds by way of diverse emotional attachments to familial and social 'objects,' which the child progressively internalizes and distinguishes from the self."[6] ORT claims that early relationships between children and their primary caregivers "leave a lasting impression. . . . These residues of past relationships, these inner object relations, shape perceptions of individuals and relationships with other individuals."[7] In this way, ORT acknowledges a more central role for relationships than was afforded by earlier psychoanalytic formulations.

Freud originally used the term *object* to refer to the target of an individual's libidinal drives. ORT, by contrast, defines an *object* as "that with which a subject *relates*. Feelings and affects have objects; for example,

---

5. Ibid., 4.
6. Calhoun, ed., "Object-Relations Theory," 342.
7. St. Clair, *Object Relations and Self Psychology*, 2.

I love my children, I fear snakes, I am angry with my neighbor."[8] Yet, within ORT, *object* also refers to the mental *representation* of important objects. My son, for instance, is an important "object" in the actual world of my social relationships, but he is also an "object" in my internal psychological world because I carry constructed representations of him in my mind. Thus, within discussions of ORT, one must be careful to distinguish between "the external person who is observable [and] the inner object, which is the mental representation of the actual observable person."[9]

One way to make this distinction clear is to use more specific terminology in reference to internal psychological objects, so as to differentiate them from actual people or things in the external world. ORT uses three key terms to describe an individual's intrapsychic objects: self-representation (SR), object-representation (OR), and object relationship (O/R). *Self-representation* simply refers to the mental representation of oneself. Self-representations may include both "narrow" and "broad" elements; narrow elements would include images of the self stored in memory, memories of the self at different points in life, or imagined images of a future self. In other words, narrow self-representations refer to direct and immediate images of the self, which may be either positive or negative. Broad self-representations, in contrast, may include images of groups or organizations that are related to the self in some important way. These may be referred to as "associated self-representations"[10] because they are not direct images of the self, but of a particular category to which the self belongs. For instance, I might have an associated SR that includes general images of seminary professors or clergy persons because I am a member of both groups.

Object-representations (ORs) signify something important to a person that is external to his or her self. Like self-representations, object-representations can appear in both narrow and broad forms. Narrow ORs would include images of other people, whereas broad ORs would include nonhuman objects such as religious entities or abstractions of various types. Furthermore, both broad and narrow ORs may include past, present, and future images of the objects in question. To return to the example I used earlier: an object-representation of my son (which

---

8. Ibid., 6, emphasis added.

9. Ibid., 7.

10. This term and its definition come from Professor Volney P. Gay's teaching on ORT. I learned the term in the context of a course entitled "Post-Freudian Theories of Religion" taught at Vanderbilt University in the fall of 2008.

would be a narrow OR) might include memories I have of him, present images of his role in my life, and how I imagine him in the future.

The term *object relationship* (O/R) refers to how a person understands the relationship between his or her SRs and ORs. The O/R thus represents a relationship that is important to the self and that describes how the self relates to a significant object. The O/R may be either positive or negative and can therefore include a sense of deep attachment to or strong reaction against the object. To carry the previous example through: because my relationship with my son is a loving one, the O/R between my self-representation and the object representation of him is primarily a positive one that creates a feeling of connection.[11] These concepts of self representation, object representation, and object relationship are central to the current discussion of splitting and projection because, as I will show below, these are *intrapsychic* mechanisms that are applied to mental representations of the self or others.

Defensive Splitting and Projection in ORT

Having established basic definitions of the intrapsychic "objects" that form the focus of ORT, it is now possible to explore how the concept of *splitting* operates within this theoretical framework. James Grotstein defines splitting as "*the activity by which the ego discerns differences within the self and its objects, or between itself and objects.*"[12] Thus, in its most basic sense, splitting is a value-neutral term that simply refers to the self's ability to make distinctions between intrapsychic phenomena. However, when used in its defensive sense, splitting refers to the self's attempt to "split itself off from the perception of an unwanted aspect of itself" or to "split an object into two or more objects in order to locate polarized, immiscible qualities separately."[13] Both of these kinds of defensive splitting tend to separate self or objects into "all good" or "all bad" categories.

Melanie Klein, considered by many to be one of the co-founders of ORT, has noted that this kind of splitting begins in the earliest days of infancy (the "pre-Oedipal"stage), and that it is initially part of normal

---

11. This is not to say that I never have any negative or conflicted feelings toward my son, but simply that the majority of my feelings toward him are positive. In fact, as I will discuss below, the inability to hold together positive and negative feelings about an important object is a major factor in splitting and projection.

12. Grotstein, *Splitting and Projective Identification*, 3, emphasis in original.

13. Ibid.

human development. At this stage, a baby will split his conception of his mother into two separate entities: the "good breast" who "satisfies all [the baby's] desires," and the "bad breast" who is held responsible for the baby's feelings of hunger, pain, or other discomfort.[14] According to Klein, the baby experiences the "good" and "bad" breasts as two completely different realities; doing so helps the baby cope with powerful contradictory feelings of love and hate toward the mother.[15] Likewise, Vamik Volkan, a contemporary psychoanalyst and psychiatrist, explains that when infants experience instances of pleasure (having a clean diaper or being held) and pain (being cold or hungry), they lack the capacity to understand that both these positive and negative aspects are contained in a unified self. As a result, they split these experiences into "the pleasant *I*" and "the unpleasant *I*," keeping the positive associations located within "the pleasant *I*," and externalizing the negative ones.[16]

As the infant matures, he or she is forced to accomplish the task of bringing dissimilar pieces of experience together—to merge the pleasant and the unpleasant "I," as well as to merge positive and negative aspects of beloved objects into singular entities: "The child attempts to create a whole object from disparate parts—to make gray from black and white."[17] This process of "gray-making" begins at about six months of age, and is typically completed around the age of thirty-six months. At that point, "the child should be able to tolerate ambivalence—to love and hate the same person or himself at any given time."[18] Thus, although splitting originates as a normal part of the child's orientation to external reality, over time it becomes unnecessary as the child learns that both good and bad qualities can be contained in the same person.

However, even in the case of "normal" human development, the process of gray-making is never totally complete. As the child grows into adolescence and then into adulthood, small remnants of "black" and "white" persist within his or her self- and object-representations. If these remnants were allowed to remain unintegrated in the self, they would become sources of perpetual internal conflict and fragmentation. Instead,

---

14. Klein, *Love, Hate and Reparation*, 59.
15. Ibid., 60.
16. Volkan, *The Need to Have Enemies and Allies*, 29, emphasis in original.
17. Ibid.
18. Ibid.

they are split off and placed on "suitable targets of externalization."[19] In this way, the intolerable or "bad" qualities can be removed from the self-representation and placed on someone else. Likewise, "bad" qualities of a beloved object can be projected onto another person, who then becomes an enemy that can be hated completely.

The notion of externalizing the "bad" qualities of the self or beloved objects points to a key characteristic of this kind of splitting: as opposed to the normal splitting that takes place in early child development, splitting that persists into adolescence and adulthood is *defensive* in nature. It is designed to defend the self against perceived threats. As I have already noted, basic threats to the self typically produce generalized anxiety within individuals; anxiety thus represents one of the most common catalysts for defensive splitting. I argue that such anxiety frequently arises in response to an encounter with *difference* that feels threatening in some way. Anxiety-producing difference may come from outside—such as experiencing another person or group as profoundly different from the self—or from inside, when a person's self-representations appear too complex or ambiguous. In this case, aspects of an individual's SRs are experienced as "different from the rest of me";[20] consequently, the person's SRs feel too heterogeneous and difficult to contain, which creates anxiety. Such intense anxiety may then cause a person to feel that his or her self is at risk of fragmenting or disintegrating. In other words, the unified self that was achieved during childhood, and that has managed to incorporate both good and bad qualities, may feel threatened by the anxiety created by the remnants of intensely positive or negative aspects within the self. Thus, when understood from an ORT perspective, the anxiety created by the remnants of all-good or all-bad qualities in self-representations can spur a person to find ways of getting rid of the unintegrated pieces. In many cases, defensive splitting may prove the most accessible remedy for the powerful discomfort generated by such threats to the self.

When individuals are unable to tolerate certain aspects of their SRs, they remove them by splitting them off from other aspects of these mental representations. The split-off qualities are then ascribed to an object external to the self, to which the self often responds with aggression. This process, known as *projection*, is recognized as a "basic and primitive ego defense," and often arises when the self feels threatened

19. Ibid., 31.
20. Edelson, "Scapegoating," 250.

in some way.²¹ Contemporary psychoanalyst Marshall Edelson describes projection as the process by which the self creates a "container" for those aspects that it cannot bear to possess: "If there is something in myself that is different from the rest of me, that I feel doesn't belong in me, you become a container in which I can throw what I want to disown in myself, just by imagining that what I feel to be not-me is in you. You can be the container in which I dispose of my garbage, which has become *nothing-to-do-with-me*."²²

Edelson's description demonstrates how projection defends the self from unwanted qualities and the uncomfortable feelings of ambiguity they produce. So, for example, if I cannot tolerate the idea that I am lazy (or sick or arrogant, etc.) I will split that trait off from my self-representation and project it onto someone else. Such splitting and projection are defensive maneuvers designed to maintain an integrated sense of self in the face of anxiety-producing threats. Yet, it is important to recognize that defensive splitting and projection are *unconscious* processes. In other words, people are not aware that they are splitting off unwanted aspects of their self-representations and projecting them onto others. Again, in early childhood such a maneuver constitutes a normal part of the developmental process; later, though, it represents a defensive mechanism that arises when a person has difficulty holding seemingly opposed traits together in his or her self-representation.

Splitting and projection may also occur when a person cannot tolerate contradictory elements within a beloved object. In this case, to cope with the anxiety produced by such contradiction, individuals may split representations of other persons or groups into separate hated or beloved entities. In *Playing Pygmalion: How People Create One Another*, psychotherapist and professor of psychology Ruthellen Josselson describes how this kind of splitting operates within the context of interpersonal relationships:

> People are bonded through their mutual creations, each carrying a part of the other that the other either can't recognize (in terms of positive aspects) or can't bear (negative ones) in the self . . . we can also enlist people to be villains and spend our lives defending ourselves against them, we can create people as needy and spend our lives enslaved to them, or, as parents,

---

21. Gay, "Glossary of Technical Terms and References," 6.
22. Edelson, "Scapegoating," 250, emphasis in original.

create children as disowned parts of ourselves and then punish or reject them for it.[23]

While Josselson does not actually use the term "splitting" in her discussion of these defensive processes, the reality she describes meshes well with the phenomenon of splitting under examination here. When Josselson speaks of "creating" others in a particular image—the villain, the dependent, the "bad" child—she is talking about the process of splitting objects into all-good or all-bad categories, to which the self can then react positively or negatively, with no uncomfortable sense of ambiguity. As Josselson notes, these categories most frequently originate from disowned parts of the self that have been split off and projected onto someone else. Yet, no matter what the origin of these categories, the goal of defensively splitting objects remains the same: to remove the uncertainty from one's relationship with important objects by refusing to acknowledge that both good and bad qualities can be contained within one person.

Collective Splitting and Scapegoating

Defensive splitting refers not only to splitting off parts of the self but also to splitting objects into two or more objects so as to divide their qualities into all-good or all-bad categories. When the object in question is a group, this process is called "collective splitting,"[24] and results in the division of the group into hated and beloved subgroups. A discussion of collective splitting proves especially relevant here, for two reasons. First, because this book addresses conflict within congregations, it is important to examine how the particular psychological concepts I am engaging might function within group settings. Second, it is important to acknowledge that within a case study approach, it is very difficult to access the internal psychological functioning and intentions of individuals. In this regard, collective splitting proves an especially helpful concept in that it moves the discussion from an intrapsychic focus on internal self- and object-representations to an exploration of the ways in which group members may utilize splitting and projection as part of interpersonal and group processes.

23. Josselson, *Playing Pygmalion*, 137.
24. This term and its definition come from Professor Volney P. Gay's teaching on ORT. I learned the term in the context of a course entitled "Post-Freudian Theories of Religion" taught at Vanderbilt University in the fall of 2008.

In *Internal World and External Reality*, contemporary psychoanalytic theorist Otto Kernberg notes that collective splitting frequently appears within the context of groups that "cannot tolerate any opposition to the 'ideology' shared by the majority of [their] members"; as a result, this kind of group "easily splits into subgroups which fight each other."[25] Similarly, pastoral theologian K. Brynolf Lyon argues that collective splitting is a common feature of conflict within communities of faith: when church members are unable to tolerate the inclusion of diverse qualities within one religious body, they split the community into subgroups that they then label as all-good or all-bad. When these dynamics occur, it becomes difficult for members of each subgroup to recognize others as unique human beings: "For both subgroups, the complexity and emotional depth of other participants in the conflict are occasionally lost. It is as if the members of the other subgroup are no longer subjects at all but rather objects or forces which are experienced as attacking or opposed to the self."[26] In such situations of intense conflict, collective splitting occurs, at its root, because the experience of too much *difference* within the group causes individuals to experience a threat to their *sense of self* or *identity*. When the self feels threatened in this way, intense anxiety develops. As a result, the individual begins to define those in the "all-bad" category in terms of how they affect the self, rather than as individuals in their own right.

Recall, too, that defensive splitting is quite frequently accompanied by projection. In a communal context, collective splitting and projection produce scapegoating, the phenomenon in which a group displaces blame and anger onto an individual or another group through defensive projective processes. Lyon studies this specific phenomenon in religious communities and describes in detail how it functions in such contexts:

> The basic process of scapegoating is this: disturbing feelings in some group members are unconsciously projected onto another individual or subgroup. In other words, as a way to protect against the pain of recognizing and managing these disturbing feelings in themselves, these group members imagine that those feelings are not present in themselves but only in those identified others. The group acts, therefore, as if it is that other

---

25. Kernberg, *Internal World and External Reality*, 213.
26. Lyon, "Paranoid-Schizoid Phenomena in Congregational Conflict," 278.

person or that subgroup of people who possess what is bad or distressing.[27]

This description clearly illustrates the processes of defensive splitting and projection that are under discussion here. In fact, many of the same characteristics that were highlighted in the previous discussion of splitting and projection appear in scapegoating as well; they simply take on new forms within a communal setting. These forms include two key elements that I discuss later in this chapter: the establishment of all-good and all-bad sub-groups, and the intolerance of complexity and ambiguity. As I will show, both of these elements function as attempts to eliminate the anxiety produced by encounters with difference in the group.

As with defensive splitting and projection in interpersonal relationships, scapegoating serves to protect the self from aspects that it experiences as intolerable, and that would create intense anxiety if they remained within a person's self-representation. Edelson describes the process this way: "Looking for some person or some group to *blame*, members put (*project*) what is unwanted in themselves into a member, subgroup, or group, already marked in some way as *different* or *other*. That is, they now perceive it to be *there*, outside themselves, where it can be extruded from their group or organization."[28] Here Edelson notes that in collective splitting, individuals not only seek to expunge negative qualities from the self but also from the *group* in which the self participates since group memberships are part of one's self-representation. Therefore, if there are qualities in a group to which one belongs that are unbearable, those qualities may also have to be removed in order for the self to feel protected. Removing such qualities through defensive splitting and projection allows an individual to simplify his or her relationship to the group, which becomes "all-good" and thereby minimizes the anxiety created by conflicted or contradictory feelings. Scapegoating thus serves to protect not only the individual self but also the "group self" to which individuals belong.[29]

Another hallmark of scapegoating involves the inability to tolerate complexity or ambiguity, either in the self or in a group to which the

---

27. Lyon, "Scapegoating in Congregational and Group Life," 143.

28. Edelson, "Scapegoating," 248, emphasis in original.

29. Lyon, "Scapegoating in Congregational and Group Life," 148. I will more fully explore the importance of group membership in identity formation from a social psychological perspective in chapter 4.

self belongs. Scapegoating begins when "disturbing feelings" arise within members of a group.[30] The need to split these feelings off and project them onto others thus seems to coincide with an inability to tolerate complexity or ambiguity within group life. The prior discussion of object relations theory showed that developing infants lack the ability to hold positive and negative qualities together in the same person. Yet, within just a few years, most children achieve this capacity and are able to recognize that the "pleasant I" and the "unpleasant I," or the "good mother" and the "bad mother," are contained within a single individual. When this capacity is not fully realized, or when the self feels threatened, individuals may respond with the unconscious defenses of splitting and projection.

Within a group context, a similar process operates: ambiguous or contradictory elements feel impossible to hold together. This generates anxiety, which drives individuals to simplify their experience by dividing the group into factions through either/or thinking, which is itself a form of splitting. For example, in a congregation, intense anxiety might cause individuals to split the group into subgroups that they then label as "supportive of the pastor" and "critical of the pastor." Such either/or thinking frequently leads to a process of scapegoating, because as positive and negative elements of experience are split off from one another, they can then be assigned to various persons or subgroups. It is important to recognize, however, that this process not only projects negative traits onto other people or subgroups but also pretends that these other people or subgroups *only* possess negative traits. In other words, in situations of scapegoating, one loses the ability to see others as complex individuals or groups with a diversity of qualities. In such situations, those doing the scapegoating lose "the ability to understand the scapegoat's behavior in terms of the scapegoat's own feelings, longings, and intentions. The scapegoat appears as having cartoonish feelings and longings rather than complex and understandable ones."[31] Subsequently, unwanted qualities of the self or the group are split off and projected onto another person or group; that person or group (the scapegoat) then becomes a flat, simplistic entity that one can wholeheartedly criticize or even hate without the discomfort of conflicted or ambiguous feelings.

Both in terms of interpersonal and group relations, the phenomenon of scapegoating proves deeply problematic because it grossly

---

30. Ibid., 143.
31. Ibid., 147.

misrepresents the true nature of human beings and the way human relationships actually work. Individuals are neither all-good nor all-bad, and every relationship—no matter how positive or negative—contains some ambiguity. This point highlights the role of *difference* in the processes of splitting and projection: when the self or beloved objects (including groups) are experienced as too complex or heterogeneous—i.e., as containing too much difference—the self (or the group to which the self belongs) begins to feel at risk of losing its cohesiveness and one's sense of identity feels deeply threatened. As a result, the defenses of splitting and projection emerge. This helps explain why conflict arises so frequently in groups like congregations, which pride themselves on cultivating intimate relationships among their members. In other words, the more we come to know others, the more complex they will seem, which in turn creates increasingly intense contradictory feelings. These contradictory feelings then generate anxiety as individuals struggle to hold together the positive and negative aspects in their representations of other individuals and of the group as a whole. If individuals are not equipped with healthy ways of handling such anxiety-producing feelings, they may resort to splitting and projection as a means of defending against them.

Application to the Case Studies

In this chapter I have established extensive definitions of defensive splitting and projection within an object-relations framework, and described some of the ways in which these mechanisms may function in communal settings. Now, I will show how these concepts illuminate the conflicts in the specific congregations described in chapter 2. I have already suggested that splitting and projection appear more obvious in the case of Grace UCC than in that of First UMC; I will explore possible reasons for this difference later in this chapter. First, though, it is important to flesh out just how defensive splitting and projection may have been operating in each of the case studies at hand. Chapter 2 clearly showed that the conflict at Grace UCC proved much more emotionally volatile than that at First UMC. At Grace UCC, the "discussions" around same-sex marriage frequently turned into heated exchanges, complete with raised voices and pointed fingers. Yet, the presence of emotional volatility does not necessarily mean that defensive psychological maneuvers like splitting and projection are operative. Indeed, because splitting and projection are, by definition, intrapsychic phenomena, there is no way to "prove" that such mechanisms were at work in this or any other particular conflict. However, if we return to some of the characteristics of collective splitting, we can begin to see that the conflict that emerged at Grace UCC displays many of these same traits.

In terms of the overall group dynamic at Grace UCC, it seems clear that "splitting" of some kind was taking place, since the congregation divided itself into two distinct groups: one that favored staying in the United Church of Christ and one that argued for leaving it. As I noted in chapter 2, I base this characterization on my own observation of how the conflict at Grace UCC played out, as well as on the perceptions of several of the individuals involved. As Jack noted in his interview, once the "sides" of the conflict were established, very little could be done to bring them together: "I don't know anyone that was on [one] side of the fence or the other that crossed over after the lines had been drawn," he stated.

Once the congregation divided into two opposing groups, they quickly began to see each other in very stark terms, based almost exclusively on their position on the issue at hand. In other words, members of each group began to identify those in the other group as "with us" or "against us," almost solely along the lines of whether or not they wanted the congregation to leave the UCC. This fact demonstrates several of the characteristics of collective splitting described above. For instance, in collective splitting, a group is divided into smaller subgroups that are labeled as "all-good" or "all-bad"; the members of the subgroups are stereotyped according to a particular trait that they ostensibly hold in common. Thus, the groups at Grace UCC were sometimes labeled as "pro-UCC" or "anti-UCC," even though individual members within the groups may have held more nuanced views toward the denomination. In some cases, members of the subgroups characterized each other with pejorative words and phrases, such as "un-Christian," "against Scripture," "liberal," "fundamentalist," "homophobic," and "irrational." Although these terms take on very different meanings depending on the context in which they are used, in this case it seemed clear that church members used them to create a sense of one's own group as "right" and the other as "wrong."

Splitting positive and negative aspects apart in this way allows individuals to get rid of unwanted characteristics within the self or the group to which the self belongs. In the case of Grace UCC, I suggest that individuals may have been deeply disturbed by a particular trait—such as tolerance of homosexuality or the appearance of bigotry—and as a result felt compelled to split that trait off and project it onto others through the use of homogeneous categories. More specifically, the passage of the UCC resolution may have caused many of the members of Grace UCC to reflect on the *self-representation* that they associated with their religious denomination. For some of them, the discovery that this associated SR contained a very powerful negative element (i.e., support of same-sex marriage) may have created so much anxiety that they felt the need to split it off from their SRs. In other words, to them it seemed impossible to maintain any SR that was still associated with the UCC; thus, the entire UCC-related SR had to go. Once this associated SR was split off from the self, its most undesirable characteristics ("un-Christian," ignorant of Scripture, etc.) could then be projected onto members of the opposing group.

In the same way, those who experienced their UCC-related self-representation in primarily positive terms (tolerant, supportive of pastors, etc.), may have also harbored some internal doubts about the issue of same-sex marriage specifically, or homosexuality more generally. Those doubts may have felt intolerable to them, and caused them to split those aspects off of their self-representations and project them onto those in the other group, labeling them as "homophobic" or as ruled by their "emotions." However, I assert that, in reality, people in both groups had more complex and nuanced ideas than what is represented in these stark categories. I know, from having been present during the conflict and from interviewing individuals who were involved, that some of those who wished to leave the UCC on theological grounds were actually wrestling with just how to understand homosexuality from a religious perspective. Likewise, some of those who wished to stay in the UCC had strong reservations about same-sex marriage and/or homosexuality, or about the denomination as a whole. Even though some of these nuances were stated publicly, the conflict continued to develop along rigid lines, with very little opportunity for productive discussion.

In addition to splitting off elements of the self and projecting them onto others, the events at Grace UCC also included splitting important objects into positive and negative categories. The clearest example of this appeared in a few parishioners' attempts to scapegoat the church's pastoral leaders as being the root cause of the conflict. Some of these parishioners felt that, because the other pastor and I had publicly voiced our loyalty to the UCC, we must also condone same-sex marriage. Others thought that by advocating continued relationship with the denomination, the pastoral staff was, at the very least, trying to force the church to be part of something with which many of its members disagreed. In short, these parishioners seem to have been unable to tolerate any theological complexity within their pastoral leaders. In other words, they could not reconcile the fact that they respected and admired many things about their pastors, while at the same time disagreeing so vehemently with the pastors' (assumed) position on same-sex marriage.

This is not to say that only those who wished to leave the denomination engaged in splitting. In fact, it is possible to understand some parishioners' staunch support of the pastors as "idealizing" behavior—i.e., imagining the pastors as all-good and splitting off any negative or ambiguous traits from their representations of their leaders. As I mentioned above, many of those who wished to remain in the UCC actually opposed same-sex marriage and/or felt conflicted about the issue of homosexuality in general. At the same time, these parishioners strongly supported the church's pastoral leaders in our advocacy for continued denominational affiliation. The awareness that the pastors might actually support same-sex marriage could have produced anxiety for some of these congregants and caused them to split that aspect off from their overall positive images of us. In fact, on more than one occasion, parishioners said things like, "It really doesn't matter what our pastors believe personally; staying in the UCC is best for the congregation, so that's what we should do." These kinds of statements imply that for some church members, it felt more comfortable not to reflect on the pastors' personal views related to same-sex marriage, because such reflection might reveal significant theological differences with which they were not prepared to cope.

This way of understanding the events at Grace UCC highlights another common characteristic of collective splitting: namely, the inability to tolerate ambiguity or complexity. Rather than seeing the opposing group as a collection of diverse individuals with varying viewpoints on a wide range of issues, the groups at Grace UCC quickly began to react to each other based on whether they wished to stay in the denomination or leave it. This kind of splitting occurs quite commonly within congregational conflict, and often results in caricaturing those with opposing viewpoints as having simplistic intentions and feelings. In fact, such splitting serves to protect the self or a beloved subgroup, not only from unwanted characteristics but also from awareness of its own bad behavior: "While each subgroup is aware of the insults it experiences from the other, it tends to be unaware of the injurious character of its own behavior toward the other subgroup or toward the pastor. The experience is more that of warding off threats to the self or valued others (including, for both subgroups, the beloved congregation) than having engaged in behavior that might potentially merit guilt or remorse."[32] Such a dynamic certainly seems to have been present at Grace UCC, in that at different times, proponents of both "sides" of the conflict used very contentious tactics and language in their approach to one another. Indeed, one member described the business meeting where the conflict initially erupted as "venomous" in its tone and in its effect on those present.

My interpretation of the events at Grace UCC—read through the lens of psychodynamic theory—is that both sides were, in effect, scapegoating each other, in that each group seemed to blame the conflict on the other's unwillingness to change. Those who wanted to stay in the UCC felt that if the others would simply "let it go" and be satisfied with writing a letter of complaint to the denomination, everything would be fine. Similarly, those who wished to dissociate argued that if the congregation left the UCC, they could keep their pastoral leaders and "nothing would have to change" other than the church's denominational affiliation. These positions fail to acknowledge any real merit in the convictions held by the other side and tend to cast the opponents as "the problem" that would be solved, if only "they" would be reasonable. As a result, the congregation began to see its conflict as a game with only one possible "winner"; we failed to imagine a way to stay together and still contain sharply opposing ideas about something as visceral as sexuality. Just as individuals, at times, struggle to contain conflicting ideas or feelings within themselves, Grace UCC was unable to contain conflicting positions within its "group self." Consequently, these positions were split apart and pitted against each other.

At First UMC, the phenomenon of splitting was still present, but in a much less virulent form. As I mentioned in chapter 2, the splitting of the congregation into three distinct groups according to worship service was most obvious at the initial meeting of the worship committee, in which individuals identified themselves physically by sitting with other members of their preferred service. Yet, at First UMC, the characterization of particular subgroups as "good" or "bad" was less apparent. Instead, the impression I got from the interviewees was that the situation felt more complex and, as a result, it was difficult to choose one service to eliminate

32. Lyon, "Paranoid-Schizoid Phenomena in Congregational Conflict," 278.

altogether. For example, in describing the committee's approach to its decision-making process, Simon, a middle-aged man who had attended the contemporary service since its inception, stated,

> I guess the main thing was we didn't want to basically just ignore a group and just say, 'hey, 8:30 and 11:00, you're identical. You've got the choir and high organ.' We just didn't want to say, 'boom, you guys are gone; just jump up to 11:00 and go,' because this other service is totally different. So I guess the feeling was you wanted to make all three groups accept a little of the pain that would be involved in consolidating services.

That said, it was also apparent from my interviews that, at least at first, members of each worship service went into the decision-making process with an inclination to fight for their particular service. Indeed, Nancy, another devoted contemporary worshipper, claimed that many of the members of the worship committee felt, "This is our chance to convince everybody that our service is the most important and the best." Such an attitude reveals some of the same in-group/out-group dynamics that frequently appear within collective splitting, since each subgroup felt compelled to advocate for its own survival. Within this process, individuals began to split off negative characteristics from their self-representation and project them onto other individuals or sub-groups as a way of protecting the self from perceived threats.

This happened at First UMC, though in a much more limited way than at Grace UCC. For instance, the senior pastor of First UMC told me that over the years, there were a few individuals in the congregation who experienced the contemporary service as an "irritant" and would have liked for it to disappear. Likewise, Roy, the founder of the contemporary service, shared that some in the congregation stereotyped the contemporary worshippers as outsiders who did not have deep roots in the congregation and who did not adequately support the congregation with financial resources. At least one person told Roy that he saw the contemporary service as practicing "cheap worship." These characterizations may be interpreted as attempts on the part of more traditional worshippers to project onto others their anxieties about something that they experienced as very different, and potentially threatening, to their sense of First UMC's identity.

Similarly, some of the contemporary worshippers I interviewed tended to describe the traditional worship service as "high church," "awestruck," or "separate." These interviewees also shared that the contemporary service felt much more "warm" to them and that they could sense God's presence much more easily in the contemporary service. While these statements do not directly characterize traditional worshippers in negative terms, they do carry a subtle implication that those in the traditional service were not as friendly and that their worship was not as closely connected with a very immanent sense of the Holy Spirit's presence. I suggest that a more subtle kind of splitting was going on through the description of the different worship services with opposing sets of terms: "warm" vs. "reverent," "casual" vs. "formal," "cozy" vs. "awestruck," "conversation" vs. "silence," etc. These pairs of opposites, though not necessarily negative, imply that each service contains only one side of the pair; thus, the contemporary service is somehow only warm, casual, and cozy, but not transcendent or reverent. Dividing the worship services into particular categories represents another form of the intolerance of complexity that so frequently accompanies collective splitting, and that may have contributed to the initial tensions between members of these different groups when it came time to address the worship issues at First UMC.

Still, although these more subtle forms of splitting were evident at First UMC, it would seem that the threat to the individuals' sense of selfhood—and, thus, their anxiety—was not nearly as powerful as at Grace UCC. People identified strongly with their preferred worship service, but by and large they identified more with the church as a whole; in fact, most of them said in their interviews that they wanted what was "best" for First UMC. For instance, "Arthur," a committed member of the 11:00 traditional service, said, "There was a sense that we're all in this together and it's not about me; it's about the church and its success. So that seemed to be the ultimate conclusion of most of the people." Similarly, Roy claimed that he would have agreed to eliminate the contemporary service altogether if it would have contributed to the overall health of the congregation: "I just felt like we were at a crossroads as a church, that it was gonna go south quick, and just—if we had to give the whole [contemporary] service up and never do it—to me, it would have been the right thing to do. You know? For the betterment of the larger church."

These reflections from members of First UMC suggest that although they felt strongly about maintaining the integrity of their own worship service, they felt even more strongly about keeping the congregation intact and resolving the conflict peacefully. In other words, the conflict at

First UMC likely posed less of a threat to parishioners' sense of self, perhaps because they ultimately identified more as members of First UMC than as members of a particular worship service. Psychodynamic psychology suggests that a decreased sense of threat to selfhood or identity means decreased anxiety, and thus less of a need for splitting and projection. This may help explain, at least in part, why First UMC experienced greater success in resolving its conflict than did Grace UCC.

The Alter Ego Need and the Desire for Sameness

The ORT concepts of defensive splitting and projection illustrate how, in a group setting, members divide the community into smaller subgroups as a means of protecting themselves against anxiety. Self-representations are closely tied to representations of the groups to which individuals belong; for this reason, people may experience too much complexity or heterogeneity within these groups as threats to their identity. If they grow too intense, such threats can generate strong splitting/projection responses. For example, suppose that a person's sense of identity is closely tied with mental representations of the congregation to which he or she belongs. If the congregation then experiences a conflict that highlights the diversity contained within it or that causes it to begin dividing into smaller subgroups, this can become a threat to that person's identity. The person may begin to ask questions like, "I thought that this congregation stood for X; now I see that many people here stand for Y instead. Where does that leave me?" As the individual's object representation of the congregation becomes more complex, or even broken into disparate parts, the person may experience increased anxiety and feel a need to identify only with one part of the object representation and reject the rest—often through processes of splitting and projection. This helps explain why congregations, which are voluntary associations of individuals who share deep relational bonds, can so quickly become embroiled in conflict characterized by either/or thinking and destructive emotional exchanges.

I have also argued that splitting and projection were more operative at Grace UCC than at First UMC. I speculated that the reason for this disparity lies in the fact that splitting and projection are defensive in nature. So, when the self feels less threatened, individuals feel less compelled to split off unwanted traits and project them onto others. Given the difference in strength of the splitting/projection responses between the case studies, I want to return to resources in psychodynamic psychology—resources less based in a framework of pathology and more rooted in the basic development of the human person. That is, rather than relying solely on concepts like splitting and projection, which are defined as "primitive" ego defense mechanisms,[33] I wish to examine the case studies through a psychological lens that views the pull toward sameness as a normal human need throughout the lifespan. In what follows, I argue that Heinz Kohut's concept of the alter ego need offers such a lens. Kohut's work "shares with object relations theories an emphasis on relationship and a retreat from the Freudian drive model."[34] However, Kohut also differs from ORT in an important way: namely, in his emphasis on how early relationships help form the structure of a person's developing *self*. As I will explain, the alter ego need represents one facet of Kohut's vision of human selfhood. Exploring this facet in more detail sheds light on the issue of congregational conflict because of its focus on the self's need for *similar others*.

Heinz Kohut and the Bipolar Self

Heinz Kohut was an Austrian-born psychoanalyst trained in the classical Freudian tradition who immigrated to the United States in 1940 to escape the Nazi regime. Although steeped in Freudian theories of the mind and the methods of psychoanalysis, Kohut eventually became convinced that traditional drive theory proved inadequate to explain the phenomena he was observing in clinical work with his patients, many of whom suffered from narcissistic disturbances.[35] Departing from Freud, Kohut ultimately theorized an understanding of the self that deemphasizes the drive to release libidinal energy and instead focuses on the cohesiveness of the self as the primary psychological goal for human beings.

Over time, Kohut also moved away from Freud's notion of the "tripartite self" (id, ego, and superego) and posited his own conceptualization

---

33. Gay, "Glossary of Technical Terms and References," 6.

34. St. Clair, *Object Relations and Self Psychology*, 145.

35. In the context of Kohut's work, the term "narcissistic disturbances" does not refer to "narcissism" as it is colloquially used, but rather to specific personality problems that Kohut believed resulted from incomplete development of the self's structure. According to Kohut, such stunted development results in a situation where "the self reacts to narcissistic injuries with temporary break-up, enfeeblement, or disharmony" (Kohut, *How Does Analysis Cure?* 9).

of the self as "the core of the personality, the nucleus of initiative for the unfolding of an individual's unique ambitions and purposes, skills, and talents, ideals and values."[36] Furthermore, through his therapeutic practice, Kohut, like ORT theorists, became convinced that the key period for healthy psychological development lay not, as psychoanalytic theory had claimed, in the oedipal phase (three to five years of age, with a focus on the mother/father/child triad), but in the pre-Oedipal phase of infancy (birth to two to three years of age, with a focus on the relationship between the primary caregiver(s) and infant). It is during this period, Kohut argued, that the fundamental processes of self-development occur.[37]

According to Kohut, the self develops primarily *in relationship* to important persons who are experienced as extensions of the self. As we have seen, psychological theorists in the school of object relations theory tend to refer to such persons as "objects," but Kohut prefers the term "selfobjects" as a way of designating that the caring persons perform vital functions for the child's developing self.[38] In this sense, these caring figures are not only "objects" in the child's psychological world, but "selfobjects" who are closely linked with the emerging selfhood of the child. Ideally, the individual's relationships with his or her selfobjects constitute an "empathic responsive matrix," which proves crucial for the person's psychological survival and maturation.[39] Kohut further theorized that within this relational matrix, the self develops within the framework of two main "poles": the pole of healthy ambitions and the pole of healthy ideals. Each of these two poles corresponds to a key need that persons experience intensely in early childhood: the "mirroring need" and the "idealizing need." The mirroring need involves the self's need to be admired, and to have an important selfobject communicate that "it is good you [the self] are here and I acknowledge your being here and I am uplifted by your presence."[40] Conversely, the idealizing need involves having "somebody strong and knowledgeable and calm around with whom I can

---

36. Randall, *Pastor and Parish*, 18.

37. Ibid., 35–36.

38. Although in his earlier works Kohut used the term "self-object" (with a hyphen), his later work—particularly *How Does Analysis Cure?*—changes the term to "selfobject," with no hyphen. Here I use the latter form of the term to reflect the development of Kohut's own usage of it over time.

39. Kohut, *Self Psychology and the Humanities*, 167.

40. Ibid., 226.

temporarily merge, who will uplift me when I am upset."[41] The idealizing need, then, focuses on the self's need to admire the selfobject, whereas the mirroring need involves the self's need for admiration *by* the selfobject.

Originally, Kohut's theory only recognized the existence of these two basic needs within the developing self. Thus Kohut proposed the model of the "bipolar self," with the mirroring and idealizing selfobject needs forming the two poles.[42] Kohut theorized that in healthy individuals, the mirroring pole leads to mature and healthy ambitions; the idealizing pole, in turn, yields mature and healthy ideals.[43] In later conceptualizations of self psychology, however, Kohut theorized that between the mirroring and idealizing poles exists a "tension gradient" (also called a "tension arc") of psychological activity that flows between the poles, and that forms the core of the self.[44] According to Kohut, this "nuclear self" represents the sense a person has of being a center of initiative that is continuous in space and time and cohesively organized.[45] Out of the tension arc develops a related set of talents and skills, which the person can use to accomplish those things toward which he or she is driven by ambition and led by ideals. As a result of this new theoretical construct, Kohut came to recognize a third narcissistic need—the need for "alter ego" or "twinship" selfobject responses. This need involves experiencing the selfobject as "essentially the same as the person's own self" or as one's "psychological twin."[46] Thus, the healthy fulfillment of the alter ego need results in the development of mature skills and talents, and the self's feeling of worth in the company of others who are experienced as "like me."

Kohut based many of his ideas about the alter ego need on his therapeutic experience with patients who had suffered severe deficits in this area. For instance, in recounting his relationship with a particular client,

41. Ibid.

42. See Kohut, *The Restoration of the Self*, 171.

43. Within this framework, ambitions and ideals both refer to a person's "basic pursuits" in life; the distinction between them lies in their origin (ibid., 180). Because ambitions arise from the mirroring pole, they are pursuits that emerge from within the person and that call out for affirmation through mirroring responses from important selfobjects. Ideals, in contrast, are pursuits toward which a person is led through the idealizing need—i.e., the need to merge with a selfobject. Thus, ambitions originate from within the self, whereas ideals originate in the selfobject that the self desires to emulate.

44. Ibid.

45. Ibid., 177.

46. Randall, *Pastor and Parish*, 39.

Kohut observes that "Her self was sustained simply by the presence of someone she knew was sufficiently *like her* to understand her and be understood by her."[47] Similarly, pastoral psychotherapist Robert Randall describes Kohut's conception of the alter ego need as follows: "Being surrounded by others the child experiences as 'the same as me' gives the child a sense of being 'normal,' anchors the child's self-continuity, and provides the sustaining power of knowing one belongs, to particular groups and to the human family."[48] In Kohut's view, the very psychological capacity for a healthy sense of belonging depends on adequate resolution of the alter ego need during the pre-Oedipal phase of development. In this sense, the alter ego need is also closely tied to a person's developing sense of *identity*. The basic feeling of belonging to a group of similar others "can help sustain a person when, by force or other circumstances, the person is placed in a foreign environment that threatens his personal and social identity."[49] In other words, the sense of belonging created by fulfilled alter ego needs can help soothe the anxiety that results from threats to one's identity. Thus, Kohut's conceptualization of the alter ego need clearly posits the desire for "essential alikeness" with others not as a pathological defect, but rather as a central, and potentially adaptive, facet of the human person.[50]

Archaic vs. Mature Alter Ego Needs

Kohut's concept of the alter ego need points to the sense of sameness with others as a vital component of normal psychic development. However, the usefulness of this concept does not end with its emphasis on the need for "similar others" in the life of the developing child.[51] In fact, Kohut's theory recognizes both "archaic" and "mature" narcissistic needs throughout the lifespan. Kohut posits the existence of both "archaic selfobjects that are the normal requirement of early life" and "the mature selfobjects that all of us need for our psychological survival from birth to death."[52] In other words, Kohut understands the needs for mirroring,

---

47. Kohut, *How Does Analysis Cure?* 196, emphasis added.
48. Randall, *Pastor and Parish,* 42.
49. Ibid., 49.
50. Kohut, *How Does Analysis Cure?* 194.
51. Randall, *Pastor and Parish,* 42.
52. Kohut, *How Does Analysis Cure?* 193.

idealizing, and alter ego responses as normal and healthy at all stages of life, with archaic needs being transformed into mature ones over time.

In terms of the alter ego need specifically, Kohut theorizes that, over the course of healthy psychological development, archaic alter ego needs become transformed into mature alter ego needs, which include "inclinations to seek out others who reflect and reinforce the essential qualities of the self."[53] Kohut describes this process as follows: "In normal development the baby's reassuring awareness of being surrounded by the voices and smells of a human environment leads to the older child's sense of strength . . . and subsequently leads to the adult's reassuring experience of being surrounded by other persons who are (nationally, professionally, etc.) *essentially identical* to him."[54] According to Kohut, then, the archaic needs for belonging experienced in childhood never disappear; instead they simply give way to more mature ones. If, however, archaic narcissistic needs are not adequately addressed in the pre-Oedipal phase, "defects, distortions, and weaknesses in the structure of the self occur."[55] When this happens, archaic alter ego needs may continue into adulthood and may manifest themselves in unhealthy ways. For instance, individuals who reach adulthood with unmet archaic alter ego needs may rigidly insist that others feel and think exactly as they do or may experience panic or rage when others "fail to function as available, empathic 'twins.'"[56] These manifestations of archaic alter ego needs in adulthood point to the intense power of such needs and carry important implications for the ways in which the need to experience sameness with others may affect human relationships across the lifespan.

Anxiety and the Alter Ego Need

Because I have chosen the concept of anxiety as the organizing principle for this project, it is important to reflect explicitly on what role anxiety may play in Kohut's understanding of the alter ego need. Admittedly, Kohut does not often use the term "anxiety" in his theorizing about the specific notion of the alter ego need. However, in *The Restoration of the Self* (1977), Kohut speaks in more general terms about the two types of

53. Randall, *Pastor and Parish*, 44.
54. Kohut, *How Does Analysis Cure?* 206, emphasis added.
55. Randall, *Pastor and Parish*, 45.
56. Ibid., 49.

anxiety that persons experience. The first, Kohut explains, occurs in an individual "whose self is more or less cohesive" and involves "fears of specific danger situations."[57] Kohut describes the second type as follows: "The second [type] comprises the anxieties experienced by a person who is becoming aware that his self is beginning to disintegrate; whatever the trigger that ushered in or reinforced the progressive dissolution of the self, the emphasis of the experience lies in essence on the precarious state of the self."[58] In his later work, *How Does Analysis Cure?* (1984), Kohut calls this latter type "disintegration anxiety," which he further defines as an intense fear of "the destruction of one's human self because of the unavailability of psychological oxygen, the response of the empathic self-object without which we cannot psychologically survive."[59]

This second type of anxiety thus has a much more diffuse quality than the first, and involves a feeling of overall threat to the self's cohesiveness.[60] It is important to reiterate that according to Kohut, disintegration anxiety arises within individuals who have suffered severe empathic failures in their early lives, and who, as a result, struggle to have any sense of a unified self. Consequently, the constant threat of the self's disintegration causes such individuals to experience depression and diffuse narcissistic rage. It seems obvious that people with such severe defects in self structure would represent only a small fraction of any given population. How, then, can we helpfully use this concept to address an issue like congregational conflict, which presumably involves persons along the entire spectrum of personality development?

Even acknowledging that "disintegration anxiety" refers to a very specific response within narcissistically disturbed individuals, it is worth

57. Kohut, *The Restoration of the Self*, 102.

58. Ibid.

59. Kohut, *How Does Analysis Cure?* 18.

60. I purposefully use the term *cohesiveness* instead of *identity* here to remain consistent with the way that Kohut talked about the self, especially in regards to disintegration anxiety. When Kohut spoke about the self, he typically did so in terms of the "nuclear self," which he defined as "an independent center of initiative and perception, integrated with our most central ambitions and ideals and with our experience that our body and mind form a unit in space and a continuum in time" (Kohut, *The Restoration of the Self*, 177–78). This is an individualized vision of the self that focuses on unity and integrity. By contrast, in this book I use the term *identity* to denote a more fluid reality—one that includes both individual and collective dimensions, which I explore more fully in chapter 4. That being said, throughout this book I acknowledge that challenges to one's identity can feel just as threatening as threats to one's individual physical or psychological self.

noting that Kohut's description of this response shares much in common with the central notion of anxiety I use throughout this book—namely, as a basic threat to the survival of the self. Building on this broader definition, I argue that the concept of anxiety contributes to a richer understanding of how the alter ego need might function within situations of congregational conflict. In what follows, I show how anxiety interlocks with the alter ego need in two specific ways in each of the case studies under consideration here. First, given that anxiety represents a basic threat to the self, it stands to reason that encountering significant differences with others in a group could intensify anxiety and make the pull toward sameness even stronger. Furthermore, recalling that Kohut theorized both archaic and mature forms of the alter ego need, one might imagine that higher levels of chronic anxiety within an organization could cause individuals to experience their needs for sameness in archaic (i.e., intense and rigid), rather than mature, forms. As I will explain, this seems to be what occurred at Grace UCC.

Alternatively, if we understand the need for similar others as a natural human need throughout life, we can see that strong, mature relationships with others "like me" might function as a way of soothing the anxiety raised by conflict or change. That is, when a group experiences an acute anxiety-producing event, one way of coping with that event is to seek the presence of similar others who reinforce the self through alter ego need fulfillment. In this sense, the need for sameness is a part of normal development, and, if it is expressed in mature forms, can contribute to human health and flourishing. If, however, something threatens to interrupt people's relationships with their similar others and thereby force more contact with difference, this can itself generate intense anxiety and cause groups to become more entrenched in their needs for "essential alikeness."[61] This description meshes well with the events that unfolded at First UMC, particularly in terms of the grief parishioners experienced at the thought of losing the similar others to whom they had become so attached.

Application to the Case Studies

The preceding section showed just how central the *desire for sameness* becomes in the overall picture of Kohut's theory. If we understand Kohut's

---

61. Kohut, *How Does Analysis Cure?* 194.

conception of the alter ego need as a powerful need for others "like me," we begin to see how this need may have operated at Grace UCC. In the events that unfolded at Grace UCC, individuals on both sides of the conflict felt most comfortable with those who shared their position and were deeply disturbed by the differences they uncovered between themselves and others in the congregation. In fact, in the midst of the conflict, one parishioner remarked to me that she was "shocked" by some of her fellow Sunday school class members' views on homosexuality because, although she had gone to church with these people for over thirty years, she had "never known they felt this way." For this parishioner, discovering such a vast difference between her own views and those of her peers felt like a threat to her own identity and to her understanding of the congregation's identity. In other words, this parishioner seemed particularly surprised and troubled by the *lack of sameness* between herself and her fellow church members.

I do not wish to suggest, however, that members of Grace UCC interpreted the desire for sameness in a purely literal way. Although those who wished to leave the UCC seemed, from the outside, completely unified in their belief that homosexuality is sinful, certain members of that group actually were not quite sure what they believed about homosexuality. Yet these same members *were* certain about their opposition to same-sex marriage and their conviction that the congregation should disassociate from the UCC. It appeared that the desire for sameness manifested itself more in terms of opposition to same-sex marriage and the preferred approach to resolving the conflict than in a unified belief about homosexuality itself.[62]

Similarly, the Grace UCC parishioners who wished to stay in the UCC actually held a wide variety of beliefs about homosexuality and same-sex marriage. However, two specific factors bound this group together and provided the "sameness" so many were seeking: commitment to a position of tolerance and a desire to retain the pastoral leadership of the congregation. First, many members of the group that wished to remain in the denomination valued a stance of tolerance over perceived exclusivity—a stance they believed could best be accomplished by remaining in the UCC. Charles summarized this commitment well: "That's why I'm happy being a part of [the] UCC . . . I believe at looking at all

---

62. As I will show in chapter 4, the reasons *why* parishioners at Grace UCC formed the particular kinds of groups they did are more helpfully explained by social psychology than by psychodynamic theories.

people the same, no matter what gender or their sexual preference. . . . I know they're God's children just like I would consider myself, and God really cares for them just as much as he does me." Others I interviewed at Grace UCC echoed Charles's perspective. For example, Christine put it this way: "I think that it's not up to us to determine who can be a part of our church and who can't. . . . I think the moment that when we stop welcoming people, we stop leading a faithful life." Evidently, for Christine and Charles, the need to believe exactly the same thing about homosexuality proved less important than the need to share a basic attitude of openness and hospitality toward others.

In addition to this shared support for a position of welcome, Grace UCC parishioners who advocated for staying in the denomination also shared a fervent desire to retain their pastoral leaders, who had made it clear that they would have to leave if the church chose to disassociate itself from the UCC. When I asked "Alice," who was fairly new to Grace UCC in 2005, what felt important to her about staying in the UCC, she replied, "I just felt like it's important to stay, because I supported Bill [the senior pastor] and I supported you." Similarly, Lily, a long-time member of Grace UCC, indicated that loyalty to the UCC itself was not the key factor in her decision to vote for remaining in the denomination, but rather loyalty to the pastoral staff: "it's not so much based on staying in the UCC as much as it was the benefit of staying with [and] having the benefits for our ministers." Thus, although the group of Grace UCC parishioners who advocated for staying in the UCC held a diversity of views on homosexuality and same-sex marriage, they seem to have found a level of comfort in the sameness they shared with others in the group by emphasizing a position of tolerance and through their commitment to retaining their pastoral leaders.

These examples from the case study of Grace UCC highlight how the alter ego need—or the need to experience sameness with others—may have been operating for each of the groups involved. In addition to Kohut's description of the alter ego need itself, his understanding of archaic and mature alter ego needs also provides a helpful analytical tool in this case. As noted above, Kohut theorized that if archaic alter ego needs are not adequately met in childhood, they may persist into adulthood in unhealthy forms. Such forms could include a rigid insistence on uniformity between the self and others, as well as expressions of panic or rage when others refuse to play the role of "available, empathic 'twins.'"[63]

63. Randall, *Pastor and Parish*, 49.

It is unrealistic to suggest, however, that all of the members of Grace UCC—or even a majority of them—would display archaic alter ego needs due to severe disorders of the self. What, then, could account for the strong needs for sameness that surfaced among parishioners at Grace UCC? Randall notes that while archaic alter ego needs are "chronically present" in individuals with severe defects of the self, they are also "passingly present in periods of special stress in those free of self pathology."[64] In other words, when individuals experience intensely stress-inducing events, they are more likely to regress to archaic forms of their alter ego needs. This way of understanding the return to archaic alter ego needs in adulthood helps to depathologize it. Instead of seeing this phenomenon as limited to persons with significant personality disorders, it is now possible to understand it as falling within the range of normal human responses to stress. Furthermore, this perspective provides a helpful tool for interpreting what happened in many of the Grace UCC meetings, particularly in terms of the extreme emotional volatility displayed in the initial business session when the conflict erupted: when parishioners encountered a lack of sameness between themselves and their peers on an issue as fundamental (from their point of view) as homosexuality, they experienced intense anxiety. As a result, their archaic alter ego needs surfaced in the form of rage and an intense desire to convert others to their point of view.

Admittedly, the powerful emotional reactions expressed during the initial meeting at Grace UCC came primarily from those who were arguing for disassociation from the UCC. It is tempting to assume that only this group experienced archaic alter ego need responses in the course of this conflict. However, the theory would suggest that those in the so-called pro-UCC group also experienced archaic alter ego needs for sameness, but along different lines. I make this suggestion based on the observation that those who wished to stay in the UCC were especially offended by remarks made by many in the other group, who stated that they would leave if the vote did not go their way. While many in the pro-UCC group were initially willing to try to work toward a compromise, the other group's threat to leave became the straw that broke the camel's back. Members of this group also seemed to experience a strong desire for sameness—not in terms of beliefs about homosexuality, but in terms of what they perceived as loyalty to the congregation itself, as well as loyalty

---

64. Ibid.

to the church's pastoral leaders. When these parishioners discovered that others did not share this loyalty, they became more anxious and were consequently more willing to sever their relational bonds.

Because the conflict at First UMC played out so differently, the expression of the alter ego need took on a very different form there. At First UMC, most people stated that they did not necessarily want everyone to be "the same" in terms of worship preferences, even as they expressed a strong desire to keep their own worship service intact. For example, when I interviewed Roy, the founder of the contemporary service, he made it clear that his intention in starting a new service was never to replace the traditional worship that was already going on at First UMC. According to Roy, his message to the leaders of the traditional service was, "I want you to have the greatest traditional [service] you can have; I'm not saying let's don't do that. . . . I don't want to compete with you." Yet, at the beginning of the period for decision making about worship changes at First UMC, individuals' anxiety seems to have risen dramatically. Why was this the case?

One could speculate that any major change has the potential to raise fears among people, particularly when that change affects the ways in which individuals experience their connection with God. It is also possible, however, that the anxiety that developed at First UMC relates specifically to the alter ego need through the fear of losing the "similar others" that congregants had found through their participation in their chosen service. In other words, by choosing their particular service, individuals managed to identify others with whom they experienced a great deal of sameness in terms of their preferred worship style. Simon, a longtime member of the contemporary service, put it this way: "We each have our own service and we go to it because that's where we've decided to go. We like the people that go to it." Also, as I noted in chapter 2, affinity for a particular worship service involved more than just superficial preferences; in many cases it reflected different ways of experiencing God's presence depending on the worship style used in those services. Worshippers shared not only preferences for particular types of music or times for worship but also strong theological resonances with others in their groups. If substantial changes were made to the worship structure, these "similar others" might disappear, which would be experienced as an important loss.

Understanding the events at First UMC in this way helps explain why those participating in the 11:00 worship service felt the lowest level of anxiety: they felt confident that a traditional, late morning service would continue to be a feature of First UMC's common life, and thus they were at less risk of losing contact with the similar others from their service. By contrast, the highest level of anxiety existed among the 8:30 worshippers, who believed they were the most likely to lose their service altogether, and, with their service, the similar others with whom they had been in relationship for so long. For their part, the contemporary worshippers also expressed grief about the potential loss of the special quality of relationships that had developed in the context of their worship service. Indeed, for many of them, these relationships were what had drawn them to that service most powerfully in the first place. When the decision was made to move the service to 5:00 on Sundays, these parishioners recognized that aspects of this service would never again be quite the same, because the mix of people would necessarily be different. Nancy captured this sense of grief well when she remarked, "The last few services of that 8:45 service when we knew we were going to nighttime, it was just sad because we just didn't like it, it was sad and we were giving up friendships and things that we'd established and it was kind of like having to leave town, move to a new city or something." In this sense, we can understand the difficulties posed by the decision-making process at First UMC not simply as resistance to change itself, but rather as resistance to the potential loss of similar others who had been fulfilling important alter ego needs for worship participants at all three of the congregation's worship services.

Conclusion

This chapter has shown that the discipline of psychodynamic psychology contributes to a deeper exploration of particular elements that may play a role in congregational conflict. From a psychodynamic perspective, the anxiety raised by difference and the desire for sameness are impulses that originate as a normal part of human development. However, these natural inclinations can also become defensive or regressive, and can often lead to the adoption of destructive behaviors designed to ward off threats to the self or to enforce uniformity throughout a group. Yet, even though these phenomena frequently produce social consequences, their nature remains intrapsychic. That is to say: the splitting/projection and alter ego responses described by psychodynamic theory ultimately originate in the minds of individual persons. Furthermore, psychodynamic psychology understands the sense of self primarily in individual terms and pays scant attention to the role of group memberships in identity formation. Because congregational conflict, by definition, is a social phenomenon, it is vital to engage additional theoretical resources that can address its communal aspects—both in terms of social identity and in terms of general group dynamics. The discipline of social psychology provides just these kinds of resources, which I explore in chapter 4.

4

Why Do Group Identities Matter?
Engaging Social Psychology

In chapter 3, I used insights from object relations theory and self psychology to show that from a psychodynamic perspective, the anxiety raised by difference begins as a normal part of human maturation. According to ORT, developing infants naturally split self- and object-representations into all-good and all-bad categories as a means of coping with the complexity of their world. Likewise, through the notion of the alter ego need, self psychology claims that the drive to seek out similar others is a fundamental requirement for developing selves throughout the lifespan. Both of these schools of thought, however, also describe ways in which the natural anxiety provoked by difference may become defensive or regressive, and thereby impairing optimal psychological functioning. Intense anxiety may produce defensive splitting and/or projection, both of which damage individuals' ability to integrate contradictory elements into cohesive images of themselves, others, or groups. Such anxiety may also cause individuals to express archaic alter ego needs through rigid demands for sameness or to react strongly against perceived differences that threaten their relationships with similar others. These psychodynamic concepts help explain why, in seemingly unified groups like congregations, conflict can erupt so suddenly among clearly defined subgroups.

Despite these important insights, however, a psychodynamic approach to congregational conflict fails to answer two important questions:

(1) *Why* do these subgroups develop in the first place? Or, put another way, what role do individuals' *group memberships* play in the development of conflict, and what does this help us see about conflict that a purely individual approach might miss? (2) Once they have formed, *why* do subgroups within a congregation choose one particular strategy over another? In other words, why do groups choose to fight, to yield, or to work together toward a mutually agreeable solution? The discussion of collective splitting in chapter 3 touched on the role of group affiliation in terms of self-representations and how they potentially contribute to protecting one's sense of identity. However, self-representations are, by definition, intrapsychic entities; as such, psychodynamic interpretations of how they function remain individualistic in their focus. In this sense, psychodynamic tools tend to examine congregational conflict as a problem that emerges primarily from dynamics related to the growth or pathology of individual selves.

By contrast, the discipline of *social psychology* helps explain what happens in the social sphere of human interaction in a way that is not adequately addressed with psychodynamic tools only. In its broadest sense, social psychology may be defined as "the branch of psychology that deals with social interactions, including their origins and their effects on the individual."[1] This definition points to the importance of looking to the realm of social contact as a key source for understanding how individuals relate to one another and to society as a whole. Like psychodynamic psychology, social psychology presents identification with groups of similar others as a natural social process, and offers theoretical explanations for the ways in which social groups behave toward one another. For instance, *social identity theory* and *self-categorization theory* offer frameworks for understanding why and how social groups form and what role group memberships play in social interaction. Similarly, *strategic choice theory* describes conflict in terms of specific behaviors and provides an explanation for why individuals and groups choose particular strategies in their relations with one another.

In this chapter, I draw on particular aspects of these social psychological resources to examine the complex relationships between anxiety, identity, and conflict in the congregational case studies. I should note from the outset that, generally speaking, the discipline of social

---

1. *Oxford Dictionaries Online*, s.v. "Social Psychology," http://www.oxforddictionaries.com/us/definition/american_english/social-psychology (accessed April 13, 2015).

psychology does not use the term *anxiety* as an analytic tool. Nonetheless, I argue that bringing the concept of anxiety into conversation with social psychological insights illuminates the issue of congregational conflict in a uniquely helpful way. For example, while identification with social groups is a normal outcome of human interaction, the development of highly polarized groups may itself function to raise levels of anxiety among group members. Increased levels of anxiety may then propel group members to react to one another in more hostile ways. Conversely, when groups are able to maintain lower levels of anxiety in their midst, they may be more likely to engage in cooperative behaviors and to seek integrative solutions to their problems.

Collective Identification

Before engaging in a detailed analysis of the case studies, I must first establish how social psychology understands the development of identity within a social context, as well as the unique characteristics of intergroup relations. The notion of *collective identification* provides a broad theoretical framework in which to understand the nuances of the case studies at hand. To illustrate the importance of collective identification within situations of intergroup conflict, I examine two major social psychological theories that have devoted sustained attention to this dimension of human life: social identity theory and self-categorization theory. According to these theories, the realm of social interaction creates a space in which social comparison is always taking place; this process not only involves individuals categorizing others but also categorizing themselves as alike or different from others. These theories further argue that social identities are no less "real" than individual identities and must always be taken into account in any kind of social interaction. The relationship between individual and collective identity is thus dialectical, with each element both reflecting and influencing the other. As I will show, these insights provide a pathway for analyzing congregational conflict from a broader perspective that addresses the social identities of the individuals involved.

Social Identity Theory

One of the earliest articulations of social identity theory appeared in a 1986 article entitled "The Social Identity Theory of Intergroup Behavior" by Henri Tajfel and John C. Turner.[2] In this article, Tajfel and Turner make two central claims that clearly distinguish their position from previous approaches to identity. First, they argue that in addition to individual traits, *identity* can also refer to the ways in which an individual identifies with a certain group. This claim stands in marked contrast to many earlier social psychological theories, which had attempted to explain intergroup dynamics in terms of intraindividual or interpersonal psychological processes.

Second, actual conflict of interest between groups is not necessary to produce "in-group bias" or "the tendency to favor the in-group over the out-group in evaluations and behavior."[3] A now-famous 1971 experiment demonstrated this concept by dividing subjects into two groups along completely arbitrary lines and asking them to allocate rewards to other individuals identified only by group membership. The results of this experiment showed that "even these most minimal of conditions were sufficient to produce in-group bias: subjects tended to assign more money to individuals who were members of the same group as themselves."[4] In other words, the fact that subjects in the study acted in accordance with their arbitrary group membership, even when they received no actual benefit for doing so, shows that "real" conflict of interest need not exist for in-group identification and bias to develop. Based on these experimental findings (which have since been replicated many times), Tajfel and Turner argue for an understanding of identity that gives adequate consideration to individuals' group identifications and that functions even in the absence of actual conflicts of interest between such groups.

This notion of in-group bias forms the core of Tajfel and Turner's articulation of social identity theory. In fact, based on the empirical study mentioned above, Tajfel and Turner claim that "in-group bias is a remarkably omnipresent feature of intergroup relations."[5] These authors further argue that "pressures to evaluate one's own group positively through in-group/out-group comparisons lead social groups to attempt to differentiate themselves from each other."[6] This statement highlights the importance of *social comparison* within social identity theory, since

---

2. This article is a slightly revised version of Tajfel and Turner's original 1979 article, "An Integrative Theory of Intergroup Conflict."

3. Tajfel and Turner, "The Social Identity Theory of Intergroup Behavior," 281.

4. Oakes et al., *Stereotyping and Social Reality*, 42.

5. Tajfel and Turner, "The Social Identity of Intergroup Behavior," 281.

6. Ibid., 284.

individuals must compare groups against one another to find the one that most appropriately matches themselves on relevant dimensions. In this way, Tajfel and Turner arrive at a definition of *social identity* as "those aspects of an individual's self-image that derive from the social categories to which he perceives himself as belonging."[7]

Given that social identity theory views identity as comprised of both individual traits and group identifications, I suggest that the conflicts described in the case studies represent not simply a clash of individual viewpoints, but rather a conflict between *collective identities*. As I have noted, at Grace UCC, the conflict quickly became polarized into a struggle between two clearly defined "sides." Although it would be tempting to characterize the identities involved in this situation as "pro same-sex marriage" and "anti same-sex marriage," this would be misleading. In fact, many of the parishioners who voted to stay in the UCC also opposed same-sex marriage but felt it was important for the congregation to maintain its covenant relationship with the UCC. Furthermore, some of the parishioners in this group actually held no particular affection for the denomination itself or its positions on social issues. Yet, these congregants still believed that being part of a larger organization would provide practical benefits, and so they advocated for continued affiliation with the UCC.

The central factor at Grace UCC therefore became identification with the larger denomination and not simply with one side of a political or theological issue. Admittedly, from the participants' perspective, the conflict probably did seem to break down along theological lines: those who wanted to stay in the UCC were seen as more "liberal" and those who wished to leave it as more "conservative." As I have noted, however, the defending group[8] actually included a significant number of people who were theologically conservative and who opposed same-sex marriage. These members' decision to identify with the defending group thus lay in their commitment to the denomination rather than to a specific political or theological perspective on same-sex marriage itself. Bearing these caveats in mind, one could therefore describe the collective identities involved in this congregational conflict as "pro-UCC" and "anti-

---

7. Ibid., 283.

8. Recall that in this context, I am using the term "defending group" to refer to those who wished to keep the congregation's existing denominational structures in place, while the term "protesting group" refers to those who wished to change the current state of affairs in the church.

UCC," with each group defining itself as the in-group and the opposing identity as the relevant out-group.

Describing the situation in this way also shows how social comparison may have been operating in this context to produce collective identification. In this particular scenario, all of the individuals involved were originally identified with the United Church of Christ by virtue of their church membership. Once the theological debate erupted, however, parishioners had to decide whether to identify with the group advocating continued UCC affiliation, or with the group urging separation from the denomination. Given that the two groups did not break down along rigid theological or political lines, one can infer that church members made comparisons between the two groups in an attempt to decide which one most closely matched the social categories to which they already perceived themselves as belonging.

At First UMC, by contrast, the group identities that emerged during the conflict were, in some sense, set up by the nature of the problem. In other words, because the congregational issue centered on changes to worship structure, people naturally divided themselves according to their participation at the 8:30, 8:45, or 11:00 service. Even though people in all three of these groups shared many important bonds (especially through Sunday school class membership), they were asked to serve on the worship committee based on their identities as participants in one of the three worship services. In this regard, it is easy to see how and why individuals ended up in the groups they did. And, at least at first, these group memberships took on great importance—so much so that at the first worship committee meeting, individuals sat with others from their same worship group and came prepared to advocate for what they saw as "their" service.

It is also important to remember, however, that these group identities tapped preexisting categories to which individuals had already committed themselves. That is, prior to the formation of the worship committee, parishioners at First UMC had already divided themselves according to the worship service they most preferred and that they attended most regularly. In this sense, parishioners had already been involved in a process of social comparison by measuring the different services against one another to find the one that most closely matched their theological commitments and personal preferences. As the case study revealed, individuals who held a more immanent understanding of God's presence in worship tended to gravitate toward the contemporary service, while those who valued transcendence and reverence chose a traditional worship style. Furthermore, individuals who valued a feeling of intimacy in worship tended to attend the smaller 8:30 or 8:45 service, while those who were attracted to a sense of being "one among many" chose the larger 11:00 worship opportunity. Though all of the parishioners at First UMC held a group identity associated with the congregation at large, they also chose to associate with particular worship groups depending on how they compared those groups with themselves on relevant dimensions. In this sense, the different worship services became not only alternatives for how to spend time on Sunday morning but also key aspects of First UMC parishioners' social identities within the context of their church membership.

Self-Categorization Theory

Social identity theory highlights the importance of social comparison processes in forming individual identity; however, it proves less successful in explaining *why* particular social categories emerge in particular contexts. In an attempt to provide a more thorough explanation of this phenomenon, John C. Turner later developed *self-categorization theory*, which built upon many of the tenets originally stipulated by social identity theory. Self-categorization theory provides a broader framework in which to understand the complexities of individual identity development within social contexts. In *Social Influence* (1991), Turner notes that

> the crucial fact about the public setting is that it is *shared with others* and provides a comparative context within which people can categorize themselves as identical to or different from others. Such contexts, therefore, change the level and content of self-identity in terms of *how people perceive themselves* and not merely how they look to others.[9]

Within self-categorization theory, then, the focus shifts from categorizing other individuals or groups, to categorizing *oneself* as like or unlike other individuals or groups. Social psychologists further characterize the theoretical shift from social identity to self-categorization in terms of moving "from Tajfel's conception of social identity as *reflecting* group affiliations, to the idea that social identity comprised social categorizations

---

9. Turner, *Social Influence*, 130, emphasis in original.

of the self which *caused* group phenomena."[10] From this perspective, then, the relationship between individual and collective identity is dialectical, with each element both reflecting and influencing the other.

Here it is important to provide a summary of key theoretical concepts that illuminate the applicability of this theory to the specific context of intergroup conflict. First, self-categorization theory "emphasizes the fact that categorization is a dynamic, context-dependent process, determined by *comparative relations within a given context*."[11] Categorization, then, is a process of social comparison not only between groups, but between *differences between* groups. This concept, known as the "meta-contrast principle," states that "a given set of items is more likely to be categorized as a single entity *to the degree that differences within that set of items are less than the differences between that set and others within the comparative context*."[12] For instance, if I am in a public place and notice a group of people who are all wearing firefighter uniforms, and another group of people wearing business suits, I am likely to categorize these groups as "firefighters" and "executives." This is because even though each group may contain differences within it (men and women, people of different ethnicities, etc.), these differences appear less important than the differences between the two groups. This principle helps to explain the process of categorization in general, and social categorization in particular, by delineating the specific criteria that are used to mark the boundaries between categories—again, the perception of greater differences *between* groups than among them.

Additionally, Oakes, Haslam, and Turner describe the notions of salience, accessibility, and fit as important determining factors in the categorization process. Category *salience* refers to the "psychological significance" of a category within a given context; thus, in order for a category to become a basis for social comparison, it must prove highly relevant for the person doing the comparing.[13] *Accessibility* refers to a perceiver's ability and readiness to use a particular category, while *fit* refers to the degree of match between perceptual input and categories that have already been stored in the perceiver's memory. Oakes, Haslam, and Turner delineate two specific kinds of fit which operate to produce

10. Oakes et al., *Stereotyping and Social Reality*, 93, emphasis in original.
11. Ibid., 95, emphasis in original.
12. Ibid., 96, emphasis in original.
13. Ibid., 43.

social category salience. *Comparative fit* refers to the conditions in which a perceiver would be likely to view persons as members of a particular group, rather than as unique individuals. Such fit often depends on a high meta-contrast ratio between intergroup and intragroup differences. Thus, if differences *between* groups are perceived as greater than differences *within* groups, social categories are more likely to become salient.

In addition to the relationship between groups, categorization also depends on the social meaning of similarities and differences between people. This concept, known as *normative fit*, refers to "the match between category and reality in terms of content."[14] In other words, simply observing that intergroup differences outweigh intragroup differences may not lead to a particular social categorization if the *content* of those differences is not congruent with the categories involved. For example, let's say I self-identify as a Democrat, but find myself in the company of a group of Democrats who all support increased defense spending and the death penalty, whereas the Republicans in the room all advocate for higher taxes and health care reform. In that scenario, I would probably find my group identification as a Democrat less relevant because the content of that identity for me does not match the content of the (ostensibly same) group identity being presented by others.

When considering the nature of the conflict that erupted at Grace UCC, one must ask: why did church members develop separate collective identities of pro-UCC versus anti-UCC, instead of maintaining the larger category of "UCC members" to which they all originally belonged? Why did the categories of pro- or anti-denomination become salient in this context? Although the two collective identities involved in this situation did not break down along strict theological or political lines, it is important to remember that this conflict arose in response to a particular action by the United Church of Christ—an action which proved highly controversial. As a result, those members of the congregation who already had ambivalent feelings about the UCC became quite hostile toward it, whereas those who were more strongly identified with the denomination—either because of their own values or their feelings toward the pastors—argued for preserving the relationship. I maintain that the very contentious and public action of the UCC made identification with it, or opposition to it, a much more *salient* category within the congregation.

14. Ibid., 118. It should be noted that Oakes et al. are using the term *reality* to denote *social* reality—that is, the reality of a given social context—and not *reality* in any philosophical or metaphysical sense.

In fact, in the midst of this congregational conflict, I was surprised by the vehemence with which certain individuals argued against continued affiliation with the UCC because, prior to that time, they had never expressed any opinion at all about the denomination. It would seem, then, that these individuals associated identity categories with the UCC, but that these categories had simply never become salient before.

The fact that the UCC's 2005 equal marriage resolution made national news and was discussed in a variety of public forums also suggests that the categories of denominational affiliation or opposition became especially accessible in the situation I described.[15] Because the unique characteristics of the UCC suddenly emerged into public view, individuals would be more likely to utilize their sense of identification with or difference from the denomination as categories for comparison with one another. The notion of fit also proves particularly helpful in analyzing the dynamics of this congregation's conflict. Recall that comparative fit often depends on a high meta-contrast ratio, in which the differences between groups appear greater than the differences within them. This principle seems to have been borne out in the situation at Grace UCC, since both the pro- and anti-UCC groups included individuals who differed greatly on many other dimensions. However, when it came to the question of whether to remain with the UCC, there was a great deal of uniformity *within* the groups, and a high level of difference *between* them.

Finally, the concept of normative fit also proves useful in examining the nature of the intergroup conflict that occurred at Grace UCC. As I have noted, normative fit refers to the "match between category and reality in terms of content."[16] Thus, for the category of denominational affiliation to become salient, the makeup of the pro- and anti-UCC groups had to match prior expectations of those categories. In this situation, both of the pastors clearly advocated for maintaining the church's relationship with the UCC, as did the majority of the congregation's lay leaders. In contrast, those who identified as anti-UCC had typically shown very little interest in denominational activities or even knowledge of the UCC's position on important issues. I contend that these factors contributed toward establishing a high degree of normative fit for the categories of denominational affiliation or opposition: if the congregation's clergy and

---

15. For an example of the media coverage of the UCC's decision, see this *New York Times* article that appeared the following day: Dewan, "United Church of Christ Backs Same-Sex Marriage."

16. Oakes et al., *Sterotyping and Social Reality*, 118.

leadership had identified as anti-UCC, or if those who had previously demonstrated little connection with the denomination had suddenly become extremely supportive of it, this likely would have contradicted expectations and decreased the overall salience of these categories for social comparison.

Again, because the nature of the conflict at First UMC differed markedly from the one at Grace UCC, the role of self-categorization in identity formation also took a different form. The fact that First UMC deliberately sought to change its worship structure meant that participation in particular worship services automatically became a relevant category for parishioners. In other words, the administrative board's directive to alter First UMC's worship structure made the category of worship participation much more salient. Prior to that time, it is unlikely that most people at First UMC would have identified themselves by saying, "I attend the contemporary service at First United Methodist." Instead, they would simply have said, "I attend First United Methodist." Before the debate about worship changes arose, then, general church membership would likely have been a more relevant category for most parishioners than participation in a particular service. Similarly, because the discussion at First UMC was focused on worship, parishioners were much more likely to use the 8:30, 8:45, and 11:00 categories to define themselves and others. This is why, when I asked the pastors for referrals for my interviews, they would say things like, "You can call Mr. X; he's an 8:30 person." Or "Ms. Y. would be a good person to talk to; she's an 8:45-er." In essence, the different services had become identity markers that took on particular meanings within the context of the congregation's struggles.

The notion of fit was also operative in shaping the group identities that came into play during the conflict at First UMC. Once the issue of worship had become salient in the congregation, differences *between* the groups became more relevant than differences *among* them. First UMC parishioners shared a variety of bonds that cut across all three groups; they also differed sharply with others in their worship group on many other issues. Yet, within the context of changes to the worship structure, the differences between the worship services were the most pronounced because that was the issue under discussion. As the case study of First UMC showed, parishioners initially identified quite strongly with the 8:30, 8:45, or 11:00 worship groups. They brought these identifications with them into the worship committee meetings and held on to them for most of the decision-making process. In the end, though, these parishioners identified more with the congregation as a whole than with their individual worship services. Why might this be so? First, as I have noted, these parishioners held preexisting relationships with each other and with others outside the committee that cut across the entire congregation. Through Sunday school classes, work on various committees, mission groups, and other church activities, these congregants had developed relationships with many other people besides those in their preferred worship service. As a result of these relationships, members of the worship committee thought a great deal about what impact their choices might have on the entire congregation.

Additionally, certain actions on the part of the pastors and the worship committee chair helped to reinforce the identity that individuals from all three services shared in common—namely, their membership in First UMC and, more broadly, in the body of Christ. The fact that each meeting began with a devotional time—including prayer, Scripture reading, and reflection—served as a reminder to committee participants of the spiritual bond they shared. This bond was even more strongly emphasized at the last committee meeting, when the devotional time included an opportunity for individuals to serve communion to one another. This sacred act of liturgy again reminded committee members of their relationships with each other as fellow church members, and as fellow Christians. Roy described the importance of the worshipful atmosphere in the last meeting as follows: "The way we did it was really good, Bob did it really good. He . . . made it sacramental, you know, did communion, let people start really having community together. But the bottom line was the power of God was unleashed in there and people were willing to step back from their own way." Over time, then, the relational bonds between parishioners at First UMC—both those forged within the worship committee and those that preexisted the conflict—mitigated the strength of the smaller identity groups that had originally formed based on allegiance to a particular worship service. As a result, the members of the worship committee ultimately identified primarily with the congregation as a whole rather than with their preferred service. This identification became especially visible through the committee's willingness to engage in problem solving and to seek a solution that they believed would most benefit the entire faith community.

Group Polarization

In addition to the notions of social identity already discussed, self-categorization theory offers a particularly helpful interpretation of *group polarization* that can also contribute to greater understanding of intergroup conflicts such as the ones that occurred within these congregations. Group polarization is "the finding that group discussion or some related group manipulation tends to strengthen the prevailing response tendency within a group. The mean response of members tends to become more extreme after group interaction in the same direction as the mean response before interaction."[17] This phenomenon, identified by James Stoner in 1961, became known as the "risky shift" and contradicted earlier assumptions that groups will typically converge on the average position of their members. Consequently, various social psychological theories developed in an attempt to explain group polarization. However, social psychologist John C. Turner maintains that none of these theories adequately explains why certain groups converge on an average position, while others polarize to an extreme.

A self-categorization theory of group polarization overcomes this problem by claiming that "people are conforming to a shared in-group norm, but that the norm is not the pre-test average but rather the prototypical position of the group."[18] In this view, the "prototype" is the position that most clearly represents the commonalities within the group as compared to members of an out-group. This approach helps explain both convergence on the mean and polarization within groups: in both cases, "members are moving towards what they see as the consensual position of their group."[19] The primary benefit of this approach is that it takes into account the importance of intergroup relations in polarization, rather than simply offering an explanation of why individuals move to one position or another within group contexts.

This interpretation of group polarization seems especially applicable to the case studies presented in chapter 2. At Grace UCC, for instance, both identity groups moved toward more extreme positions than they had displayed before the conflict erupted, thereby providing a classic example of polarization. While the members of the pro-UCC

---

17. Turner, *Social Influence*, 49.
18. Ibid., 76.
19. Ibid., 77.

group identified positively with the denomination before the conflict, these identifications became much stronger as they compared themselves against and entered into conflict with the out-group. Similarly, many of the anti-UCC group members had previously exhibited ambivalent or slightly negative feelings toward the denomination, but when the congregation became embroiled in debate, they moved to a much more extreme, hostile position—one that insisted on disassociation from the UCC as the only viable solution. Using Turner's perspective on polarization, one could argue that each group was moving toward what their members perceived as the "prototypical" position—namely, the position that most clearly represented each group's commonalities as compared to the relevant out-group. Since the main issue at stake for both groups revolved around denominational affiliation, each group moved toward an extreme position at opposite ends of the spectrum.

Similarly, at First UMC, polarization was operating in the early part of the decision-making process. Considering that the issue under discussion focused on worship changes, the various subgroups formed according to their commonalities—i.e., their worship preferences. This helps explain why the three worship groups were so clearly defined at the first committee meeting, to the point where individuals physically identified themselves by sitting with members from their own service. Nancy, a devoted member of the 8:45 service, noted that from her perspective, each group went into the process thinking, "This is our chance to convince everybody that our service is the most important and the best." However, many interviewees observed that as the decision-making process went on, group identities softened as individuals began to understand and appreciate one another more.

When it came time to make actual decisions about worship changes, however, these group identities surfaced again and caused sharp divisions between members of the different services. These divisions became especially apparent at the penultimate committee meeting, when many of the members began to "dig in their heels" and resist agreeing to any major changes to their own services. Again, a self-categorization approach to group polarization explains this movement back toward more rigid positions by showing how individuals move toward what they see as the prototypical position of their group as compared to a relevant out-group. So, if a person identifies primarily with the 8:30 traditional service and perceives the consensual position of his or her group as an insistence on maintaining an early worship time with traditional liturgical elements, he or she will move more strongly in that direction rather than moving toward a more middle-ground position. This happened at the third committee meeting, to the point where many members left the meeting feeling hopeless about the possibility of ever reaching a solution.

As the case study showed, however, the final committee meeting ended with all members agreeing to an integrative solution that involved both gains and losses for all parties. How can we explain this outcome given the polarization that occurred at the previous meeting? Self-categorization theory suggests that the key factor in both cases is the notion of the prototypical group position. When polarization was happening among the First UMC committee members, individuals were likely conforming to what they saw as the prototypical position of their group as opposed to the other two out-groups. Yet, the committee members at First UMC ultimately identified more strongly with the congregation as a whole than with their individual worship services. This means that, in the end, a more encompassing social identity took precedence for committee members, and they were able to move toward a solution that was located at the intersection of all three groups' interests, rather than remaining rigidly focused on an extreme position that refused to give any ground.

Collective Identification, Polarization, and Anxiety

In this chapter, I have utilized concepts from both social identity theory and self-categorization theory to illustrate how collective identification and group polarization may have been operating in the conflicts I described in the case studies. Such concepts shed light on the ways in which individuals within these congregations acted according to their group identities, rather than simply as unique individuals with a variety of diverse viewpoints. While this analysis is useful in its own right, returning to the theme of anxiety at this point provides another helpful lens through which to understand the events that unfolded in these faith communities. Throughout this book I have advanced a definition of anxiety as diffuse fear related to feelings of threat to the self. I now argue that just as threats to one's individual identity create anxiety, so do threats to one's social identity.

Recall from chapter 3 that self-representations include representations of groups to which the self belongs; consequently, when those groups become too heterogeneous and thus too threatening, anxiety develops. In the same way, social identity theory and self-categorization theory help explain why particular groups form in specific social settings and why individuals may affiliate with particular groups at any given time. According to social psychological theorists, these dimensions of social identity are no less "real" than individual identity. It stands to reason, then, that if people experience significant challenges to their social identities through conflict, they could interpret such challenges as threats to their selfhood and, as a result, experience anxiety.

Given that anxiety is such a pervasive social force, one also wonders what role it might play in situations of group polarization such as those described in the case studies. I suggest that although anxiety does not necessarily cause group polarization,[20] it is reasonable to assume that *group polarization causes anxiety*. After all, group polarization essentially means that a larger group splits into two or more subgroups that take increasingly extreme positions against one another. Particularly in a setting like a congregation, where members have a certain expectation of unity, such polarization feels very uncomfortable. For instance, Lily, a member of Grace UCC, described her experience of the conflict as follows: "It was just the thought that everybody that I felt was family was getting ready to split. It was kind of intimidating, scary." Lily's words encapsulate the anxiety that members of groups often experience when they see smaller, more rigid subgroups forming in their midst. When such anxiety runs rampant in a communal setting, destructive behaviors frequently result. Conversely, if group members manage to contain their anxiety, they may feel less threatened and be able to work together more cooperatively. This distinction helps us understand why different groups take different approaches to one another in the midst of conflict. In the final section of this chapter, I draw on strategic choice theory to explore more deeply why social groups choose their preferred modes of relating to one another, as well as what role anxiety might play in those choices.

Conflict and Strategic Choice

One way of defining "conflict" from a social psychological perspective is as a *"perceived divergence of interest*, a belief that the parties' current

---

20. As I have already discussed, self-categorization theory offers a convincing explanation for why, under certain circumstances, groups within social settings polarize to extremes rather than converging on a mean.

aspirations are incompatible."[21] Throughout this section, I use this definition as a guide for understanding the events presented in the case studies, since the elements of *perception* and *incompatibility* played key roles in these congregational struggles. In fact, the form that the two conflicts took represents a complete divergence of interest because it was impossible for all parties to achieve their stated goals. In the case of Grace UCC, the congregation had to make a clear choice between staying in the denomination and leaving it. For First UMC, the choice was a bit more complex since it required reducing the number of worship services from three to two. In this sense, the choice was not "either-or" in nature, but the choice still meant that at least one of the three worship services would cease to exist in the same form. In both of these congregations, then, a divergence of interest arose that required action to resolve. As the case studies showed, these two communities of faith took very different approaches toward the conflicts that emerged in their midst. Social psychological theories related to *strategic choice* describe these varied approaches and illuminate some of the reasons these congregations may have acted as they did.

One of the most pressing questions raised by the case studies presented in chapter 2 is "Why did the involved parties choose to approach the conflict in a particular way?" In other words, why did the members of Grace UCC choose such a contentious approach, while the members of First UMC chose something much closer to cooperation? Parties in a given conflict may choose between at least four basic strategies: contending, yielding, avoiding, or problem solving.[22] *Contending* involves trying to resolve a conflict on one's own terms without considering the interests of the other party. *Yielding*, in contrast, occurs when one lowers one's own aspirations, and makes partial or total concessions to the other in order to keep the peace. *Avoiding* refers to the choice not to engage the conflict at all, whereas *problem solving* "entails an effort to identify the issues dividing the parties and to develop and move toward a solution that appeals to both sides."[23] When parties choose either contending or problem solving as their preferred strategy, the result is "overt confrontation, a behavioral form of conflict."[24] Such confrontation need not be

---

21. Pruitt and Kim, *Social Conflict*, 7–8, emphasis in original.
22. Ibid., 38.
23. Ibid.
24. Ibid., 13.

destructive and may actually serve many positive functions unless it is allowed to escalate. Based on the case studies presented in chapter 2, the members of Grace UCC appeared to choose a strategy of contending that escalated to the point of destructiveness. In contrast, the parishioners at First UMC chose problem solving as their primary approach. In what follows, I describe the various group behaviors exhibited by each congregation, and then analyze them as a means for understanding why each church chose its preferred strategy. Alongside this social psychological analysis, I again introduce the theme of anxiety as a conceptual tool that clarifies the particular choices made by the members of Grace UCC and First UMC in the midst of their respective conflicts.

Grace UCC

As the case studies in chapter 2 made clear, the conflict at Grace UCC became extremely hostile and divisive. In view of this fact, I argue that the members of Grace UCC (including those on both sides of the conflict) made a strategic choice to engage primarily in contending, rather than yielding, avoiding, or problem solving. This choice is evident in the particular conflict behaviors—especially the adoption of contentious tactics and the development of escalation—that emerged during the course of the conflict. In this section I describe the specific conflict behaviors that emerged at Grace UCC, supporting my argument that contending became the strategy of choice there. I then turn to social psychological frameworks involving the dual concern model and departures from rational choice to explore *why* the members of Grace UCC chose to contend with one another.

Contentious Tactics

When an individual or group chooses contending as its primary strategy in a conflict, the aim is very clear: namely, to impose one's own wishes on the other. To accomplish this aim, one can select from a wide variety of "contentious tactics," all of which are designed to persuade or force the other party in the conflict to yield. Contentious tactics include a wide range of behavioral responses, which exist along a continuum from "light" to "heavy." "Light" tactics refer to acts "whose consequences for Other[25]

---

25. In their text, Pruitt and Kim note that they focus on "dyadic conflict," or conflict

are favorable or neutral," while "heavy" tactics "impose, or threaten to impose, unfavorable or costly consequences on Other."[26] In the conflict at Grace UCC, both groups employed light and heavy tactics in an effort to achieve their goals.

For instance, one light tactic is *promises*, which are "messages from Party announcing its intention to reward Other if Other complies with Party's wishes."[27] At Grace UCC, each side used promises in an attempt to convince the other side to yield. When arguing for disassociation from the denomination, the protesting group promised that the professional staff would keep their jobs, along with their retirement and insurance benefits, and that "nothing would have to change" within the congregation's day-to-day life. Conversely, the defending group promised that if the complainants agreed to stay in the UCC, they would be supported in their desire to voice their grievances to regional and national church bodies.

Promises are considered "preparatory tactics" because they "erode Other's resistance to lowering aspirations."[28] Other tactics, however, aim to lower the other party's aspirations in a direct and forceful manner. *Persuasive argumentation* represents one such tactic, which uses logical appeals in an attempt to convince the other party to back away from its objectives.[29] In the conflict described above, the light tactic of promises failed to achieve the desired result for either party. Consequently, each side turned to persuasive argumentation to challenge the other's goals more directly. The protesting group for example, made arguments closely related to their promises: they argued that even if the congregation left the UCC, it would still be feasible to pay the ministers their current salary and benefits. Additionally, this group asked parishioners to consider the moral consequences of remaining within a theologically radical denomination, and the effects such a choice might have on future church membership and giving.

The defending party responded primarily with logical arguments about practical matters, such as how difficult it would be for the congregation to function without pastors or denominational support. They

---

between two parties. Consequently, in their discussion these authors use the terms "Party" and "Other" to differentiate between the two sides of a given conflict. Ibid.

26. Ibid., 64.
27. Ibid., 66.
28. Ibid., 68.
29. Ibid.

also argued that since same-sex marriage was not recognized by the state, the Synod resolution would have no actual effect on the congregation's functioning. As such, the Synod resolution was essentially a non-issue for Grace UCC. Considerable skill is required to achieve success through persuasive argumentation, because "Party must convince Other to surrender something that it holds dear and that Party covets."[30] In the case of Grace UCC, the "something" that each party held dear was the power to determine the direction that the church would go in terms of its denominational affiliation. Not surprisingly, neither party in the conflict at Grace UCC was able to use persuasive argumentation successfully. As a result, both parties moved toward heavier contentious tactics aimed at levying specific costs on each other.

Threats represent one of the "classic" heavy tactics used within social conflict. Whereas persuasive argumentation relies on facts in an effort to convince others of one's own position, threats move beyond logical appeals to communicate "the intention to hurt Other if Other fails to comply with Party's wishes."[31] Threats are considered "heavy" tactics because the threatening party is asserting its own right to control the situation; thus, threats are, by nature, coercive. In the situation at Grace UCC, both groups engaged in threats in different ways. For those who wished to leave the denomination, the threat was clear: if they did not achieve this goal, they would leave the congregation. This threat made a strong impression on those in the opposing party, many of whom mentioned it in their interviews with me.

By contrast, those who thought Grace UCC should remain in the denomination expressed threats in a slightly different way. A few members of this group did threaten to move their membership if Grace UCC voted to leave the denomination. However, most of these parishioners seemed unwilling to make such a threat, perhaps in part because they had been so offended by the protesting group's use of it. Instead of direct threats, members of this group instead expressed a *warning*, which is "a prediction that Other will get hurt if it fails to act in a particular way."[32] This group expressed warnings mainly by emphasizing what they saw as the inevitable consequences of a choice to leave the UCC—namely, the loss of the congregation's ministers. In other words, instead of say-

30. Ibid.
31. Ibid., 71.
32. Ibid.

ing, "If you make this choice, I will impose this punishment on you," the pro-UCC group communicated something more akin to: "If you make this choice, we will lose our ministers, and we will all suffer." The key difference between threats and warnings is that unlike threats, the party issuing the warning does not control whether the other party gets hurt. Nonetheless, within the context of social conflict, warnings may also fall into the category of contentious tactics. Although the parishioners in the defending group may not have thought they were using contentious tactics, those in the opposing group clearly experienced their behavior as threatening, which made them become even more rigid in their position. Within the conflict at Grace UCC, then, both groups first used lighter tactics such as promises and persuasive argumentation, but when these approaches failed, they began using threats and warnings to lower each other's aspirations. This movement from lighter to heavier tactics reveals a pattern of *escalation*, or an increase in the conflict's intensity, over time.

Escalation

Overt confrontation that results from the use of contending strategies is not necessarily destructive, and may serve many positive functions within a community by providing a catalyst for change. However, when such confrontation escalates, these positive functions are often overshadowed by the negative consequences that result. During the escalation of a conflict, various kinds of "incremental transformations" take place.[33] These transformations typically are mirrored by each party involved and frequently cause the conflict to intensify "in ways that are sometimes exceedingly difficult to undo."[34] In addition to the progression from light to heavy tactics described above, three other transformations may be identified within the conflict depicted in the case study.

The first of these involves the movement from *specific to general* issues. For example, the protesting group moved from particular grievances about the equal marriage resolution toward more general complaints about the denomination as a whole. Similarly, the defending group progressed from arguing against the protesting group's wish to leave the UCC to discussing the complainants' role in previous church conflicts. In other words, both groups moved from focusing on the matter

33. Ibid., 89.
34. Ibid.

at hand to a much wider variety of contested issues. Unfortunately, when this kind of transformation takes place, "the overall relationship between the parties deteriorates" and is often replaced with "a general intolerance of the other side."[35] The complete lack of communication that ultimately developed between the two parties in this conflict implies that such deterioration did occur as a result of specific-to-general transformations within the relationship.

Another kind of transformation that may take place during escalation involves each party's progression from *wanting to do well, to wanting to win, to wanting to hurt the other*. This pattern appears clearly in both sides of this congregational conflict, since both groups originally focused on having their perspectives heard and respected. As the debate continued and grew more heated, however, the atmosphere became more contentious, and each side became more determined to win. Ultimately, with the use of threats and warnings intended to impose costs on the other side, the transformation to a desire to hurt the other party was achieved.

One final transformation that may occur during escalation is the movement from *few to many* participants. Although this conflict began with a significant number of parishioners involved, over time it came to encompass many other people who were not present at the original business meeting. In fact, members of both parties in the conflict attempted to enlist previously uncommitted parishioners in their cause, hoping that their side would ultimately have the largest number of votes. The purpose of this kind of transformation is for each group to draw neutral third parties into the fray in an effort to ensure that its own aspirations will prevail.

The Dual Concern Model

In an effort to understand why individuals or groups choose one strategy over another, social psychologists have proposed the *dual concern model*, which asserts that the relative strength of self-concern or other-concern will contribute significantly to strategic choice. According to this model, when self-concern is high and other-concern is low, contending will be the preferred strategy; when both self- and other-concern are high, problem solving will usually take place.[36] Given this model, one must wonder

---

35. Ibid.
36. Ibid., 40–41.

why, in a congregation of people who ostensibly cared about each other, contending quickly overtook problem solving as the strategy of choice.

One answer to this question may lie in the four conditions that tend to promote high self-concern: fear, a high value on the outcome of the conflict, a high emotional investment in the conflict, and the involvement of social identities.[37] I suggest that all of these conditions were met in the case of Grace UCC. First of all, fear seems to have been operating on both sides of the conflict: the protesting group feared the moral and social consequences of remaining in the UCC, while the defending group feared what would happen if the congregation severed its denominational ties. Both parties consequently placed a high value on the outcome of the conflict, so much so that at least some members in each group were willing to leave the congregation altogether if they did not achieve their goals. As evidenced by the tone of the initial business meeting, as well as the conflict that took place in subsequent weeks, both groups were emotionally invested in the conflict itself. Finally, both groups seemed to be operating out of a sense of social identity—as either pro- or anti-denomination—that took precedence over the identity they both shared (i.e., as members of the same congregation).

One must bear in mind, however, that the dual concern model also takes other-concern into consideration; thus, even if self-concern is high, a simultaneously high other-concern will typically lead to problem solving rather than contending. Given the fact that the two groups involved in this conflict were members of the same congregation, and that many church members were also related by blood or marriage, one would assume that the level of other-concern between the groups would have remained fairly high. What, then, could account for the lack of problem solving strategies within this conflict? According to Pruitt and Kim, "Although [interpersonal] bonds and dependencies usually foster other-concern, under certain conditions they can produce exactly the opposite reaction: antagonism toward Other and the use of contentious tactics. This reaction is especially likely when people to whom we are bonded . . . fail to fulfill their minimum obligations or severely frustrate us."[38] This observation offers a clue to why the parties involved in this conflict quickly adopted contending, rather than problem solving, as

---

37. Ibid., 43.
38. Ibid., 46.

their preferred strategy: namely, because members of both groups felt intensely disappointed or frustrated by those in the opposing group.

While frustration and disappointment undoubtedly played a role in how the conflict at Grace UCC developed, I suggest that *anxiety* provides an additional tool for understanding why members of this congregation chose contending over problem solving. First, recall that according to the dual concern model, two of the conditions that typically produce contending behavior are fear and the involvement of social identities, both of which were met at Grace UCC. In fact, the fears that surfaced in the conflict at Grace UCC—i.e., fears about what would happen if the congregation chose to stay in or leave the denomination—appear to be closely linked with both anxiety *and* social identity. For instance, the protesting group at Grace UCC feared the moral and social consequences of remaining within the denomination. Likewise, the defending group feared what would happen if the congregation were to have to function without the organizing structure of the UCC. These fears, though understandable, took the form of diffuse anxiety because they primarily involved fears of the *unknown*. Neither group could know exactly what would happen if Grace UCC chose one course of action over another; as a result, their fears focused on what *might* happen in particular sets of circumstances.

Furthermore, for both groups, this generalized anxiety was closely linked to their social identities. Members of the protesting group were deeply disturbed about the prospect of being part of an organization that was perceived in the community as supporting same-sex marriage. In their view, remaining within the UCC would mean espousing values to which they were deeply opposed and would reflect badly on them as persons. In contrast, members of the defending group worried about how the congregation would define itself in the absence of a denominational identity. At one meeting, someone asked, "Well, if we stop being UCC, what will we be? Nothing?" Additionally, many members of the defending group did not want to be associated with what they saw as bigoted attitudes or with disrespectful behavior toward the pastors. Because these social identities took on such importance in the midst of the conflict at Grace UCC, it stands to reason that having those identities repeatedly challenged by others in the community would create more intense feelings of threat, and thus more anxiety for all involved. And, as I discussed in chapter 3, the greater the sense of threat to the self, the more likely it is that destructive behaviors will result. In the case of Grace UCC, then, fears of the unknown and threats to social identity caused members' anxiety to be raised. This anxiety then contributed to the opposing groups' adoption of contentious tactics and to the pattern of escalation that ultimately developed—both of which, in turn, created additional anxiety and made the conflict even more intractable.

Departures from Rational Choice

In addition to the dual concern model, social psychology offers another way to understand the move toward contending and away from problem solving: namely, as *departures from rational choice* within the decision maker. In other words, simply because problem solving seems like the "rational" strategy to adopt within a group that shares social and religious bonds, this does not mean that the actors involved will necessarily choose that strategy. Instead, individuals and groups often choose less rational strategies because of certain biases that exist within decision-making processes, and these choices affect the relative strength of self- or other-concern. The concept of *framing* as a particularly powerful bias within the context of conflict negotiation is useful here.

Framing involves "evaluating an alternative (vis à vis some referent point) as a potential gain or a potential loss. Negotiators behave in a more risk-averse fashion when evaluating potential gains and in a more risk-seeking manner when evaluating potential losses."[39] Negative framing tends to generate more self-concern than does positive framing.[40] I suggest that in the conflict at Grace UCC, both parties were framing the dispute in terms of potential *losses*—the protesting group focused on moral concessions and a loss of face in the community, while the defending group emphasized the loss of their clergy and the benefits of denominational support. As a result of this negative framing, both sides seemed more willing to engage in the "risky" behavior of using contentious tactics, despite the potential for destroying their relationships with church members in the opposing group.

An additional factor that may influence individuals or groups to depart from rational choices in decision making is the "fixed-pie myth," also known as "zero-sum thinking." According to the fixed-pie myth,

---

39. Neale and Bazerman, *Cognition and Rationality in Negotiation*, 44.
40. Pruitt and Kim, *Social Conflict*, 44.

any gain for one party represents a loss for the other and vice versa.[41] Admittedly, in cases of scarce physical resources, the fixed-pie model is accurate; however, in many conflicts that involve less tangible stakes, zero-sum thinking simply represents the way in which the parties have chosen to view the conflict. In this case, zero-sum thinking is actually "a *faulty* belief. In actuality, the parties do have compatible interests, but they are blind to this fact."[42] At Grace UCC, both sides of the conflict engaged in negative framing, which led them to view the dispute in terms of a fixed-pie model. Once this had happened, each side began to see any gain for the other as a loss for itself, which blinded them both to the common interests they shared: namely, the benefits of keeping the congregation intact. If this common interest had remained at the forefront of the discussion, perhaps both groups would have been more willing to move toward an integrative solution.

The "departures from rational choice" framework is useful because it allows us to understand conflict through the lens of cognitive biases. However, like the dual concern model, this framework becomes even more valuable when viewed through the lens of anxiety. Notions such as negative framing and zero-sum thinking helpfully explain why certain social groups may choose contending over problem solving, but they do not explain *why* such groups engage in negative framing and zero-sum thinking in the first place. We know, for example, that people tend to behave in a more risk-seeking manner when evaluating potential losses.[43] This raises the question: why, at Grace UCC, did parishioners frame the conflict in terms of potential losses instead of potential gains?

I suggest that because the congregation was experiencing such an elevated level of anxiety members tended to focus on only what they stood to lose from any given outcome. In other words, they were functioning in a self-protective manner that sought to keep intact those things about the congregation that felt most important to them. Any perceived threat to keeping those things intact consequently raised individuals' anxiety even further and made the conflict escalate. In the same way, I argue that increased levels of anxiety also contributed to parishioners' tendency to rely on zero-sum thinking. As the conflict developed, social identities were increasingly threatened and anxiety continued to increase. Over

---

41. Ibid., 22.
42. Ibid., emphasis in original.
43. See Neale and Bazerman, *Cognition and Rationality in Negotiation*.

time, a process of polarization took place, increasing anxiety levels even further and widening the gap between the two groups. In such a situation, it is not difficult to understand why members of each group would have begun thinking of the situation as a zero-sum game. After all, if individuals are experiencing increased levels of threat to their personal or social identities, it is less likely that they will attempt to problem-solve with those who are threatening them. Instead, they will likely adopt a self-protective stance designed to hold on to the social resources they feel they need to maintain their group identifications.

First UMC

Clearly, the conflict at Grace UCC proved deeply divisive. Both parties engaged in contentious tactics such as promises, persuasive argumentation, and threats; and both parties seem to have operated primarily from a position of high self-concern driven by increased levels of anxiety within the congregation. At First UMC, though, the picture was quite different. Admittedly, some of the same tactics were used, though in a more indirect way than at Grace UCC. Judith Murray, the chair of the worship committee at First UMC, told me that although the actual committee meetings were always respectful in tone, some individuals still sent e-mail messages to her and others expressing their displeasure with the process. Judith described these e-mails as "motivated out of frustration and fear," and as "devastating" for those who received them. Also, according to other interviewees, some of the worship committee meetings were quite tense, and all three groups seem to have come to the negotiating table with fairly rigid aspirations—namely, to keep their particular worship services intact.

Ultimately, though, the process at First UMC was much more akin to problem solving than contending. Within the context of social conflict, problem solving may be described as follows: "At its best, problem solving involves a joint effort to find a mutually acceptable solution. The parties or their representatives talk freely to one another. They exchange information about their interests and priorities, work together to identify the true issues dividing them, brainstorm in search of alternatives that bridge their opposing interests, and collectively evaluate these alternatives from the viewpoint of their mutual welfare."[44] The events that unfolded at First

---

44. Pruitt and Kim, *Social Conflict*, 190.

UMC match this description quite well. When the administrative board decided to reduce the number of worship services at First UMC, the pastors put into place an intentional decision-making process that they hoped would lead to an integrative solution. This process was developed in conversation with a professional church consultant and was designed to allow representatives from each of the three worship services to participate equally.

According to the committee members that I interviewed, the aim of the process was to allow each person to voice his or her preferences and concerns, and ultimately to move the group toward finding a solution with which they could all live. Despite the tensions that occasionally developed, interviewees described the overall experience as deeply respectful and rewarding. Judith, the chair of the worship committee, described the process as follows: "And there were some tense moments, but never was anything said out of hatred or out of disdain for each other. . . . The actual process was a process of integrity, I feel, in that one group was not favored over the other and we sat together as the body." Similarly, Ann, who was new to First UMC at the time of the conflict, said, "And I think the key to the whole meeting and the key to the whole change was that people were listened to. Every single person was listened to. And whether it turned out how they wanted it to turn out or not, I think that was secondary to the fact that they had a chance to say what they needed to say and they were listened to without interruption." These characteristics of the process at First UMC, along with the relative lack of contentious tactics used during the process, suggest that the committee members were able to focus on problem solving as their primary strategy for coping with a potentially divisive change in their worship structure.

One particular approach to problem solving that proves especially applicable in this case is the concept of *bridging*. In bridging, "neither party achieves its initial demands, but a new option is devised that satisfies the most important interests underlying those demands."[45] Each group at First UMC started out with the desire to keep its own service intact with no major changes to it; clearly, then, no group was able to obtain its original goal. Yet, the worship committee at First UMC was able to settle on a solution that was acceptable to all parties involved, even though it required all parties to make certain sacrifices. The committee was able to achieve this result because it found an integrative solution that still

---

45. Ibid., 197–98.

satisfied all parties' major interests. From my interviews with First UMC parishioners, I would describe the key interests for all three groups as follows: access to a worship service that contained elements (particularly music) with which they were familiar; the opportunity to worship in a style that helped them feel close to God; and the maintenance of strong relational bonds with others in their preferred worship service and in the wider church. From this perspective, the solution reached by the First UMC worship committee bridged all of these interests by integrating worship elements important to all three groups into the two new services, and by making sure to provide both traditional and contemporary opportunities for worship every Sunday. In this way, all three groups got many of their needs met, although no group got everything it wanted.

As I noted in the case study, a crucial element in the worship committee's ability to move toward this integrative solution was Roy Sanderson's suggestion to move the contemporary service to 5:00 p.m. Some would interpret Roy's action as an instance of yielding rather than problem solving, since it seemed to involve lowering the aspirations of the contemporary worshippers as a way of making peace with the other two groups. In fact, at least one of the individuals I interviewed stated that he believed Roy made this choice in order to avoid further conflict with others on the committee. However, considering the key interests that I noted above, the "out of the box" solution Roy devised helped to meet all of those criteria. The contemporary worshippers would still have access to a worship service that fit their style and theological commitments, while maintaining a positive relationship with others in the congregation. Each of the contemporary worshippers I interviewed—even those who did not like the 5:00 p.m. worship time—agreed that it was important for the contemporary-service-goers to show their willingness to "sacrifice" along with everyone else. These interviewees stated that if they had "dug in their heels" and refused to make any concessions, they would have damaged the relational fabric of the church. This shows that for many of the worship committee members, maintaining relationships with others in their church proved just as important as their theological understanding of worship.

The events that unfolded at First UMC show that this congregation chose to approach conflict through problem solving rather than contending. Why would this be the case? First, in terms of the dual concern model, the parishioners at First UMC demonstrated both high self-concern *and* high other-concern. Like Grace UCC, First UMC met the criteria for conditions that tend to produce high self-concern: fear, a high value on the outcome of the conflict, high emotional investment in the conflict, and the involvement of social identities. As the case study revealed, interviewees from First UMC cared a great deal about the outcome of this conflict because of its potential effect on their participation in worship, which they defined as an activity with deep spiritual relevance. Many of the people I interviewed at First UMC experienced much fear and anxiety related to the prospect of losing their preferred worship service, and they identified strongly with the particular group of worshippers with whom they had come to associate.

However, the dual concern model also predicts that when high self-concern is accompanied by high other-concern, problem solving will usually prevail as the preferred strategy for addressing conflict. At First UMC, almost everyone I interviewed—even those who felt very strongly about keeping their worship service intact—expressed deep concern about how any proposed worship changes might affect others in the congregation. This strong other-concern was grounded in the relationships First UMC parishioners shared with each other, both within and outside the confines of the worship committee. For instance, several of the individuals I interviewed noted that although they primarily identified with one particular worship service, they shared important bonds with people from other services through their participation in other aspects of congregational life—especially Sunday school classes. Esther, a devoted contemporary worshipper, highlighted the importance of such bonds when she stated, "I think that's probably what kept our church successful at having two kinds of worship, because in individual Sunday school classes there were people from both services. It was people from the church, not from the service."

In addition to the relationships that already existed among parishioners throughout First UMC, further bonds were built in the context of the worship committee itself. Roy described the relational impact of the committee's meetings this way: "Well, when people started hearing—oh, man! These are just, these are good folk, who just worship in a different way . . . people were starting to understand each other, and people were starting to like each other, there was a closeness." This "closeness" was instrumental in moving the parishioners at First UMC toward a position of problem solving rather than contending. Although members of all three services were deeply concerned about maintaining the integrity of their worship experience, this self-concern was balanced by a concern for those who worshipped somewhat differently, but were still valued members of the same faith community. In fact, throughout the process at First UMC, parishioners expressed concern not only for other individual members but also for the well-being of the congregation as a whole. It was out of such concern that the leaders of the 8:45 contemporary service made the decision to volunteer to move their worship to the evening. Simon, a middle-aged man who had been part of the contemporary service since its inception, described that decision as follows: "So basically, the group of us that went to the contemporary service got together and said, hey, we've got to think of what's best for the church, not for us." Roy even went so far as to say that he would have agreed to the complete elimination of the contemporary service if he thought it would contribute positively to the health of First UMC:

> You know there's a quote says that "The needs of the many outweigh the needs of the few." And, I just felt like we were at a crossroads as a church, that it was gonna go south quick, and just—if we had to give the whole service up and never do it—to me, it would have been the right thing to do. You know? For the betterment of the larger church.

One could argue, however, that prior to the conflict, members at Grace UCC also shared high levels of closeness, especially since many of them were related to one another through blood or marriage and had been attending church together for decades. Yet, this closeness ultimately was not enough to produce the other-concern needed to lead that congregation toward problem solving and away from contending. As I have already discussed, the notion of anxiety helps explain why members at Grace UCC engaged in specific behaviors—such as negative framing and zero-sum thinking—that social psychology understands in terms of "departures from rational choice." Likewise, at First UMC, lower levels of anxiety allowed parishioners to build on the strength of their relationships and develop additional closeness, which helped to mitigate the conflict and make it more manageable. In other words, because First UMC members felt less threatened, they were able to focus on their common interests and to engage in problem-solving techniques to further those interests.

Lower levels of anxiety at First UMC also contributed to that congregation's ability to embrace the opposite approach represented by the departures from rational choice exhibited at Grace UCC. For instance, instead of negative framing, members of First UMC were able to engage in positive framing as a means of approaching the conflict in their midst. Admittedly, at the beginning of the process, members of the First UMC worship committee experienced a great deal of anxiety, and many of them told me about their fear of "losing" their worship service. In this sense, many of them began the decision-making process with negative framing, focusing primarily on what they stood to lose. However, as the intentional decision-making process was implemented within the committee, more emphasis was placed on preserving and honoring those elements of the different worship services that parishioners most valued. "Simon" noted the importance of this emphasis when he said,

> To me it was important that everyone laid out why they liked each of their services and then what we could do to continue to do those things that made you feel at home at this church, made you want to come to this church. We don't want to lose any of that. We don't want to drive people away because we're making time changes. So we wanted to make sure that everyone was able to get those ideas out, those reasons out as to why they wanted to come to their service.

I suggest that this focus on keeping the most valued aspects of the various worship services intact helped lower anxiety among First UMC members because they experienced less threat to the social identities involved with their preferred services. As a result, instead of focusing on what they might lose from their worship services, parishioners became able to think about their situation in terms of potential gains—i.e., retaining important elements of worship as well as keeping the relational fabric of the congregation intact.

Finally, because they were able to maintain relatively low levels of anxiety during the conflict, members at First UMC moved *away* from zero-sum thinking and *toward* positive-sum thinking. Positive-sum thinking is "the view that the two parties' interests are not totally opposed and hence that problem solving is feasible."[46] Because the committee members at First UMC experienced lower levels of personal and communal threat, they were able to engage in problem solving strategies and ultimately agree on a solution that involved both gains and losses for all parties involved. Indeed, almost every person I interviewed from First UMC mentioned how important it was that participants from each of

---

46. Ibid., 50.

the three worship services make some "sacrifices" in order for the group to move toward an acceptable resolution to the conflict. In this sense, the committee members became able to see that a fixed-pie approach would actually overlook the fact that they all shared an interest in maintaining the health and well-being of the church as a whole. This move toward positive-sum thinking is especially evident in the "out of the box" solution suggested by Roy and other members of the contemporary service. By proposing an approach that had not yet been entertained in the committee, the contemporary worshippers moved the discussion from a focus on what each service would lose to a reframing of the entire issue in terms of the common interests that all parishioners shared.

Conclusion

In this chapter I have broadened my analysis of the congregational case studies to include social psychological as well as psychodynamic resources. Admittedly, these case studies are highly complex, and many different factors likely contributed to the disputes that occurred within these congregations. Yet, my contention remains that the discipline of social psychology—particularly through its understandings of collective identification, polarization, and strategic choice—offers new frameworks in which to examine the patterns of interaction between groups. Theories related to collective identification and group polarization, for instance, shed light on how and why social groups form, while concepts related to strategic choice help explain why groups select particular approaches for engaging each other in conflict. Such theories make it possible to see intergroup conflicts not simply as products of individual disagreements, but rather as a complex intermingling of interpersonal and social processes in which collective identities become strongly engaged.

I have further argued that viewing these social psychological theories through the basic lens of *anxiety* clarifies why the intergroup conflicts under discussion here developed as they did. I have suggested that, at Grace UCC, threats to parishioners' social identities and the resulting group polarization raised anxiety levels and propelled subgroups toward contentious tactics with one another. At First UMC, by contrast, lower levels of anxiety allowed members to focus on the social identity they shared, and thus to move more easily toward problem solving and integrative solutions. As helpful as these resources are, they are primarily intended to be descriptive in nature; that is, they seek to describe how individuals and groups actually behave, but not necessarily the way they "should" behave. For prescriptive reflection on the nature of healing and transformation within congregations, a different set of resources is required. Those resources may be found in the language of theology, which provides ways of talking about brokenness, health, and community that include both the "is" and the "ought" dimensions of human life. Thus, in the next chapter, I take up theology as another lens through which to explore congregational conflict.

5

Where Is God in All This?
Engaging Christian Theology

In the last two chapters I have brought the resources of psychodynamic psychology and social psychology to bear on the problem of congregational conflict in an effort to understand how and why such conflict originates. Both of these disciplines claim that the tendency to resist difference and gravitate toward similar others and groups is a natural part of human development. In certain circumstances, though, these tendencies become intensely defensive or aggressive, resulting in destructive behaviors like splitting and projection, rigid demands for sameness, polarization, or contentious tactics. I have argued that anxiety plays a key role in such developments, either as a catalyst for or as a result of their emergence. More specifically, I have suggested that increased anxiety produces an increased sense of threat, and that destructive behaviors frequently result. In contrast, lower levels of anxiety yield a decreased sense of threat, and a greater likelihood of problem solving within conflicted communities.

When combined with the insights provided by family systems theory, these social scientific resources help clarify how human beings relate to one another, both interpersonally and as members of groups. These resources also offer very concrete descriptions of how interpersonal and communal relationships become disordered and damaged in response to the anxiety stirred by difference. Additionally, each of the theoretical frameworks I have engaged in this book gestures toward ways in which this basic anxiety might be soothed. Such ways include managing anxiety, resisting splitting, developing tolerance for ambiguity, releasing rigid needs for sameness, and adopting cooperative or problem-solving approaches to conflict. Despite these important suggestions, however, in each case the default assumption remains the same: human beings seek to protect themselves from the anxiety produced by encounters with difference. As I have shown, this idea seems completely justified, based on what social scientific theory tells us about human functioning. Yet, such an assumption also implies that difference represents, at best, a basic challenge with which human beings must cope, rather than an important resource for the self's development and relationships.

Given the anthropology implied by the social scientific resources I have engaged, I suggest that an additional step is needed here: namely, a theological reframing of difference and conflict. In this chapter I argue that theology provides a way to see difference as both challenge *and* gift. In this way of thinking, resisting difference is, as social science suggests, a fundamental aspect of the way human beings operate. At the same time, however, resources in theology also make it possible to see difference as a result of God's enlivening, creative power. Reframing difference in this way serves to normalize the anxiety provoked by the diversity encountered in community, but also goes a step further to claim diversity *itself* as a good created and intended by God. Within this framework, then, difference becomes a resource to be cherished rather than a blight to be eradicated. This alternative theological perspective could help lower levels of anxiety in conflicted congregations and contribute to communal healing.

To build my argument, I make the following theological moves. First, I argue that conflicting human aims and needs represent a basic fact of human existence. As a result, individuals and communities will always experience a certain amount of incompatibility, which is part of the "tragic" structure of human life.[1] I then argue that such "irreducibility"[2] is not *only* a tragic feature of existence but *also* an outgrowth of God's creative power, which reveals itself through diversity in nature and theological diversity within faith traditions. In other words, diversity represents not only the way things are but also the way things should be. To eradicate difference, then, is to eradicate a part of the diversity that God

---

1. Farley, *Good and Evil*, 36.
2. Ibid.

intended for the world and for the church. In this way, it becomes possible to understand diversity theologically as *gift* rather than problem.

I recognize that presenting a theological argument for diversity as a desirable norm does not necessarily make it less anxiety provoking. Consequently, I suggest that the way forward for congregations torn by conflict lies in learning to sit with the anxiety generated by encounters with difference. I frame this idea theologically by adopting a notion of *vulnerability* to difference—i.e., remaining open to difference despite the anxiety and discomfort it produces. Building on this theme, I then argue for a vision of ecclesial hospitality that aims toward finding ways to *remain connected* across difference without attempting to change it. By establishing strong theological rationales for vulnerability and hospitality, I lay the groundwork for exploring, in the final chapter, what these commitments might look like within the concrete context of congregational conflict.

Human Being and the "Tragic"

In addressing the problem of congregational conflict in this book, I have sought to maintain a focus on the *anxiety raised by encounters with difference*. As a means of exploring this anxiety theologically, I draw upon the work of philosophical theologian Edward Farley, who specifically addresses the role that difference plays in human life. In fact, Farley offers a theological answer to the question of why conflict is so common in human communities: because it is part of the "tragic" structure of human existence, which will always include an element of basic incompatibility. In his 1990 text *Good and Evil: Interpreting a Human Condition*, Farley offers a compelling framework for understanding the fundamental brokenness of human existence. However, instead of "brokenness," Farley uses the term "the tragic" to describe the nature of human life, which he further characterizes with words like *vulnerability, incompatibility,* and *alienation*. In fact, the tragic proves the "most general and unifying feature"[3] of the human condition and provides the basic structure for all human experience. Within this conceptual structure, the tragic is "a situation in which the conditions of well-being require and are interdependent with situations of limitation, frustration, challenge, and

---

3. Farley, *Good and Evil*, 28.

suffering."[4] Yet, the presence of suffering itself is not what renders human existence tragic; instead, it is tragic "because sufferings of various sorts are *necessary conditions* of creativity, affection, the experience of beauty, etc."[5] Farley thus uses the term *tragic* not simply to acknowledge the reality of suffering in human life but also to signal that the positive goods human beings experience cannot be achieved without some suffering. The structure of existence means that humans can never be freed from their limitations as created beings and that to experience joy, hope, and peace they must also expect, at times, to experience sadness, despair, and turmoil.

While Farley describes the human condition primarily in terms of "the tragic," this does not mean that he neglects the category of sin. Indeed, later in the text, Farley analyzes sin through a variety of conceptual lenses, including bondage of the will, idolatry, and oppression. These lenses all contribute to an understanding of sin as something that distorts human agency in myriad ways. However, inclinations to sin are not the same as basic human vulnerabilities and limitations. Instead, sin is a "distinctive dynamic," while "the tragic character of our condition" provides the "primary motivating background of sin's origin."[6] Thus, in Farley's view, the tragic—not sin—is the most basic feature of human being. In fact, the tragic is the backdrop against which the realities of sin are played out among individuals and throughout human societies.

This way of understanding the human condition differs quite markedly from more traditional theological approaches, which tend to identify sin—as symbolized by Adam and Eve's transgression in Eden—as the origin of all that ails humanity. Within Farley's framework, by contrast, the potential for such transgression is written into the structure of created beings who have been given the freedom to make their own choices. Of course, too often these choices increase suffering through acts of violation or oppression, and therefore are sinful. Yet, the tragic structure of existence means that human beings will be subject to a certain amount of suffering no matter what choices they make. Suffering, then, is simply part of being human. How human beings deal with suffering, however, sets the stage for experiencing both the burden of sin and the release of redemption.

4. Ibid., 29.
5. Ibid., emphasis in original.
6. Ibid., 121.

To see how this perspective applies to the issue of congregational conflict, we must delve more deeply into its theological framework. In this text, Farley sketches a view of human reality as made up of three main elements: individual agents, the social, and the "interhuman," which he defines as "the sphere of face-to-face relation or being-together in relation."[7] While all three of these elements form interlocking components of human existence, the interhuman remains primary because it is the sphere that forms the foundation for the workings of the others. That is, individual agents cannot be known to one another without the dimension of the interhuman, and, likewise, the sphere of the social is made up of many different interhuman relationships.

Furthermore, within each of these three spheres of reality, the tragic structure of human life creates particular types of vulnerability, defined as "the capacity of a living creature to undergo harm. Harm means both the frustration of the needs and desires of that creature and the pain and suffering that accompany that frustration."[8] Further, the interhuman sphere of relations includes two distinctive kinds of vulnerability: interpersonal suffering and benign alienation. The first of these, interpersonal suffering, "occurs in two primary forms: the suffering that comes from commiseration with the other's suffering; and, the suffering that occurs when interpersonal relations themselves are wounded."[9] This, then, is suffering experienced within the context of specific interpersonal relationships, whether as a result of compassionate empathy or of the grief that accompanies death, discord, or any other form of human fragility.

Unlike interpersonal suffering, which occurs within particular human relationships, benign alienation refers to the more general "incompatibility" between individuals, which results in the "impossibility of harmonizing the perspectives, aims, desires, and agendas of self-initiating persons."[10] In other words, because each person is a unique and irreducible center of needs, thoughts, and experiences, there will inevitably arise occasions in which these elements come into conflict with one another and cannot be easily resolved. In making this claim, Farley wishes to paint a realistic picture of the human condition as falling along a spectrum between the extremes of sentimental goodness, on the one hand,

---

7. Ibid., 33.
8. Ibid., 43.
9. Ibid.
10. Ibid., 45.

and complete destructiveness, on the other.[11] Instead, individuals' needs and desires are profoundly shaped by the tragic nature of human being, and as such they often lead to brokenness in human relationships—not because of evil intentions, but because of the basic given-ness of human incompatibility.

To the reader, the relevance of this theological framework for a discussion of congregational conflict may not be immediately clear. I claim, however, that this understanding of the human condition contributes to a pastoral theological approach to this issue in three particular ways. First of all, Farley offers a view of human being that is neither all-good nor all-bad; rather, it is both complex and ambiguous. Such a vision of the human condition is more true to lived human experience and therefore more relevant to any attempt to reflect on what makes people act the way they do toward one another. This recognition of complexity proves especially important in an investigation of conflict, in which increased anxiety may spur individuals to identify contending groups as either "good" or "bad." This theological framework offers a more nuanced approach to human being that troubles these neat categories and highlights the basic fragility and finitude that likely contribute to all instances of human conflict.

Second, Farley's work offers a way of understanding conflict not as an "evil" to be avoided but as a foreseeable consequence of living in relationship with one another. The description of the human condition as basically tragic, with the potential to move toward good or evil, maps well onto what I wish to claim about conflict: namely, that it is a given part of human relationships that, depending on how it is engaged, can produce positive or negative results. That is, within the basic incompatibility of human life, people can make particular choices about how to engage conflict in ways that either increase or decrease individual and communal suffering. It is on this basis that I will later argue for an approach to congregational conflict that emphasizes vulnerability and hospitality.

Finally, by emphasizing the interhuman dimension of experience, Farley's theology complements my desire to focus on the space between

---

11. In this sense, Farley offers a theological middle ground between the approaches of certain traditional schools of psychology, which tend to describe human nature as either harmonious or antagonistic. As Don Browning and Terry Cooper have argued, humanistic psychology "sees human wants and needs as easily reconciled and coordinated in almost frictionless compatibility," while the Freudian model "sees the world as basically hostile and humans as largely self-absorbed creatures with only small amounts of energy for larger altruistic ventures" (*Religious Thought and the Modern Psychologies*, 5).

individuals (and, by extension, between members of a community) as a key place where human beings experience brokenness. As I explained in chapter 1, pastoral theology as an academic discipline has only recently begun to reclaim its historic roots by refocusing on the experience of ecclesial communities as an important source for new theological knowledge. Farley's focus on the interhuman—which might be described as a "middle" area between an individual care-seeker and society as a whole—meshes well with my interest in the brokenness that can occur through conflict in congregational settings.

Despite these important contributions, however, Farley's description of the nature of human being also invites some constructive critique. I have already noted the helpfulness of understanding human beings as individual centers of needs and desires, which are, by definition, incompatible with one another at times. In this sense, Farley's theological anthropology confirms what we already know through conventional wisdom—namely, that conflict is simply a fact of human life, and that attempts to eradicate it completely are doomed to failure. However, in framing his theological vision of humanity with terms like "tragic" and "incompatible," Farley implies that these are essentially negative realities with which human beings must cope. The fact that human beings are all unique, and possess unique needs and desires that cannot all be easily reconciled, is simply a given that must be tolerated. Farley's view suggests, then, that negotiating the diversity of human life is part of the *cost* for attaining other, more positive aspects of life—such as joy, beauty, and creativity.

For instance, Farley claims that the acknowledgment of difference involves not only an awareness of our inability to understand fully what is in another's mind but also a recognition of the other's basic autonomy in the face of our own—a recognition that brings with it a specific kind of vulnerability. Farley further claims that the reality of alterity brings with it suffering in the form of alienation. This alienation arises from each person's awareness that his or her worldview conflicts with the worldview held by others. Here, again, Farley names a reality that resonates with much of human experience: it is, indeed, painful to recognize that one is not the center of the universe and that one's understandings of the world are limited. In framing human alterity and incompatibility primarily in terms of fragility and loss, however, Farley indirectly suggests that it would be preferable for all human beings *not* to be irreducibly unique. In other words, Farley implies that the radical differences between human beings contribute *only* to human brokenness, and not to human healing.

This is not to say that Farley recognizes no positive value at all in human differences. In fact, he acknowledges that without an "other," the interhuman sphere itself would not exist, since "dialogue, intimacy, and empathy all require a genuine other."[12] Despite this acknowledgment, however, Farley continues to speak of alterity primarily in terms of the tragic nature of human life, rather than in terms of a condition that makes the joys of human relationship possible. This perspective overlooks the possibility that the negotiation of difference through conflict—which many people experience as a form of suffering—may *itself* become a source of creativity and renewed relationship.

That is, instead of seeing humans' unique needs and desires *only* as incompatible, and thus *only* as a challenge to be negotiated through compromise, it is possible *also* to see such diversity as a good created by God—a good that can itself yield further goods of creativity, joy, and beauty. Further, as practical theologian James Poling argues, differences among human beings provide a critical impetus for self-reflection and spiritual growth:

> Difference provokes thought.... Self-conscious lived experience is filled with the tensions of similarity and difference, and identity becomes stronger as these tensions are faced and worked through. We become enlarged spiritual persons as we face the contradictions in our lives and our social setting.... This means that otherness must be preserved as a window into the depths of ultimate reality. Without difference and contrast, there can be no self-conscious experience.[13]

This is not to minimize the power of conflicting human aims to wreak division and brokenness in relationships and communities. Indeed, one of the case studies I have described in this book shows just how damaging such conflicting aims can be. I fully agree that in one sense, the nature of human beings as having vastly diverse goals and desires, which cannot all be smoothly reconciled, represents a tragic dimension of our existence. Yet, to limit our understanding of human being such that the tragic becomes its most essential characteristic also seems to close down the possibilities of human potential.

---

12. Farley, *Good and Evil*, 34–35.
13. Poling, *Rethinking Faith*, 161.

Instead, I propose a theological anthropology that is paradoxical in nature—one that sees human being as both profoundly broken *and* participating in healing at any given moment. This vision understands human beings as individual centers of needs and desires that are often incompatible with one another, a fact which constitutes a tragic dimension to human life. At the same time, this tragic dimension may also contain within it the source for healing and wholeness. The fact that all of our needs and desires are incompatible is, in one sense, tragic; the fact that we all *have* unique needs and desires is a result of God's creative process, which values difference over sameness or seamless agreement. In what follows, I argue for diversity as both a created good and as a desirable norm for faith communities. Such an understanding of diversity creates a pathway for understanding the friction created by difference as both challenge and gift.

Diversity as a Created Good

The theological anthropology advanced in this chapter contributes meaningfully to an understanding of congregational conflict because it moves the discussion from a view of conflict as rooted only in human selfishness and greed (sinfulness) to seeing conflict as an inevitable consequence of life among a diverse human population (the tragic). Within this framework, conflict becomes a reality that is, in some sense, unavoidable. In other words, if one understands conflict as part of the "tragic" structure of human existence, one can no longer say that conflict could be eradicated if everyone would simply cultivate kindness and compassion. To be sure, some forms of *violent* conflict might be avoided this way, but recall that within this conceptual structure, violence falls into the category of sinfulness. It is played out against the backdrop of the tragic, but violence goes a step further. That is, violence does not constitute a foregone conclusion in the same way as incompatibility among conflicting human needs. This is an important theological point because it dispels the illusion that conflict is, by definition, terribly destructive.

Yet, a theological anthropology that sees conflicting human aims as *only* a part of the tragic structure of human existence misses an opportunity to explore the notion that conflict could represent both challenge *and* gift to human beings. I argue instead for a theological understanding of diversity both as a good created by God and as a desirable norm for faith communities. To build this argument, I present a way of interpreting diversity—as it is seen in creation and in theological diversity within faith traditions and communities—not only as a fact of life on this planet but also as a vital part of God's will for the world. In this way, I make a specific case for recognizing such diversity as a desirable norm which congregations are called not only to tolerate but also to embrace as a defining feature of the ecclesia.

Diversity in Creation

Within Christian theology, the concept of diversity as a created good is most commonly found in discussions of creation as a whole. Such discussions frequently describe the sheer teeming diversity of the world as the incarnation of God's "power of differentiation and relationship."[14] Novelty and difference are thus cherished as illustrations of God's never-ending ability to create increasingly varied forms of life. This view has its origins in the early Trinitarian theology of the Christian church. More specifically, the importance of the Trinity to a discussion of creation lies in the *relationality* shared among the three Trinitarian persons. This relationality becomes the wellspring from which flow the abundant and interdependent forms of life on earth.

This Trinitarian basis for understanding the created order entails the recognition of relationship—both among the persons of the Trinity and between God and the world—as "the *primary* metaphysical category."[15] By extension, then, difference and diversity become positive theological attributes because relationship cannot exist without distinctions. Put simply, relating to another person or creature requires that the other be different from oneself. For God to love the world, then, the world must be—in some significant sense—distinguishable from God's own being. Such distinction constitutes a theological good, since it is what makes possible an intimate, loving relationship between God and world. Ultimately, diversity lies at the heart of God's good creation; without difference, there would be no creation at all.

One can also argue for diversity as a created good by focusing on the intimate relationship between the Creator and the world. For instance, process theologians like Marjorie Suchocki have proposed an

---

14. Hodgson, *Winds of the Spirit*, 175.
15. Yordy, "Biodiversity and the Kingdom of God," 170, emphasis in original.

understanding of creation that involves a "call and response" relationship between God and the world: "God calls the world into being, and the world's order exists in and through its response to God. God responds to the world, evaluating and integrating what the world has done with the last call into the divine self. God then calls a new form into existence, with this new form made possible by the last response."[16] In this way of thinking, the relationship between Creator and created becomes a never-ending cycle of mutual response—a cycle originally initiated by God, but the shape of whose progression crucially depends on the many and varied responses of the created order. Within this model, the teeming diversity of the world is not an accident or a divergence from God's intentions, but rather a direct *result* of God's invitation.[17] In this sense, the diversity of creation is not only a theological good, but also a logical inevitability given the way that God has chosen to create the world. That is, God's decision to engage the world in a call-and-response relationship means that the world will necessarily include increasingly diverse forms of life. Since this system is one of God's own choosing, it must, by definition, be good.

Theological Diversity in Faith Communities

The inherent goodness of creation's variety implies an inherent goodness in the diversity of humanity as well. After all, if the innumerable differences among all life forms on the planet point to the goodness of God, it stands to reason that the differences among human beings point to this same goodness. If it is good that God created so many different species of plants and animals, it must also be good that God created human beings with different genders and with a wide variety of skin tones, body types, cultures, and languages. But what about *theological* diversity—including theological diversity within religious traditions, or even within individual congregations? As the case studies in chapter 2 showed, it seemed just as difficult for people to accept differences within their own congregations as it might have been for them to talk about religion with practitioners of completely different faiths. Yet, in researching the topic of congregational conflict, I discovered that very few resources address the dilemma caused by theological pluralism within a single religious

---

16. Suchocki, *Divinity and Diversity*, 28.
17. Ibid., 30–31.

tradition, denomination, or congregation. Many theological texts now grapple with how Christians should approach people of other faiths, and much practical literature exists to help congregations cope with conflict of various types. Still, very few resources reflect on the unique problem experienced by the parishioners in the case studies: namely, how best to enter into *theological* conversation with members of their own faith communities. Why would this be?

One way to explain this gap in the literature is that when it comes to practitioners of other religions, individuals *expect* to encounter difference; but, within their own faith communities, they do not expect to find much theological dissimilarity. Could it be, then, that theological diversity within faith communities is so threatening because it reveals difference where there appeared to be only sameness? After all, as I showed in chapter 3, the basic human desire for sameness often compels individuals to seek others who can function as "psychological twins." It is possible that this desire leads many religious practitioners to seek out communities where they expect to experience a high degree of theological sameness between themselves and their fellow parishioners. As the case studies revealed, even when such sameness is not truly present, many parishioners assume that it is and are both surprised and dismayed to discover significant theological differences between themselves and other members of the faith community.

Closely related to this desire for and/or assumption of sameness within congregations is a pervasive tendency for Christians to cling to a particular notion of unity that seeks to smooth over or eliminate differences in the interest of getting along or keeping the peace. For instance, in the conflict that I witnessed at Grace UCC, several members told me that they wished that Peter Vance—who put forward the original motion to leave the UCC—would simply "drop" his request or "let it go." Such sentiments imply that it would have been better to pretend that disagreement did not exist between the members of Grace UCC than to engage the very real differences of opinion that surfaced within the congregation. This kind of approach, though very common in faith communities, puts forward a vision of unity that really means undifferentiated sameness, or that simply ignores true differences in an effort to maintain the congregation's status quo.

In the remainder of this section I argue for an understanding of theological diversity within faith communities as both fact and norm. First, I make a general case for conceptualizing identity as hybrid and pluralistic. Such a perspective opens a path toward recognizing the ways in which all religious communities and the individuals within them are shaped by multiple forces and contain pluralities. I then argue that such multiplicity is not only the way things are but also the way things *ought* to be. I make this claim by extending the argument for diversity as a created good to apply to differences experienced within individual religious traditions and communities.

Identity as Hybrid and Plural

Encountering difference can prove especially threatening when it occurs in unexpected places, such as within faith communities that were previously assumed to be homogeneous. Contemporary theologian Michele Saracino explores this idea in her book entitled *Being about Borders: A Christian Anthropology of Difference*. In this work, Saracino observes that within postmodern culture, people generally assume that borders are constantly disappearing. The advent of globalization and the rapid development of certain technologies (such as the Internet) are interpreted to mean that boundaries have been broken down and that "in the midst of human diversity we are all part of one unified world."[18] However, such an interpretation "obscures the lived reality that borders are present everywhere—within interpersonal relationships, interreligious communities, and the international panorama."[19]

For many people, the idea of living in a "borderless" world holds strong appeal, because in such a world no one would ever have to engage troubling differences. However, differences *do* exist among human beings, and coping with such difference, even within faith communities, proves extremely difficult at times. Part of what made the experiences of Grace UCC and First UMC so challenging was the discovery of differences where people thought there were none. Because individuals belonged to the same religious community and held certain beliefs and practices in common, they assumed that they would also agree on other theological issues like homosexuality or worship. When they realized that they did not, the resulting differences felt like border lines dividing community members from one another. As a result, people experienced

---

18. Saracino, *Being about Borders*, 1.
19. Ibid.

increased levels of anxiety and began to see these differences as threats to be eradicated.

One way to help Christians cope with the reality of anxiety-provoking differences in their midst is to encourage an understanding of "hybrid existence."[20] Such an understanding recognizes that "our identities are comprised of many different stories, including those related to our gender, ethnicity, class, race, sexual orientation, ability, and religion."[21] All human beings experience such hybrid existence; yet, individuals may not truly appreciate the nature of this hybridity until they come face-to-face with a person whose stories differ dramatically from their own. When this happens, the stories that previously seemed like unassailable truth are suddenly called into question, and the boundaries that had once existed between individuals' identities begin to overlap or disappear.

For most people, recognizing one's own existence as hybrid feels threatening because neat categories of identity abruptly become messy. As a result, relationships with others also become much more complicated. In chapter 3, I noted that the more intimate a relationship is, the more complex and ambiguous parties will seem to one another. In turn, increased complexity and ambiguity create increased anxiety, which makes it more challenging for individuals to maintain integrated images of themselves or those with whom they frequently relate. Consequently, human beings need ways to acknowledge hybridity—both within their own personal identities and within the identities of their religious communities. Recognizing the theological diversity that exists within communities of faith might help parishioners be more comfortable with, and less "emotionally undone," by the differences they discover there.[22]

This requires recognizing religious traditions as containing a plurality of theological positions, rather than as monolithic entities. In my experience, individuals tend to view theological differences *among* Christians as negligible when compared to differences *between* Christians and adherents of other faiths. As a result, people may assume that there is a single "Christian viewpoint" (or "Protestant viewpoint" or "UCC viewpoint," etc.) that decisively defines the parameters for theological conversation. In contrast to such a view of religious communities as unitary, "self-contained" entities, I argue that, in actuality, faith

20. Ibid., 14.
21. Ibid., 14–15.
22. Ibid., 14.

communities "constantly interact, overlap, and modify one another."[23] In this sense, the continual interaction among congregations, denominations, and the wider culture highlights the multi-traditioned nature of all religious communities and all individual adherents within them. This is a crucial point because it dispels rigid notions of doctrinal "purity" or loyalty to a tradition, and exposes such doctrines and traditions as themselves shaped by a variety of factors.

Closely related to a view of religious communities as fluid and multiply formed is the notion of internal pluralism. This term points to the fact that, all too frequently, "differences *within* [religious] traditions are as sharp as differences *across* them."[24] The reality of internal pluralism is borne out in the prevalence of theological conflict within individual denominations and congregations, as in the case studies presented earlier in this book. Given the irrefutable fact of theological diversity within religious communities, an internally pluralistic understanding of traditions is more in keeping with the actual circumstances in which congregational conflict takes place. Recognizing individual and communal identity as hybrid and pluralistic provides a basis for acknowledging the real theological differences that exist in the midst of faith communities, even in those that seem quite homogeneous in other important ways.

Diversity as Theological Norm

I have argued that faith communities are multiply formed and internally pluralistic, and that they are made up of individuals whose identities are similarly hybrid. Such an understanding of identity serves an important purpose within a discussion of theological diversity: it helps explain why discovering theological differences within a single tradition or faith community can be so disorienting. Encountering difference in unexpected places can profoundly threaten an individual or group's sense of identity; consequently, embracing notions of hybridity and pluralism might mitigate the impact of difference when it arises in surprising contexts. Within the argument I am making in this chapter, however, the theological differences within religious traditions and communities not only represent what is but also what *ought to be*. The prescriptive tone of my argument

---

23. Neville, *On the Scope and Truth of Theology*, 17.
24. Thatamanil, *The Immanent Divine*, 5, emphasis in original.

here is necessary to avoid idealizing theological uniformity as God's true intention for the church.

The groundwork for this argument has already been laid by theologians who maintain that differences among creatures permit a fuller representation of God's being. For instance, Sallie McFague has argued that "It is not the oneness or unity that causes us to marvel at creation, but the age, size, diversity, complexity that the common creation story tells us about. If God . . . [is] the empowering, continuing breath of life throughout [creation's] billions of years of history and in each and every entity and life-form on every star and planet, then it is in the *differences* that we see the glory of God."[25] In the same way, it is possible to affirm diversity as part of God's will for the world as it is realized within the specific context of the Christian church. The church has, from its very birth, included a diversity of outlooks—a diversity created by God's abundant Spirit, which has been poured out and enacted through a multiplicity of beliefs and practices that ultimately enrich the church as a whole.[26] Such a vision of the church lends theological weight to the notion of diversity as *gift*: because God has created diversity, an encounter with difference means an encounter with a unique part of God's creation. Thus, human diversity points not to a departure from God's intention for the world, but rather to a concrete embodiment of it.

From this perspective, the theological plurality that inevitably exists within Christianity serves a vital purpose: it empowers the church to incarnate its identity as the body of Christ. As evangelical theologian John R. Franke argues, God has created and sustained this complex identity for the purpose of doing God's work in the world:

> The diversity of the Christian faith is not, as some approaches to church and theology might seem to suggest, a problem that needs to be overcome. Instead, this diversity is part of the divine design and intention for the church as the image of God and the body of Christ in the world. Christian plurality is a good thing, not something that needs to be struggled against and overturned.[27]

Indeed, given the church's status as the living body of Christ in the world, all of the different "parts" of the body are needed in order for God's

---

25. McFague, *The Body of God*, 155, emphasis in original.
26. See Yong, *Hospitality and the Other*.
27. Franke, *Manifold Witness*, 7–8.

purposes to be accomplished. To exclude any of these parts (i.e., particular Christian traditions or understandings) from the church's identity and mission is to hamper the ability of the body to participate fully in "the plurality of truth lived out in the eternal life of God."[28] Without the multiplicity contained within the different parts of Christianity, the church would no longer represent the living body of Christ, but only individual pieces that no longer constitute a whole. Instead, the church is called to be a manifold reality that contains plural understandings of truth and that bases its unity not in uniformity of belief or practice but in its commitment to the "liberating and reconciling mission of God."[29] In turn, this makes it possible to understand the diversity within Christianity as an inherent good, created by God and reflective of the relational multiplicity contained within the divine life itself.

This approach contributes helpfully to a discussion of theological diversity within faith communities because it extends the argument for diversity as a created good and applies it to practitioners within one particular religious tradition. Given that the focus of this book is theological disagreement between members of a single faith community, it makes sense to extend this argument even further. I argue for a robust ecclesiology founded on the metaphor of Christ's body—a body made up of many different parts, all of which are required for the body to function properly. Seeing theological diversity *within* individual faith communities as a created good affirms that God intentionally created all the parts of the body to function differently. In other words, God never intended that all parts of the body would eventually become the same.

Of course, this idea has its origin in the words of Scripture, which offers a powerful image of the importance of diversity among the parts of Christ's body: "If the whole body were an eye, where would the hearing be? If the whole body were hearing, where would the sense of smell be? But as it is, God arranged the members in the body, each one of them, as he chose. If all were a single member, where would the body be?"[30] This New Testament image has profound implications for a discussion of congregational conflict because it allows us to shift our understanding of what actually poses the greatest threat to the body's continued cohesion. Perhaps what breaks Christ's body is not conflict itself, but the attempt to

---

28. Ibid., 137.
29. Ibid., 131.
30. 1 Cor 12:17–19 (NRSV).

erase difference—difference which is, by definition, part of being human and part of living in Christian community. What breaks Christ's body is trying to make all of its parts look exactly the same. In this way of thinking, then, theological diversity represents not only a reality with which we must cope but also an inherent good that, when eliminated from our common life together, harms churches' ability faithfully to incarnate Christ's body in the world.

For those in congregations torn by conflict, however, this position may appear naïve at best and completely untenable at worst. After all, to claim that theological diversity within communities of faith is a good created by God suggests that there is no final answer to the complex questions with which such communities currently wrestle. At Grace UCC, for example, the crux of the conflict rested on individuals' understanding of homosexuality within the context of Christian faith. It is not possible, some might say, for homosexuality to be both wrong and right at the same time. Is it not important, then, for communities of faith to strive toward theological uniformity on particularly important issues?

In response to this question, I offer two observations. First, even within communities that seem to have achieved such uniformity, theological diversity likely still exists. Indeed, as I have already argued, religious traditions are both internally pluralistic and influenced by multiple factors, including a variety of cultures in which the traditions themselves may be situated. Thus, it cannot be assumed that the established doctrines and practices of a particular religious community are "givens" that no longer require critical scrutiny. The example of slavery offers an illustration of how previous givens within a faith tradition may later be recognized as theologically indefensible:

> There may, indeed, at any one point in time be certain practices that all Christians immediately perceive to be incompatible with their faith (for instance, judgments about slavery are now of that sort).... One cannot assume from these easy cases that hard ones are rare. Nor can one assume that easy cases now were not hard ones earlier. These easy cases in fact became so by way of earlier disputations among Christians who deliberated differently about what their faith required.[31]

In emphasizing the importance of "disputations" to the process of refining Christian practices over time, this example points to the crucial roles

---

31. Tanner, *Theories of Culture*, 141.

of dialogue and debate, even within one particular tradition or congregation. In ecclesial terms, this is known as discernment, in which members of a faith community work together to assess whether previous theological commitments still seem to reflect the will of God and faithfulness to the church's mission.

Second, I suggest that it is still possible to understand theology as a search for truth without demanding theological uniformity within a faith community. As we have seen, the quest for uniformity in congregations often translates into an attempt to extinguish real theological differences between individuals. Such an attempt actually results in a diminishment of the church because it masks the true diversity of Christ's body—a diversity which, I contend, represents God's will for creation in general and for human beings in particular. Yet, to affirm the goodness of theological diversity within faith communities does not necessarily entail a relativistic, "anything goes" mentality. In fact, wrestling with theological claims in the context of a congregation involves testing those claims against the historic witness of the tradition. While at times that witness may itself require correction, a respect for theological diversity must also include willingness to accord generosity to one's own spiritual ancestors. Within this process, the theological judgments one ultimately makes must in turn render themselves vulnerable to the same kind of correction. In this way, Christians within a given faith community may submit their theological claims to one another for scrutiny and correction, while remaining flexible enough to maintain normative claims that their religious forebears have tested and refined over time. This approach makes it possible for congregations to hold in tension the notion of theological diversity as a desirable norm, on the one hand, and the commitment to theology as a search for truth, on the other.

In order to see internal theological pluralism as a positive resource for congregations coping with conflict, it is now vital to redefine the ultimate goal of theological reflection. In many religious contexts the assumed goal of theology is uniform *agreement* on a set of beliefs or doctrines that are normative for the community. In this view, theology's task lies simply in articulating the concepts that already implicitly define the community's perceived boundaries. While such articulation may play a pivotal role in faith groups' identity formation, the true task of theology is not the achievement of agreement, but rather, reflection on "what is ultimately important and valuable."[32] This definition of theology remains purposefully vague; in so doing, it allows for a maximum number of viewpoints to contend with one another about what qualifies as ultimately important or valuable. In this process, truth is ever more closely approximated as theological propositions are systematically weighed and tested against each other. In other words, this understanding of theology allows for theological perspectives to converse with one another on the same level, but *without necessarily coming to full agreement*. Indeed, the very notion of theology as reflection on "what is ultimately important and valuable" marks out space for interpretation and argument rather than easy consensus.[33]

Despite the importance of redefining theology's goal away from notions of complete agreement, however, it is also important to avoid the opposite extreme of complete fragmentation. Such fragmentation is often what religious practitioners fear when they consider engaging theological diversity within their own faith communities. As the congregational case studies showed, the threat of fragmentation is real, and preventing its emergence is not always possible. I propose that the primary goal of theology as a search for truth must now be modified to include the related goals of productive dialogue and openness to disagreement. Such an understanding means that parishioners will inevitably face the fact of theological pluralism and will be challenged to assume a posture of remaining open to the differences in their midst—a posture that itself requires a solid theological foundation. In what follows, I argue that a theological vision of *vulnerability to difference* can provide just such a foundation and can help create solidarity in the midst of irreducible diversity.

Vulnerability to Difference

In this chapter I have argued for understanding individual and communal identity as hybrid and pluralistic, and for viewing such diversity within faith communities as a good created by God. Yet, acknowledging that difference exists in faith communities and embracing the idea that God intended the church to contain a "plurality of truth"[34] are only

---

32. Neville, *On the Scope and Truth of Theology*, 1.
33. Ibid.
34. Franke, *Manifold Witness*, 137.

the first steps toward a vision of theological diversity. While these are important ideas, they do not necessarily temper the visceral reaction that so often arises in the encounter with difference, especially when it emerges in unexpected places. As a means of addressing the anxiety often produced by such encounters, I propose a theological understanding of *vulnerability to difference* as key to the creation of true community. This vision of vulnerability supplements the theological anthropology already advanced in this chapter by framing contingency not only as part of the tragic structure of human existence but also as that which makes loving relationships and hospitable communities possible.

As Farley has suggested, vulnerability represents a primary component of the tragic nature of human life. The fact that human beings have the power to hurt one another—whether through overt acts of sinfulness or through the incompatibility of competing needs and desires—is simply part of the way we are made. Our freedom carries with it the capacity to harm; likewise, our ability to experience joy and beauty also opens us to the possibility of experiencing sorrow and loss. Vulnerability is thus a defining condition of human being that is more akin to brokenness than to sinfulness or evil. As I have noted, however, this understanding of vulnerability emphasizes its role in human pain and suffering.

A different way of understanding vulnerability is to see it less as a condition that simply must be endured and more as a crucial factor in the relatedness that is at the core of being human. Of course, this way of framing vulnerability is not new within the field of constructive theology. Numerous contemporary theologians—including Rita Nakashima Brock, Thomas E. Reynolds, Kristine A. Culp, and Elizabeth O'Donnell Gandolfo—have engaged vulnerability as a key part of their thinking about the nature of human being.[35] These writers, and others like them, highlight the two-edged nature of vulnerability. Vulnerability, after all, includes both the ability to be harmed and the ability to be fully known. In fact, for intimacy to be established in relationships, vulnerability is crucial. Vulnerability provides a space for each person to encounter another in all his or her uniqueness. Yet vulnerability also opens the real possibility of being hurt or disappointed. It is the source both of human connectedness and of the damage human beings experience in relationships.[36]

---

35. See Brock, *Journeys by Heart*; Reynolds, *Vulnerable Communion*; Culp, *Vulnerability and Glory*; and Gandolfo, *The Power and Vulnerability of Love*.

36. See Brock, *Journeys by Heart*, 7.

Here it is important not to understate the risk that comes with vulnerability. For those who have experienced violence or mistreatment at the hands of another, talking about vulnerability may sound trite at best or dangerous at worst. I am not suggesting that people willingly put themselves in harm's way or submit quietly to victimization in the name of vulnerability. Rather, what I wish to communicate through this concept is just the basic, paradoxical element of human nature: that the condition that allows us to be hurt by one another is the very same condition that makes intimacy and community possible. As Gandolfo has observed, "as unattractive as our exposure to harm may be, vulnerability is also the condition for the possibility of existence itself, along with the possibility of goodness and flourishing. Human life and happiness are only achievable within the contours of our fragile, finite existence."[37]

Yet, within relationships and communities, people often do resist vulnerability, and often for good reason. If individuals have been hurt by others or feel threatened in some way, it is perfectly natural for them to want to protect themselves. Further, as pastoral theologian Melinda McGarrah Sharp has written, "Human beings simply do not desire vulnerability in the precise moments that they experience destabilization of a sense of self and communal identity."[38] In a situation of protracted conflict within a faith community, it is likely that people will be experiencing destabilization in many different ways, so they will probably be more inclined to think of vulnerability as a weakness that others can exploit rather than a strength that can enliven and enrich relationships.

Even so, an understanding of human vulnerability that includes the potential for *both* "devastation" and "transformation"[39] is crucial for this exploration of conflict in faith communities because of how it connects with the themes of anxiety and identity with which I have been working throughout this book. As we have seen, the encounter with difference frequently produces anxiety because, as human beings, difference subjects us to the ways others may disagree with us, hurt us, or contest our views of the world. Our natural human inclination is to defend against the threats produced by vulnerability, either by gravitating toward sameness in our relationships and communities, and/or by behaving defensively or aggressively toward those we experience as different and strange. If

37. Gandolfo, *The Power and Vulnerability of Love*, 25.
38. Sharp, *Misunderstanding Stories*, 111.
39. I owe this way of naming the different aspects of vulnerability to theologian Kristine Culp (*Vulnerability and Glory*, 3).

we understand vulnerability *only* in terms of our capacity to be harmed, we will continue to operate in a defensive mode that seeks to protect our sense of self from anxiety-producing encounters with difference. But this is a double-edged sword: if we protect ourselves from the disconcerting presence of difference, we also close ourselves off from the ways in which we might be enriched or enlivened through relationship with those who do not necessarily think, believe, or act as we do.

The vision of vulnerability I am commending here, then, seeks not to eliminate difference but to recognize it as the "starting point" for all true relationship.[40] Instead of assuming sameness, vulnerability involves stepping back and trying to see the other for who he or she truly is. Vulnerability thus requires a willingness to be hurt, challenged, or changed by difference. It also requires a willingness to endure the anxiety produced by difference, which can threaten our perceptions that our own ways of living and thinking may not be the only right ways. From this perspective then, it is no longer adequate simply to acknowledge and tolerate the existence of difference. Instead, this theology demands a posture of "embrace" that "receives the other's difference as contributive, valuable, and good."[41] In a very real sense, to try to avoid the vulnerability generated by an encounter with difference is to avoid relationship altogether. It is, in fact, to avoid the possibility of giving and receiving love.[42]

Within the context of the church, loving relationships between individuals contribute to the relationality experienced throughout the community of faith. Therefore, trying to erase the conditions that lead to vulnerability (i.e., difference) actually erases the conditions that create and define the Christian community. Indeed, as I have argued above, what breaks Christ's body is not the existence of difference itself, nor even the conflict that inevitably arises in the midst of differences. Instead, what breaks Christ's body is the attempt to eliminate difference because such an attempt impairs the church's ability to function in the way that God intended—namely, as an embodiment of God's love for the world. Instead of resisting vulnerability, Christians are called to embrace it and remain open to true relationship with one another, even across serious theological differences. Bringing such a vision to fruition is no easy task. Yet, as I will argue in the final section of this chapter, remaining connected across differences through ecclesial hospitality is one vitally important way of doing so.

40. Reynolds, *Vulnerable Communion*, 14.
41. Reynolds, *The Broken Whole*, 189.
42. Reynolds, *Vulnerable Communion*, 123.

Remaining Connected across Difference: Ecclesial Hospitality

Through case studies and theoretical analysis, this book has illustrated just how powerfully human beings resist becoming vulnerable to difference. The disciplines of psychodynamic psychology, social psychology, and theology all help explain the origins and development of such resistance. Consequently, congregations in conflict need ways to counteract this tendency and to move *toward* vulnerability as part of becoming more fully human and more fully connected in community. I suggest that congregations might achieve this through a vision of ecclesial hospitality that seeks to *remain connected across difference*—even significant theological difference. In the concluding section of this chapter, I offer a brief sketch of how we might understand such hospitality theologically.

Within the Jewish and Christian traditions, hospitality is an ancient concept rooted in the religious experience of the people of Israel. This tradition of hospitality continued to grow and thrive in the context of early Christianity, appearing as a central theme in the writings of St. Paul, John Chyrsostom, Martin Luther, John Calvin, and many other Christian leaders.[43] In the context of this discussion, I use the term *hospitality* to denote a posture of relationship that recognizes the basic human dignity of others and that embraces apparent differences. Such a posture of dignity entails "a welcoming of one's neighbor that bears and invites him or her into a shared space of mutuality, a household."[44] I ground this understanding of hospitality in a concept for which I have already argued in this chapter: namely, *vulnerability to difference* as central to the creation of community. In so doing, I argue for a theological understanding of hospitality that sees difference not as a difficulty to be overcome, but as a defining mark of the church that embodies loving relationship.

To make this argument, I advance an ecclesiology that sees vulnerability to difference as the heart of Christian community. Within the context of the church, difference should not be seen as a problem to be overcome or eradicated. Instead, it should become "constitutive of the new community, which is a *koinonia* [communion] through and not in spite of diversity."[45] In making this claim, I reinforce my arguments for

---

43. Pohl, *Making Room*, 5–6.
44. Reynolds, *Vulnerable Communion*, 241.
45. Ibid., 235.

diversity as a desirable norm and put forward a vision of hospitality that could help make the acceptance of such diversity a reality within faith communities. Committing to this vision of hospitality—one that seeks to remain connected across difference, rather than ignoring or trying to erase it—provides an important theological resource for congregations experiencing conflict in their midst. Such a vision points the way toward an understanding of community that, through shared vulnerability, "creates space for identifying with and receiving the stranger as oneself."[46]

Here, I intentionally use the language of "remaining connected across difference" as a way of theologically reframing the concept of differentiation from family systems theory. As I noted in chapter 1, family systems theory (FST) identifies anxiety as the primary social force operating within families and organizations, and differentiation as the primary path toward soothing anxiety and reducing emotional volatility. According to FST, differentiation involves the ability to "maintain a position and still stay in touch."[47] In other words, it is the capacity to define one's own values and goals clearly and to do so in a way that enhances, rather than destroys, connections with others. Because it represents a way of holding in tension two competing human needs (i.e., the needs for individuality and togetherness), differentiation proves a useful starting point for imagining what relationships of hospitality might look like within religious communities.

Theologically speaking, members of faith communities experience competing needs that demonstrate parallels with the needs for individuality and togetherness: the need to stand firmly on one's deeply held religious truths and values, and the need to experience connection within a religious community that embodies welcome through its diversity. On the surface, these needs seem diametrically opposed; yet, many religious resources understand paradox and complexity as basic facts of human life. In the same way, I argue that *both* the quest for truth *and* the celebration of diversity can be affirmed at the same time within faith communities. In fact, both are required if congregations wish to use conflict as a resource for growth and creativity. Admittedly, as the congregational case studies showed, keeping these two elements in balance is no easy task. Too much emphasis on diversity can cause people to feel as if their fundamental religious convictions are being disrespected or ignored, and

---

46. Ibid., 242.
47. Friedman, *Generation to Generation*, 230.

contribute to fragmentation. Conversely, too much emphasis on theological agreement can push some community members to the margins and make them feel unwelcome.

As a means of bridging this gap, I put forward a vision of ecclesial hospitality that seeks to remain connected across differences. Such hospitality requires neither watering down one's own convictions in an attempt to establish "peace" within the community, nor considering others' differences as threats to be eradicated. Instead, within this vision of hospitality, Christians are invited to recognize diversity as a good intended by God and thus to welcome each person as a unique embodiment of the divine creative power. In this way, individuals can remain committed to the expression of their own theological principles, but are challenged to do so in ways that resist cutting off or castigating those who disagree. Instead, members of the faith community must seek ways of understanding the search for theological truth as a shared venture that requires compassion, openness, and a willingness to remain vulnerable to the discomfort that comes with encountering difference.

Again, I do not suggest that embodying such hospitality within congregations is simple or effortless. Bringing such loving communion to fruition in the midst of real human communities is often much more easily said than done. However, in addition to recognizing the difficulty of achieving true hospitality, it is also important to emphasize its nature as nonhierarchical. In recent years, numerous writers have problematized the use of hospitality as a theological category because of its implication of inequality between guest and host, since the guest depends on the host for generosity or even survival. Conventional understandings of hospitality remain inadequate because they rely on simply assimilating "others" into unaltered systems of power.[48] Such views of hospitality, which ostensibly aim toward "inclusion," continue to keep the "host" in the powerful position of extending or denying welcome, without critically examining the system in which this dynamic operates.[49] Others have criticized engaging hospitality theologically because of the term's association with the hospitality industry. Within that context, the relationship between guest and host remains unequal, but the guest is the one holding special power because of the economic arrangements involved.[50] Despite

---

48. See Fulkerson, *Changing the Subject*.

49. Streufert, "An Affinity for Difference," 34.

50. Feminist writers have noted that the notion of hospitality becomes even more problematic when it is used in certain contexts to contribute to the exploitation and

these important critiques of hospitality, however, I contend that it still proves useful for a discussion of congregational conflict, as long as it is imagined as a relationship of mutuality that seeks to remain connected across difference.[51]

The acts of Jesus as recounted in Scripture also make a powerful contribution to the nonhierarchical vision of hospitality I wish to commend here. Indeed, in any discussion of Christian hospitality, Jesus must serve as the central model because he "represents and embodies the hospitality of God."[52] As ethicist Luke Bretherton has argued, in the New Testament (and especially in the Luke–Acts tradition) Jesus becomes a paradigm of hospitality not only by offering it to those whom society deemed least deserving but also by *receiving* it from the most unlikely places. In this sense, Jesus constantly plays the role of the "journeying guest/host,"[53] and in so doing, breaks down the hierarchy that might ordinarily characterize these roles. Jesus thus becomes a living representation of God's abundant welcome to all who receive him. Because Jesus has set such a powerful example of hospitality through his simultaneous roles as guest and host, Christians are now called to emulate him by both receiving and offering hospitality to others.

Ideally, then, hospitality is a nonhierarchical reality that makes space for difference. Furthermore, it is possible to overcome the potential pitfalls of inequality between guest and host by emphasizing shared vulnerability as that which draws human beings into relationship with one another in the context of community. Even though the traditional understanding of hospitality sees the guest as dependent on the host, hospitality also makes the host vulnerable in important ways: "Once the stranger is invited in, the host yields stability and control, adjusting the household to accommodate and attend to the guest's unique needs as they became apparent."[54] This vision of hospitality suggests that members of

---

oppression of women. For example, in some countries, the term "hospitality girls" is used as a euphemism for prostitutes within the industry of international sex trafficking. See, for instance, Mirkinson, "Red Light, Green Light," lines 1–3.

51. Indeed, as ethicist Luke Bretherton convincingly argues, it is important to maintain hospitality as a theological category because of its "antecedents in Christian social practice" and its grounding in "explicitly biblical and theological imperatives" (*Hospitality as Holiness*, 125).

52. Yong, *Hospitality and the Other*, 101.

53. Bretherton, *Hospitality as Holiness*, 135.

54. Reynolds, *Vulnerable Communion*, 243.

faith communities remain connected across their differences, but not in a unidirectional way, by assuming that the other must be fixed or tolerated. Instead, such hospitality challenges each person to recognize the ways in which one's own certainties are challenged by another's presence and to welcome others as they are without needing to change them. Within the context of the faith community, then, all are called to be guests *and* hosts to one another, in a perpetual relationship of giving and receiving welcome.

This is not to say that there are no limits to hospitality or that being hospitable means excusing unacceptable behavior in the name of "welcome." If I extend hospitality to guests in my home, for instance, I can welcome them as they are, but I can also ask them to join me in a commitment to keeping our shared environment free of certain kinds of destructive behavior (e.g., violence against or verbal abuse of persons). Similarly, communities of faith can welcome the expression of a variety of theological points of view but can also protect the dignity of all their members by agreeing to maintain respectful modes of communication and action at all times. In the event that this agreement is violated, community members must find ways to hold one another accountable to the shared behavioral norms of the group. From this perspective, then, hospitality is not a wishy-washy, "anything goes" approach to community, but rather a true openness to difference that simultaneously maintains standards of respect and care, rooted in God's grace.[55]

Opening oneself to difference in this way goes against many natural human inclinations. Throughout this book, I have emphasized that the encounter with difference frequently provokes anxiety and can lead to destructive behaviors designed to protect the self from threats. Despite the difficulty of remaining open to difference without becoming defensive, I suggest that it is only through such vulnerability that we can begin to embody the kind of hospitality I have attempted to describe here. In this view, hospitality does not pride itself on its generosity or on its ability to include others who are defined as deviating from a norm. Instead, those who practice this type of hospitality decenter themselves and are willing to be changed by the encounter with difference, recognizing that their own dearly held beliefs may be questioned in the process. Those who seek to embody the hospitality modeled by Jesus assume the roles of both

---

55. For further reflections about the limits of hospitality, particularly within the context of multiculturalism, see Miller-McLemore and Sharp, "Are There Limits to Multicultural Inclusion?"

guest and host, understanding that in doing so they make themselves vulnerable to others in a variety of ways. It is just this kind of vulnerability that can provide the basis for cohesion within faith communities, even in the midst of what may feel like intractable differences. As Bretherton writes, "Openness to the stranger requires constant remembrance of our strangeness to God and God's hospitality of us. Thus hospitality to the stranger is an evangelical imperative: it is a mark of the truthful disclosure of God's nature by a people who themselves are guests of God."[56] The cohesion that emerges from our shared vulnerability or "strangeness" can, in turn, become the unity that Christians so often seek with one another—not a unity that depends on strict theological uniformity, but a unity that draws the faithful together in community, sustained by the love of God and by the power of the Holy Spirit.

Conclusion

In this chapter, I have argued that the discipline of theology provides vital resources for reflection on congregational conflict. While social scientific theories demonstrate that the anxiety stirred by difference represents a natural part of human development, they offer few resources for reframing difference itself. Building on a broad affirmation of diversity as a created good, I have argued that difference represents *both* an aspect of basic human incompatibility *and* a good that God intended. Furthermore, I have suggested that such difference proves necessary for human beings to be in relationship with one another, and for the church fully to incarnate the body of Christ. Based on these theological proposals, I have commended vulnerability and hospitality as pathways through which members of congregations torn by conflict might seek to remain connected to one another across their differences. As always, however, the question remains: *how*? How, exactly, can churches and their leaders embrace diversity as part of God's overall creative project, even as they acknowledge its anxiety-producing qualities? To answer this question, I turn in the final chapter to a description of particular practices that may help communities of faith navigate significant theological conflict in their midst.

---

56. Bretherton, *Hospitality as Holiness*, 138.

6

What Can Conflicted Congregations Do?
Practices for Faith Communities and Their Leaders

In this book, I have engaged the resources of psychodynamic psychology, social psychology, and theology to show that the anxiety raised by encounters with difference is a natural part of being human. The social sciences do a particularly good job of describing what happens when this normal dimension of human life becomes too powerful: it produces destructive behaviors like splitting and projection, rigid needs for sameness, or contentious tactics within a group setting. For its part, theology is especially well-suited to offer a remedy to these destructive effects by reframing conflict and difference in ways that can soothe anxiety within a group and point toward a new understanding of being together in community. To this end, I have made a case for diversity as a desirable theological norm within faith communities, and for a vision of ecclesial hospitality that seeks to help members of congregations be vulnerable to and remain connected across difference.

With these new psychological and theological understandings in place, I return to the realm of practice. Now that we can see more clearly what is happening in conflicted congregations—psychologically, social psychologically, and theologically—we must ask: what difference does this make? How do these understandings help us imagine what faith communities and their leaders might do differently when they encounter conflict in their midst? Before attempting to answer these questions, I reflect on an observation practical theologian Joyce Ann Mercer once made in a public lecture.[1] In presenting her ethnographic research on congregations experiencing conflict around issues of human sexuality, Mercer noted that these situations seem to bear little resemblance to the kind of "interest-based conflicts"—such as divorce disputes or disagreements about business practices—that are typically addressed through conflict mediation services. Instead, congregational conflicts around sexuality are much more similar to the "identity-based" conflicts seen in the realm of international peace-making efforts. Such identity-based conflicts are "fueled by a group's sense that their very ability to *be* is at stake."[2] In other words, people begin to fear that if they are on the "losing" side of the conflict, their basic sense of identity or selfhood will be at risk of annihilation.

Mercer's insights connect with much that I have been saying in this book—namely, that congregational conflict is frequently driven by anxiety raised by encounters with difference. Since anxiety represents a basic sense of threat to one's selfhood or identity, it stands to reason that in congregations experiencing high levels of chronic anxiety, individuals may feel that their identities as persons and as members of groups are at risk in some fundamental way. When this happens, the conflict—which may have originally arisen as a disagreement about a specific issue—instead begins to take on the character of identity-based conflicts. Such conflicts tend to be "intractable in their amenability to intervention" and "extraordinarily difficult to heal."[3] Furthermore, most resources currently available to help congregations cope with conflict are based in problem-solving or mediation models that are designed to deal with interest-based, not identity-based, conflicts. As a result, many of these models simply do not work for the kinds of volatile and divisive conflicts that many congregations are now experiencing. Also, as I have already discussed, congregational conflicts around issues of theology touch on deep dimensions of individual and collective identity. For this reason, understanding such conflicts through an identity-based framework may be more helpful than the typical interest-based approach that most current resources offer. Therefore, I focus in this chapter on practices designed to soothe anxiety and facilitate healing and transformation in communities,

1. Mercer, "Drama, Trauma, and Comma."
2. Ibid.
3. Ibid.

rather than on task-oriented approaches that may not address the larger identity issues involved.

At this point, I return to reflection on the case studies as a means of moving toward concrete proposals for congregations in conflict. As I argued in chapter 2, examining the two case studies side by side is instructive because it reveals similarities that help clarify the dynamics of congregational conflict. However, this method is also useful because of the differences it unearths—differences that led to very different outcomes in each of the congregations under consideration here. In this concluding chapter, I reflect further on these varied outcomes and build on them to suggest three broad practices for helping conflicted congregations embody ecclesial hospitality: (1) acknowledge difference and the anxiety it produces; (2) redefine unity and strengthen relationships; and (3) cultivate calm, connected leadership.

Acknowledging Difference and Anxiety

Much of this book has been devoted to sketching the ways in which individuals and groups respond to the anxiety produced by encounters with difference. I have argued that this anxiety is a normal part of being human; as such, it is not something that can ever be completely eliminated from group life. However, I have also argued that *how* congregations respond to this anxiety has significant implications for whether conflict in their midst proves creative or destructive. My observation of Grace UCC, and many other congregations with which I have been associated over the years, has convinced me that most faith communities tend to avoid acknowledging the differences in their midst, particularly if those differences are about "important" things. These kinds of differences produce anxiety among church members, who frequently respond in one of two ways: either trying to pretend that the differences do not really matter, or trying to "convert" others to one's point of view so that the group will share a high level of sameness on important issues. In either case, the differences are not fully acknowledged and, as a result, the anxiety is never fully relieved. Instead, individuals and groups simply cover up the underlying anxiety and, in many cases, they make this anxiety worse through their attempts to ignore or eradicate the real differences that exist among them.

In light of this observation, it seems to me that the first step for congregations in conflict is to acknowledge the differences in their midst, as well as the anxiety that frequently accompanies those differences. At first glance, this may seem like an unusual suggestion. After all, if a congregation is in conflict, don't members already know that there are differences of opinion within the group? The answer to this question, I believe, is both yes and no. Obviously, in a situation of conflict, people are aware that there is a disagreement afoot. Yet, in such situations individuals often believe that there is only one solution to the problem or one "right" way to think or believe, and thus their job is to convince those on the other side to change their minds. This way of dealing with conflict actually refuses to acknowledge the real differences within a faith community because it assumes that, ultimately, the goal is for everyone to start thinking the same way about a problem or issue. This is a standard of sameness, not diversity. As such, in my view, it is not the most effective way of handling conflict within a group, which necessarily contains a myriad of different ways of thinking about matters of faith and human life. Thus, instead of coping with conflict by trying to ignore difference or enforce uniformity, I suggest that congregations start by intentionally acknowledging the important distinctions that exist within the group.

Provide Opportunities for All Voices to Be Heard

One of the most effective ways of acknowledging differences within a group setting is to provide everyone the opportunity to be heard. This kind of open, honest discussion helps dispel the perception of unanimity on any particular issue and reveals the internal diversity that is almost certain to exist in any community of faith. In other words, by allowing everyone the opportunity to speak his or her mind in an environment that feels safe, the group facilitates the expression of differences in a way that is less threatening than the argumentative, adversarial model so frequently used in congregations. Furthermore, creating this kind of environment promotes the kind of healthy vulnerability within a community necessary for wholeness: "When we listen in this way, it shows our willingness not only to be known in our vulnerability but also to hear others with respect and care for their vulnerability."[4] It seems, then, that one of the best ways to help congregations reduce anxiety in their midst

---

4. Hunsinger and Latini, *Transforming Church Conflict*, 16.

is simply to encourage them to talk to one another in ways that facilitate understanding rather than animosity.

The question then becomes: *how*? Exactly how does one create an environment where varying perspectives can be shared in a nonthreatening way? One of the most striking differences that emerged in the case studies of Grace UCC and First UMC was the ways in which their respective opportunities for conversation were structured. At Grace UCC, the senior pastor and I were taken aback by the conflict, and thus were put in a position of reacting rather than responding to the turmoil unfolding in the church. Although we attempted to plan a series of events designed to facilitate "dialogue" among parishioners, these large-group conversations ended up being more like verbal wars with very little opportunity for authentic interchange. Our goal was to create a calm environment where individuals could listen to one another carefully and speak without fear of being attacked. Instead, these gatherings felt tense and anxious, and many participants seemed more focused on making their argument as forcefully as possible than on truly understanding what others were saying.

In fact, many of the Grace UCC parishioners I interviewed commented on how ineffective these meetings were. Leah, for instance, remembered the gatherings this way: "I think people did a lot of talking, but I don't think people did a lot of listening. . . . People stood up and made their point, but there wasn't a dialogue." "Stephanie" also found these meetings to be ineffective because even with so much "talk" going on, most people ultimately did not feel that they had truly been heard:

> I think some of these people that actually did [leave the church], I don't feel like their thoughts and their feelings on the subject matter was really addressed—their fears. . . . I don't think the meetings were helpful because to me it flared tempers, it raised a lot of tempers . . . that was no different than a brawl. . . . I don't think our process was helpful.

It seems that because the process at Grace UCC was hastily planned with little formal structure, it proved ineffective in facilitating the kind of conversations for which we had hoped. As a result, parishioners felt disappointed, frustrated, and angry because they did not get the chance to be heard on an issue that was extremely important to them.

At First UMC, the picture was quite different. Roy described *listening* to others' perspectives as central to the process Rev. Fisher used to facilitate the worship committee meetings: "[The senior pastor] did a great job.... He did it scripturally, prayerfully—just started letting people talk about this process, you know, to talk about—hearing the other person. Why does [the 11:00 service] mean so much to you? You're eighty years old, and been singing in the choir for sixty years. Tell us why it means so much to you." Ann, a new member at First UMC at the time of the conflict, identified this focus on hearing all voices as the key to the congregation's ability to find a resolution to their problem:

> And I think the key to the whole meeting and the key to the whole change was that people were listened to. *Every single person was listened to.* And whether it turned out how they wanted it to turn out or not, I think that was secondary to the fact that they had a chance to say what they needed to say and they were listened to without interruption.[5]

Ann added that allowing everyone's voice to be heard helped First UMC avoid being split into rigid factions or "camps" because people felt less threatened and thus less compelled to stick only with members of their own group. As she put it, "there wasn't really a need to go into a camp because you got to say what you needed to say. And the other people got to say that I understand you; I hear you."

Based on the experience of these two congregations, it seems clear that healthy conflict in communities of faith requires finding a way for all to have their voices heard so that differences can be surfaced and engaged in constructive ways. However, this admonition is not only a logistical one; it carries psychological and theological weight as well. As I have argued throughout this book, people become more anxious in the presence of difference because at a basic level, their very sense of selfhood feels threatened. Thus, if parishioners are effectively excluded from conversations about matters that are of personal and communal import, they feel as if their selves are not being fully recognized by the community of which they are a part. When this happens, congregations

---

5. Emphasis added. Interestingly, Ann's point is also supported by current social psychological research. In a study that examined citizens' attitudes about and experiences with law enforcement, social psychologist Tom R. Tyler found that "People have more favorable attitudes toward legal authorities if they are allowed to state their case. The increase in favorability is as great when people do not think that what they say influences the decision as it is when they think that it does" (*Why People Obey the Law*, 127). In other words, it seems that *being heard*—regardless of the outcome—is an extremely important factor in helping people to accept a decision with which they might disagree.

both literally and metaphorically fail to see the differences in their midst because they do not recognize them in any formal way. This feeling of being unseen in the midst of one's own community can be extraordinarily painful for church members, who may come to believe that their very personhood is not valued and that ultimately their only option is to leave the congregation.

Recognition is an extremely powerful theme in both psychological and theological understandings of the human person. As I showed in chapter 3, the "mirroring need" is one of the most basic requirements for healthy human development. This is the need that reaches out for affirmation of the self's goodness from an important other, who, ideally, responds by saying, "I acknowledge your being here and I am uplifted by your presence."[6] It is through this kind of mirroring response from important people in a child's emotional world that the self begins to gain strength and to create internal structures forming the core of the personality. Similarly, Scripture contains many stories that emphasize the importance of recognition from the divine Other for human selfhood and purpose—such as when God looks upon human beings and calls them good or when God chooses Moses as the leader of the Israelites or when God's voice speaks from heaven saying, "This is my Son, the Beloved, with whom I am well pleased."[7] In all of these stories and many more, human beings come to understand their value and vocation more fully when they are afforded the gift of recognition.

Conversely, when individuals go unrecognized by people or institutions that are important to them, their sense of self is diminished and deep woundedness may result. Mercer observed that in her research with conflicted congregations, "the sense of not being acknowledged" proved "so central and so primary" in the stories of many of the people she had interviewed in these communities of faith.[8] This theme struck her powerfully as a researcher because it revealed just how traumatic congregational conflicts can be and how harmful their effects often are in the emotional and spiritual lives of those who live through them. It seems to me, then, that in situations of congregational conflict, it is crucial to provide ways to ensure that all church members have the opportunity to bring their concerns to voice—not only as a means of practical problem

6. Kohut, *Self Psychology and the Humanities*, 226.

7. These biblical references may be found in Gen 1; Exod 3–4; and Matt 3:17, respectively (NRSV).

8. Mercer, "Drama, Trauma, and Comma."

solving but also as a way of formally recognizing the uniquely diverse collection of selves that make up any community of faith.

It is important to note here that providing space for all voices to be heard does not mean allowing people to act abusively toward one another. Unfortunately, the risk for such abuse in congregations is very real; as a result, it is even more important that church leaders be well-differentiated and skilled at staying connected to all parts of the system. In some cases, embodying these traits will involve setting limits on some individuals' actions and words so that others can be heard and respected.[9] In fact, fostering an environment for honest conversation within a community of faith may initially involve additional conflict as these kinds of behavioral boundaries are negotiated within the group. Creating the kind of space that can adequately hold such conflict is a complex task, and again points to the need for skilled, connected leaders within congregations—a need about which I will say more later in this chapter.

Structured, Small-Group Processes

Designing a process that allows everyone to be heard proves a major challenge for congregations experiencing conflict. However, members at both Grace UCC and First UMC agreed that having a small-group component to any conflict resolution process is vital. Grace UCC did not have such a component; all "discussion" meetings were in a large-group format which, almost by definition, meant that a large proportion of the individuals present did not get a chance to speak. Even if the opportunity to speak was available, some parishioners simply did not feel comfortable doing so because the atmosphere of the meetings was so hostile. For instance, "Rita" told me that she often was not able to stay through the end of the meetings because she became so uneasy. She said, "It was pretty heated, and I liked to make my exit." Rita seems like a person who could have benefited from a structured, small-group process that would have allowed her to state her views without fear of being attacked.

Likewise, when I asked Stephanie, also a member of Grace UCC, what she thought the church could have done to handle the conflict more effectively, she said, "I think it would have been helpful if we had like little small meetings, small-group meetings and maybe taking a couple

---

9. This would be a concrete example of the limits of hospitality discussed in chapter 5.

people over here that had this opinion . . . and people over here and let them discuss why they thought what they were thinking." This is not to say, however, that all small-group processes are created equal. If a small-group process degenerates into the same kind of arguing and name calling that happened during the large-group meetings at Grace UCC, it will probably not be effective and may actually make matters worse. For this reason, congregations must design processes that allow differences within a group to be expressed clearly and openly, but in a way that minimizes people's sense of threat.

The pastors at First UMC accomplished this by meeting with a professional church consultant who recommended a process based on a technique known as "functional subgrouping." This technique was created within the broader framework of systems-centered therapy (SCT), a particular form of group therapy developed by Yvonne Agazarian.[10] Functional subgrouping is a strategy that provides opportunities for individuals who already agree with one another to talk together, while those who hold a different perspective listen in on the conversation. Then, those who were on the "outside" of the circle have a chance to talk together, while the others listen. The value of this approach lies in its ability to promote free-flowing communication since many group discussions tend to volley back and forth between contending ideas without fully addressing the concerns of either side. As a result, participants in such groups become frustrated because they are constantly interrupted or contradicted.[11] By contrast, functional subgrouping surfaces the different ideas present within a group by allowing those who feel similarly on an issue to talk to each other in subgroups without interruption. This method halts the "tendency to contend with or convert the differences" in a group by encouraging participants to see their differences as an important "resource" that everyone can use.[12]

At First UMC, the worship committee used an adapted version of functional subgrouping to structure its dialogical process. The process began with asking members of each worship service to converse with each other, while those from other services simply listened to the conversation. In turn, each worship group had the opportunity to converse together and to be listened to by the members of the other groups. Many

10. See Gantt and Agazarian, "Systems-Centered Emotional Intelligence."
11. Ibid., 159.
12. Ibid.

of the people I interviewed from First UMC commented on how helpful they found this aspect of the congregation's process to be. Because the conversation began with members of each service talking with others *from their own group*, the anxiety level remained lower and they were able to express their views without trying to convince or argue against anyone.

As Arthur noted, those who were in the outside circle listening in on these conversations "were able to ask clarifying questions but not to make comments about what the people in the inner circle were saying, so that it was to allow dialogue and not commentary or criticism." Nancy, a longtime member of the 8:45 service, explained that for her the chance to talk first with members of her own service proved important in laying the groundwork for later conversations with those who felt differently: "So we all sat down and wrote what we liked and what we disliked about that service. And then from there, we broadened that format into mixing it up. So then you got in another small group, but this time it wasn't just with your buddies that you were comfortable with, it was now you got to chat with people about other issues and questions."

Ann reiterated the key value of a process like this one: namely, the opportunity for everyone to be heard without being interrupted or debated. She said, "So everybody in the whole room that wanted to have a chance to talk was given that opportunity," adding that "That was probably the best church meeting that I've ever been to in my entire life, and I've been to a lot of church meetings." Of course, this is not to suggest that functional subgrouping is the only technique that could or should be used in a situation of congregational conflict. I simply offer it here as one strategy that seems to hold great potential for conflicted faith communities because of its ability to keep anxiety levels low, promote open communication, and provide opportunities for all voices to be heard and affirmed. What seems most important for congregations in conflict— even more so than the particular technique they may choose—is to think carefully about the process they will use to engage differences in their midst and to plan accordingly.

Skilled, Non-anxious Facilitators

In addition to the importance of a structured, small-group process, numerous people at First UMC spoke highly of the facilitation skills of both Bob Fisher, the senior pastor, and Judith Murray, the chair of the worship committee. For instance, Ann said, "Bob was the one that basically had the model for the evening and for the conversation. He's the one that presented it and guided us through it. And I think he did an excellent, excellent job. I think that kind of a meeting and that kind of process and that kind of model takes somebody very skilled." Likewise, Nancy stated that Rev. Fisher "did an absolutely incredible job of being the moderator of all the committee meetings. . . . I've never been in a situation where I've seen someone trying as hard as he tried to be fair, diplomatic, letting everyone's opinions be heard, not cutting anybody off, not showing his own prejudices." Simon had similar praise for Judith Murray's leadership throughout the committee's decision-making process: "I really liked how Judith ran the meetings. She was very orderly and very intent in what we did in making sure that everybody had the opportunity to speak."

These comments make clear that both Bob and Judith's skills in group facilitation contributed to First UMC's ability to resolve their conflict peacefully. Yet, many conflicted congregations have members and leaders who are skilled in group facilitation, but who are unable to exercise those skills calmly in the midst of a highly anxious group. How, then, did Bob and Judith do it? As I have mentioned, prior to the start of this process, Rev. Fisher had received coaching from a professional church consultant about how to design and lead a decision-making process that began with a functional subgrouping model. Rev. Fisher then shared insights from this coaching with Judith, which seems to have helped them both gain confidence in their ability to lead this process from start to finish. Additionally, Bob and Judith worked together to implement spiritual focal points at the beginning of each meeting. These short devotional times were designed to help break down the barriers between the different groups and to center their attention on common elements of their faith through Scripture, prayer, reflection, and ritual. My interviews with members at First UMC revealed that this combination of practical skill and spiritual focus helped participants feel more at ease with one another and allowed them to talk about their differences with one another in ways that felt safe, though not necessarily free from tension or struggle.

Here, then, is what I believe we can learn from First UMC about resolving congregational conflict: not only is it important to have a well-planned, structured small-group process, but it is also crucial to have skilled, non-anxious facilitators available to lead such a process. Because the conflict at First UMC was less volatile, the congregation was able to draw on its own clergy and lay leaders to moderate their meetings, and these leaders wisely sought counsel from a professional consultant to prepare for that responsibility. At Grace UCC, however, the pastoral leaders' attempts to facilitate gatherings proved ineffective at best and detrimental at worst. This was due to the fact that because of the nature of the conflict (namely, a decision about whether or not to leave the denomination), the pastors were unable to remain neutral. Because of our denominational commitments, the senior pastor and I were unable to refrain from "taking sides" in the conflict. In fact, many parishioners experienced our support for the congregation's continued denominational affiliation as a sort of ultimatum—i.e., they felt that we were saying, "If you don't vote to stay in the UCC, we'll leave." From our perspective, the senior pastor and I were simply stating the logical consequences of a congregational decision to disaffiliate, but some of our parishioners did not see it that way. This damaged our ability to lead the church through its decision-making process because we were seen as trying to influence the outcome unfairly.

Even if the conflict at Grace UCC had centered on an issue that was less clear-cut for the clergy, the sheer level of volatility and divisiveness there probably would have made it difficult for the pastoral staff to provide the kind of non-anxious leadership needed without seeking outside help. In fact, when conflict reaches these kinds of levels, "it is usually beyond the ability of the congregational leadership to manage by themselves" and they should seek outside assistance.[13] When I interviewed Grace UCC members five years after the conflict, one of the questions I asked them was, "Looking back, what, if anything, would you like the church to have done differently as it approached this important decision?" Several individuals suggested that if professional help had been sought early on in Grace UCC's process, it might have made a difference. Leah, for instance, said "perhaps if we had more experience at negotiation. Perhaps if we had had someone who could've acted as a mediator, it would've helped us work together through it instead of allowing it to be something that tore us apart." Similarly, Noelle reflected on the potential usefulness of the entire congregation receiving training in skills related to conflict:

> So the other thing I can think of that would be helpful is that we could really use, if we could figure out how to do it . . . some training in managing conflict. Understanding conflict, what is it about, how do you work them through, how does everybody try to get a little piece of the pie so they go away feeling like they were a winner, instead of there was a winner and a loser.

13. Leas, *Moving Your Church through Conflict*, 55.

These comments highlight the fact that parishioners at Grace UCC experienced the leadership of the congregation's conflict resolution process as ineffective and unhelpful. As a result, the process seems to have increased, rather than relieved, the high levels of anxiety already present within the congregation.

Sitting with Anxiety

Noelle's language of "winners" and "losers" raises another important insight from these two case studies: namely, that at times it may be necessary to encourage congregations to sit with their anxiety for a while rather than trying to resolve it immediately. This is not to suggest that congregations should (or even could) put off difficult decisions indefinitely to avoid making conflict more intense. Indeed, as important as it is to facilitate parishioners' ability to have their voices heard, at some point decisions do have to be made for the good of the church's common life. Simply letting every person have his or her say does not necessarily help a congregation move forward in its decision-making process. In fact, this is where many faith communities end up feeling stuck as they try to navigate conflict.

Even at First UMC, there came a point during the final meeting when committee members began to despair about ever finding a mutually acceptable solution to their problem. Roy summarized it this way: "So, we had four [meetings], and it was really good. But you could see we weren't coming to—people were starting to understand each other, and people were starting to like each other, there was a closeness. When it got down to it, though, we still had this big elephant in the room: what are we gonna do?" Roy's comment highlights the fact that at certain critical junctures in a congregation's life, it is important for a church to be able to make clear decisions. At First UMC, that critical juncture came at the end of an intentional and structured group process, which included four meetings spread over several months. In contrast to First UMC's experience, most churches tend to move very quickly toward eliminating conflict, usually through a voting process that relies on majority rule. The problem with this approach—particularly when it concerns a highly controversial issue—is that it often does not allow enough time for all members to have their voices heard. Furthermore, as Noelle pointed out, a vote automatically creates divisions between "winners" and "losers," and if the issue at hand is an important one, the "losers" may feel as if they can no longer remain in the congregation.

At this point I return to the theme of anxiety, since anxiety within a congregation is especially likely to rise when people feel that a decision has to be made about something. I suggest that this spike in anxiety occurs because as a significant congregational decision looms, individuals begin associating with the group or side with which they agree. This surfaces important differences within the group, and, as I have shown throughout this book, encounters with difference naturally produce anxiety. One way that congregations attempt to soothe this anxiety is by having a vote; voting, they believe, will settle the issue, and those who lose will simply have to accept the majority's decision. What this perspective misses, though, is that even after a vote, anxiety continues to circulate because the differences within the group have often not been sufficiently surfaced or engaged, and individuals feel that their voices were not truly heard in the process. Furthermore, the "losers" often feel angry and betrayed as well, and may come to believe that they have no choice but to discontinue fellowship with other church members.

When I asked interview subjects at Grace UCC what they thought the church could have done differently, some of them said that they thought the congregation should have tried to avoid having a vote, or at least postponed it for several more months. Sean put it this way: "Votes tend to, obviously, split things. If it were left up to me, and if I saw a vote was inevitable . . . I'd push it back as long as I could, like six months or a year even maybe." Tom agreed, stating, "regardless of how [the vote] came out, there was going to be a split." Tom added that Grace UCC might also have benefited from a different understanding of conflict—not as a purely negative reality but as holding the potential for positive change: "On the surface anyway, conflict-avoidance is sort of the name of the game, you know, and that's not always healthy. Sometimes conflict is good and can be creative, but I think at Grace UCC there has been a tendency to avoid it."

These reflections again point to the importance of asking congregations to sit with their anxiety for a period of time, rather than trying to relieve it prematurely. Grace UCC attempted to relieve its anxiety through a voting process that many thought would eliminate the conflict by virtue of making a decision about denominational affiliation, one way or the other. The result, however, was not a decrease in anxiety, but rather the rapid exit of most of those who lost the vote—an event which, in itself, created additional anxiety (as well as pain, anger, and grief) among those who "won." In contrast, at First UMC members engaged in an intentional process of "sitting together as the body."[14] This allowed them to tolerate their discomfort long enough to be able to hear one another clearly, to engage the differences that surfaced in the group, and to move toward a solution that, while not perfect, felt acceptable to almost everyone involved.

Redefining Unity and Strengthening Relationships

I have argued that a healthy approach to conflict within congregations begins with acknowledging the diversity already contained within communities of faith, as well as the natural anxiety that awareness of such diversity produces. However, the question remains: once a congregation has fully acknowledged the differences in its midst, what should it do with them? This question proves particularly important in those cases where diversity (particularly theological diversity) is experienced as a threat to be eradicated rather than simply a natural part of living together in community.

In chapter 5, I made an extended argument for a theological reframing of diversity—not only as an existing attribute of the created order but also as a quality that God intends and values for creation in general, and for the church in particular. I argued that such a theological reframing can lower anxiety in conflicted congregations because it shifts the perception of diversity from a fall away from God's true intentions to a vital aspect of God's will for the world and for the church. Furthermore, such reframing can potentially transform the vision of what binds the church together from an ideal of undifferentiated sameness to a goal of remaining vulnerable to and connected across differences. In this way, the concept of church "unity" can be reimagined as "solidarity" that is "forged from honest confrontation and mutual confidence amid struggle."[15] In this sense, church unity can become a way of speaking about what binds members together in the presence of their differences rather than that

---

14. Judith Murray, the chair of First UMC's worship committee, coined this phrase to describe how she understood the committee's process: "But the actual process was a process of integrity, I feel, in that there were not—one group was not favored over the other, and we sat together as the body."

15. Brock, "On Remembering What Is Impossible to Forget," 11.

which eliminates all difference or seeks to reduce the community to the lowest common theological denominator.

But what might these new understandings of diversity and unity look like in practice? In other words, how might one bring such understandings to life in the day-to-day existence of congregations? Building on the arguments I have already made for reframing diversity as a desirable theological norm, I further suggest that conflicted congregations must wrestle with the question of what Christian "unity" might mean in the face of internal theological diversity. Unfortunately, many congregations currently understand the goal of community as striving toward a standard of "harmonious/homogeneous unity" that stresses sameness or agreement over any kind of conflict or struggle.[16] Indeed, as I have argued throughout this book, denying or avoiding potential areas of conflict represent attempts to ignore the internal pluralism that always and necessarily exists within congregations, because acknowledging such differences creates increased anxiety. Consequently, Christians tend to understand diversity as a problem to be eliminated, rather than as a creative gift of God's Spirit.

Yet, as the case study from Grace UCC demonstrated, even when communication between theological perspectives does occur within faith communities, it often takes unhealthy or unhelpful forms. As I noted in chapter 3, such forms often include destructive behaviors like splitting/projection or rigid needs for sameness, resulting in the caricature of opposing viewpoints as devoid of theological integrity. Instead of these sorts of attempts to establish complete theological uniformity within a faith community (a clearly impossible task), congregations could focus on other ways in which their members might affirm their commonalities.[17] One strategy for accomplishing this task involves using denominational resources, such as creeds or statements of faith, as fodder for theological conversation rather than as litmus tests for community membership.

At First UMC, the worship committee members did not use specific denominational resources as a basis for reflection. However, they seemed to have accomplished the same goal by engaging in a shared devotional time at the beginning of each meeting. As I noted above, each committee meeting began with a structured devotional time—led by Judith Murray—that allowed participants to focus on common elements of their

---

16. Ibid., 9.
17. See Kliewer, *How to Live with Diversity in the Local Church*.

faith. Judith understood the purpose of this time as follows: "my role in the group was to set the scene each night by having a devotional that I felt was going to help us set our sights on what we had to accomplish that night and get the right mind-set going in all of us. So we had prayer and a devotional each of the nights.... Praying together was a really important part of what we did." Interviewees described this part of the process as vital to the committee's ultimate ability to find a solution that would be acceptable to all involved. As Arthur put it, "it was helpful that people that were there were prayerfully considering their responses and trying to provide their input." It would seem, then, that a common spiritual emphasis for committee members at the beginning of each meeting helped break down the barriers that existed between the various groups and encouraged participants to focus on the spiritual values they all shared—regardless of what particular worship service they attended.

In addition to the notion of shared religious resources, "interdependence" is a helpful notion that supplements and enhances understandings of unity, particularly in faith communities that are experiencing open conflict.[18] In this view, interdependence refers to strategies designed to help diverse groups within a congregation work together toward a common goal, such as a specific service project within the wider community. In the process, the opportunity for polarization is minimized, and "relationships can be built which are very helpful in the management of the existing pluralism."[19] Thus, by joining together in shared acts of service and hospitality in the wider world, Christians may develop stronger hospitable inclinations toward each other as well, thus creating more unity within their congregations and denominations.

This emphasis on commonality and interdependence highlights the role of relationships between church members as key to the dialogical process and as a possible resource for mitigating conflict. In terms of the congregational case studies under consideration here, it is important to remember that although individuals in both churches identified with specific positions or groups, the conflict at Grace UCC ultimately proved much more intense than that at First UMC. This is where interpersonal relationships within the congregations seem to have played important though differing roles. While virtually all the individuals I interviewed from Grace UCC expressed deep regret about the relational ruptures that

18. Ibid., 37.
19. Ibid., 38.

resulted from the conflict, in the end, these interpersonal relationships were not enough to keep the congregation from splitting.

At First UMC, however, many of the individuals I interviewed talked about how the strength of the interpersonal relationships within the church helped to ease the intensity of the conflict. Specifically, interviewees mentioned the importance of First UMC's Sunday school classes, which met between the early and late worship services. Esther, a faithful 8:45 participant, said, "I think that's probably what kept our church successful at having two kinds of worship, because in individual Sunday school classes there were people from both services. It was people from the church, not from the service." Bart, another contemporary worshipper, agreed with Esther's assessment: "We have a very strong Sunday school component within the church. And to be honest with you, church revolves around that Sunday school component . . . because most of our Sunday school—a lot of our Sunday school—classes were made up of people from all of the services. And so that's where we'd really meet."

In addition to the importance of Sunday school, others that I interviewed from First UMC emphasized the general quality of relationships within the congregation as key to the ultimate resolution of the worship dilemma. Roy put it this way: "It came down, to me, to this issue of my church is fixin' to blow up over this. And so, OK, we'll get the worship times like we want them, and we got a lot of folks hurt, and it's gonna take a long time to repair that—it just is not worth it." He then added, "I know that the kingdom of God has gotta be bigger than what time we worship. It's got to be bigger. And that these people, and their relationship with each other, and their relationship with Christ, is bigger than what time we worship."

It would appear that at First UMC, members' relationships with one another helped keep the conflict from becoming more divisive. By contrast, at Grace UCC, many of these relationships were ultimately ruptured, which continues to cause a great deal of pain for the members there. This is not to say that the relationships at Grace UCC were not strong. However, it appears that once the sides of the conflict had been formed there, it proved very difficult for members from opposing sides to find common ground or to approach each other in any way. Indeed, many of the members who wished to leave the UCC all belonged to the same Sunday school class, so they literally did not have to converse with people of different perspectives during class time on Sunday mornings.

At First UMC, in contrast, the Sunday school classes provided an important forum for individuals in different services to be together and to strengthen what we might call "cross-cutting" relationships[20]—that is, relationships that cut across the divisions of the three different worship services and that brought members together in shared conversation and projects. Such relationships help lower anxiety within a congregation because they dilute the sharp differences that are drawn between major identity groups. In other words, when parishioners can see others not only as members of opposing groups but also as individuals who share common interests and commitments within the congregation, they are less threatened by the differences they experience in those relationships. And, as I have emphasized throughout this book, a lower sense of threat yields lower levels of anxiety and an increased ability to remain calm and connected in the face of conflict.

From a social psychological perspective, strengthening cross-cutting relationships within conflicted congregations makes sense as well because such a strategy could help decrease intense group polarization. Recall that group polarization typically occurs when members move toward what they perceive as the "prototypical" position of their identity group—that is, the position that most clearly represents the commonalities within the group as compared to members of an out-group. When this happens, groups define themselves solely in contrast to a specific out-group on particular dimensions, and the groups then polarize toward opposite extremes. However, if individuals within a congregation were encouraged to define themselves in a variety of ways—not simply by which side of the conflict they embraced—they might be less inclined to move toward an extreme prototypical position. This seems to be what happened at First UMC: although the conflict initially pushed individuals to define themselves according to their preferred worship service, the

20. I first encountered the notion of "cross-cutting" social categories through my study of social psychology. Marilynn Brewer, a social psychologist who has written extensively about this concept, notes that "societies are differentiated along a number of different dimensions of social identity—ethnicity, religion, region, occupation, gender—each of which subdivides the whole into different sub-groupings with overlapping memberships. In such a system, individuals may belong to, and identify with, multiple ingroups *at the same level of inclusion*" ("Reducing Prejudice through Cross-Categorization," 169, emphasis in original). Although Brewer is speaking here about large social categories such as gender or ethnicity, the concept of cross-cutting memberships seems to apply equally well to a congregation, where individuals might simultaneously identify with a particular worship group, a Sunday school class, and a fellowship group.

Sunday school classes cut across these categories and made the worship divisions less important and less prone to produce polarization. Perhaps if members at Grace UCC had found ways to strengthen their relationships with one another across the fault lines of the conflict, they might have discovered important commonalities that would have made their disagreements on denominational affiliation feel less powerful.

Admittedly, once a conflict in a faith community has reached the level of emotional volatility experienced at Grace UCC, finding ways to strengthen relationships and foster unity across differences can prove extremely challenging. Here I have simply pointed to a few ideas that need to be developed further—ideas such as using a common spiritual or theological focus to remind the group of its shared commitments and redefine unity; inviting members to participate together in shared acts of service as a means of breaking down barriers; and strengthening cross-cutting relationships in the congregation through educational opportunities or other activities. The key to all of these suggestions is finding ways to counteract the natural human tendency to gather together in like-minded groups. As I have argued throughout this book, this tendency is a normal part of human development, but in the context of groups experiencing high levels of anxiety it often produces rigid group identifications and polarization. Instead, congregations need strategies that help them focus on their shared identity as a community of faith and value their theological diversity as an energizing resource for establishing solidarity, common goals, and productive conversation.

Cultivating Calm, Connected Leadership

In this chapter, I have reflected on the importance of acknowledging differences and anxiety, and redefining unity and strengthening relationships within congregations that are facing conflict. For each of these broad categories I have suggested specific practices that congregations might undertake to make these ideas a reality. Yet, all of these practices require a basic element that now invites more detailed reflection: namely, the presence of calm, connected leaders in the community of faith. As I noted in chapter 1, many practical resources are already available to help congregations develop such leadership in their midst. It is not my intention to duplicate those efforts here. However, in light of the crucial role that leaders play in the shape of congregational conflict, it is worth

WHAT CAN CONFLICTED CONGREGATIONS DO? 187

making a few specific suggestions about what leaders can do to contribute toward healing in their organizations.

Remaining Non-anxious

The first thing leaders in conflicted communities can do is to remain as non-anxious as possible in the midst of conflict—even conflict that is highly volatile and infused with a great deal of affect. This is a very difficult task, and I do not wish to suggest otherwise. As many family systems theorists have noted, the ability to remain nonreactive in the face of intense anxiety is acquired over time through the process of differentiation. In other words, it may not always be possible to decide, in the heat of the moment, to differentiate. Yet, if we recall the definition of *differentiation* as a leader's capacity to "maintain a position and still stay in touch,"[21] we begin to see glimpses of ways in which church leaders might begin to develop practices that could lead them down the path toward differentiation, even in the midst of very difficult situations.

Yet for many pastoral leaders, the avoidance of conflict tends to be the "default" mode of operating because it seems to be a way of decreasing anxiety in the short term. Consequently, many ministers and congregational leaders prefer to ignore a problem (rather than deal with the anxiety it generates) until it can no longer be ignored. This seems to have been one of the factors at Grace UCC that caused the conflict to gain such momentum and to be so explosive when it was finally brought out into the open. For several weeks before the summer business meeting, the senior pastor and I had been hearing rumors about Peter Vance's Sunday school class and their members' outrage over the General Synod equal marriage resolution. Perhaps, if the class members had brought their concerns to the pastoral staff, or if we had inquired directly about what was happening in the class, the conflict could have been dealt with more effectively. Instead, neither party approached the other, and a volatile conflict was the result.

Indeed, as Jack observed, "I think that possibly, looking back, the way to have helped solve [the conflict] would have [been to] attack it right up front and said okay, let's discuss what you're talking about. But after it got momentum, there was no discussing to it." Tom also commented on the importance of pastoral leadership in dealing with conflict before it

---

21. Friedman, *Generation to Generation*, 230.

gets out of hand: "I've come to feel very strongly about the role of the pastor in church leadership.... When you become aware of conflict, it needs to be dealt with early before it boils over and there was, looking back on this issue, there was a lot of tension in the church, before the gay marriage issue ever became known. And it wasn't being handled effectively."

Looking back, it seems to me that one of the key mistakes the pastoral and lay leaders made at Grace UCC was our failure to stay in touch with all parts of our congregational system. Although the senior pastor and I and most of the lay leadership had a clear position on remaining within the denomination, our anxiety kept us from staying in close touch with those in our congregation who disagreed with us. In so doing, we allowed other parishioners to convince themselves that we did not care about their views, and by the time the conflict came into the open, many of these individuals were no longer willing to listen to what we had to say. "Adam," a deacon and lifelong member of Grace UCC, summed this failure up succinctly when he observed, "From a leadership standpoint, we missed it." In contrast, at First UMC, the structured, small-group process that was put into place seems to have convinced the committee members that their pastors and other leaders were hearing them and striving to understand their points of view. This does not mean that the leaders did not have their own opinions, but they were able to maintain their positions while *at the same time* remaining connected to those in the system who held different perspectives.

Modeling Attempts to Connect across Difference

Remaining connected across differences is no easy task, especially if parishioners become so upset that they cut off all communication with their leaders. Still, non-anxious leaders can continue to promote healing within the congregation by modeling attempts to stay in touch with those who disagree. Frequently, in situations of congregational discord, both pastoral and lay leaders are tempted to identify a few "troublemakers" and place all of the responsibility for the conflict onto them. As I noted in chapter 3, this tendency is actually a form of scapegoating designed to split off the negative aspects of the group's life and locate them in a few individuals. Psychologically, this approach is appealing because it convinces leaders that if they could simply get rid of the troublemakers— either by converting them to a different point of view or having them leave the group altogether—peace and harmony would be restored to the community.

However, as in all cases of splitting, the "negative" traits that the group wishes to expel actually exist in much more ambiguous and complex forms throughout the community. Getting rid of a few members will not solve the problem. In fact, at Grace UCC, the exodus of a sizable group of parishioners left a trail of pain, grief, and brokenness in its wake that persists in the congregation even now. Instead of succumbing to the temptation to scapegoat those perceived as troublemakers, calm leaders can acknowledge individuals with different points of view and seek ways to connect with them across differences. In practice, this might mean inviting persons on the opposite side of the conflict to have one-on-one or small-group conversations with individual leaders. Or, it might simply mean designing a small-group process that ensures that all perspectives are heard and affirmed so that leaders are not tempted to discount or ignore the voices of those with whom they disagree. It is important to recall here that remaining connected across difference does not mean abdicating one's own position in an attempt to restore "peace" to troubled relationships. Instead, it involves exhibiting a posture of differentiation—that is, claiming one's own position clearly, while also staying in touch with all parts of the system.

Seeking Professional Support

Modeling differentiation in the ways I have described may be very difficult to do, especially if those with different viewpoints cut off communication or categorically refuse to acknowledge leaders' attempts at connection. In such cases, leaders may need to ask for help sooner than later. When I conducted my interviews with my former parishioners at Grace UCC, almost every one of them asked me, "So, what do you think we should have done differently?" Each time, I replied that I wished that the senior pastor and I had recognized that we were not equipped to deal with such an intense conflict and that we had sought professional consultation. Traditional conflict mediation services simply may not be well-suited for handling these kinds of congregational conflicts; consequently, leaders will have to think deeply about what kind of consultation will be most helpful to them.[22] Fortunately, there are now many avenues available for

---

22. Mercer, "Drama, Trauma, and Comma."

finding consultants who are specially trained to work with congregations. I believe that such resources could have been immensely helpful to us at Grace UCC.[23]

This is not to say that this approach will not involve costs for the congregation, however. Seeking professional help first requires leaders to admit that they cannot handle the situation on their own, which can be difficult—especially for clergy who may feel that they should be able to cope with conflicts themselves. It also requires parishioners to agree to the presence of an outsider in their midst, which can feel very unsettling for communities in open conflict. Finally, there are substantial financial costs involved, which may limit congregations' ability or willingness to seek such help. Nonetheless, it seems clear from the case studies that First UMC benefitted greatly from their pastors' consultation with a professional, and that Grace UCC might have benefitted from such services if it had sought them out.

Conclusion

In this chapter I have sketched the contours of specific practices that could help congregations cope more effectively with conflict in their midst. These practices include acknowledging difference and the anxiety it produces; redefining unity and strengthening relationships; and cultivating calm, connected leadership. These practical recommendations flow from two main sources: first, from the insights I gained from talking with parishioners about their experiences with conflict in their congregations; and second, from my own analysis of those experiences using psychodynamic, social psychological, and theological tools. In this regard, my approach to this subject has been unequivocally pastoral theological. As I noted in chapter 1, pastoral theology distinguishes itself as a discipline through its use of lived experience as a starting point for theological reflection, its engagement with the social sciences (especially psychology), and its ever-present commitment to transformed religious practice. It is in the spirit of this last commitment that I have offered these concrete suggestions for transforming congregational approaches to conflict.

---

23. Such resources include the Turner Center for Church Leadership and Congregational Development at Vanderbilt Divinity School and the Center for Congregational Health in Winston-Salem, North Carolina, among others.

It is also important to note here one other hallmark of pastoral theology: namely, its keen attention to the individual shape of human suffering. In this book, I have argued that the phenomenon of congregational conflict can prove intensely painful both for individual parishioners and for faith communities as a whole. Indeed, as the case studies showed, persons often experience deep suffering in the midst of congregational discord. In this sense, congregational conflict provides a prime example of "human suffering [that] evokes or calls for a religious response."[24] As such, it is a phenomenon that possesses inherently theological dimensions. As practical theologian Mary McClintock Fulkerson has noted, "theological reflection is not something brought in after a situation has been described; it is a sensibility that initiates the inquiry at the outset."[25] This statement resonates deeply with my own approach to the problem of congregational conflict because, from the very beginning of my interest in this topic, I had a sense that it carried theological import. Fulkerson further describes this theological sensibility in terms of "theology as response to a wound":

> Wounds generate new thinking. Disjunctions birth invention—from a disjuncture in logic, where reasoning is compelled to find new connections in thought, to brokenness in existence, where creativity is compelled to search for possibilities of reconciliation. Like a wound, theological thinking is generated by a sometimes inchoate sense that something *must* be addressed.[26]

In this case, the wound is the kind of conflict that I witnessed in the congregation I served. That conflict propelled me into an investigation of the other shapes conflict may take in communities of faith, like the conflict I have researched at First UMC. The fact that these conflicts played out in such different ways led me to many more questions.

In fact, in attempting to answer some of those questions, I became convinced that the resources of theology alone would not be sufficient to address such a complex reality. Although, in one sense, this book begins and ends with theology, I have argued that in order to address the specific problem of conflict within faith communities—as well as the general human problem of negotiating difference—additional tools are needed. While particular theological frameworks offer broad understandings of

---

24. Miller-McLemore, "The Subject and Practice of Pastoral Theology," 179.
25. Fulkerson, *Places of Redemption*, 13.
26. Ibid., 13–14, emphasis in original.

human being as marked by frailty and incompatibility, the resources of the social sciences cast that frailty in much sharper relief, and illustrate the ways in which specific intrapsychic and social phenomena are tied to the anxiety raised by encounters with difference. In other words, though theology may, at root, be a response to a wound, the social sciences are vital for diagnosing and describing the specific nature of the wound itself.

At the same time, I have argued that the social sciences still need to be balanced by the insights of theology—insights that offer a more robust picture of individual and communal healing than the social sciences provide. Additionally, I have made the case that while the social sciences prove critical in describing the anxiety-producing impact of difference on individuals and social groups, they offer few resources for reframing difference itself as a resource for human development or relationality. By contrast, through the notion of diversity as a created good, theology offers a way of understanding difference both as the most basic challenge with which human beings must cope *and* as a core aspect of God's intentions for the church and the world. This understanding opens a pathway toward seeing vulnerability to difference and ecclesial hospitality as postures that Christians are called to embrace as ways of remaining connected across the differences that threaten to divide and destroy the unity of Christ's body.

Finally, I offer a more specific reason why an approach like mine is vital for communities of faith: recognizing the role of anxiety and threats to self or identity might help congregations—and particularly their leaders—become more compassionate about conflict. As I have noted, it is tempting to understand congregational conflict as resulting primarily from the behavior of a few "troublemakers" who want to control things. To adopt such an idea, however, would just be another form of splitting and projection. Furthermore, this approach misses the opportunity to understand more deeply what might be happening within all individuals in a congregation, as well as the dynamics of the group as a whole. Instead of seeing conflict as the result of a few "bad apples," the approach I am commending here recognizes conflict as rooted in deep truths about who we are as human beings: diverse individuals with incompatible needs, wishes, and desires, and, at the same time, part of a diverse creation whose very variability is part of God's intention for the world.

Bringing psychological and theological insights together to address congregational conflict proves a vitally important task—not only because it sheds light on the way human beings are but also because it calls us toward a new way that we could be. Additionally, when we understand the specific role of anxiety in conflict, we can take steps to address it and move toward reframing conflict theologically. In this way of thinking, difference does not have to remain a problem to be eliminated. Instead, it can become a source of growth and creativity for congregations and a way of incarnating the body of Christ. May it be so.

Appendix

Reflecting on Lived Experience:
Case Study as Pastoral Theological Method

In a 2004 essay titled "Contemporary Pastoral Theology: A Wider Vision for the Practice of Love," pastoral theologian Nancy Ramsay writes, "In contrast to systematic theology or ethics, pastoral theology... begins with the concrete particularity of experience and intends a useful response for that situation."[1] Ramsay's observation highlights the key element of *lived experience* that has always been a hallmark of pastoral theology. In fact, reflection on human needs and struggles is a core component of pastoral theological method, which distinguishes it from other theological approaches. Since this is a pastoral theological project addressing theological conflict in congregations, it is especially important to include and reflect on the lived experience of communities of faith struggling with such conflict. One way that I have done this is to provide, at the beginning of this chapter, quantitative data from congregational studies that paint a detailed picture of the pervasiveness of conflict in congregations. Yet this kind of data only allows us to see the larger shape of these congregations, rather than the ways in which individual members may be affected by conflict. Indeed, as this chapter has explained, pastoral theology is not only concerned with the broad outlines of communal problems, like racism, poverty, or conflict, but also seeks to reflect deeply on the *individual* needs and suffering that arise in the context of such problems.

This concern with hearing the unique voice of the suffering person emerged very early in the development of pastoral theology as a field, perhaps most strikingly in the work of Anton Boisen. Boisen was a chaplain and psychologist of religion who had himself suffered serious mental

---

1. Ramsay, "Contemporary Pastoral Theology," 157.

breakdowns, and had experienced powerful spiritual awakenings in the midst of his mental illness. Boisen insisted that in order to understand the relationship between religious experience and psychological health, pastoral care practitioners must learn to study "living human documents" and reflect on the needs and suffering expressed there. As Boisen wrote in *The Exploration of the Inner World*, "I have sought to begin not with the ready-made formulations contained in books but with the living human documents and with actual social conditions in all their complexity."[2]

As a means to helping his students study living human documents more effectively, Boisen pioneered a clinical case study method designed to help religious practitioners understand individual persons in all of their depth and complexity. Building on case study methods that had long been in use in the fields of law and medicine, Boisen developed detailed case study forms that theological students could use to gather relevant information about their patients.[3] These forms included questions about a patient's social and religious background, personal history, particular problems and struggles, and theological understandings. As pastoral theologian Glenn Asquith has noted, the "basic goal" of Boisen's method was to "study and understand religious experience as well as to stimulate the formation of the student's own theology. As part of his case discussions, Boisen prepared many questions which forced students to think theologically about human experience."[4] Thus, in developing and using this case study method with his students, Boisen revolutionized theological education and the field of pastoral theology by drawing attention to the needs and struggles of individual human persons in their unique particularity.

As the field of pastoral theology progressed, it continued to emphasize the importance of "living human documents" and of reflecting on their needs through the inclusion of case material in pastoral theological texts. However, more recent critiques of this methodology have pointed out that traditional pastoral theology was done from the point of view of the pastor alone. In other words, cases were typically presented from the practitioner's perspective without fully including the voices of those receiving care. Furthermore, within pastoral theology there has been a growing awareness that within communities of faith, the clergy person is

---

2. Boisen, *Exploration of the Inner World*, 185.
3. Asquith Jr., "Case Study Method of Anton T. Boisen," 85.
4. Ibid., 94.

not the only practitioner of care; instead, all members of the community are called to care for one another in a variety of ways.⁵

Concerns about the apparent hierarchy of the traditional approach eventually led to the emergence of the "communal contextual paradigm" for pastoral care, which continues to be developed in pastoral theological writing today. Pastoral theologian John Patton notes that this paradigm "broadens the clinical pastoral's focus beyond the clergy to include the caring community of clergy *and* laity. It also calls attention to contextual factors affecting both the message of care and those bringing it and receiving it."⁶ The emerging communal-contextual paradigm thus emphasizes not only the importance of including voices other than that of the ordained person but also of allowing those voices to shape the formulation of new pastoral theological ideas. In addition, this model retains pastoral theology's focus on individual needs and suffering, but insists that these aspects be placed within the context of real, living communities of faith and the particular social and cultural frameworks in which they are situated.

As a pastoral theologian, it is important to me to ensure that my exploration of theological conflict remains intimately connected with the actual life and practices of specific communities of faith. Thus, building on the tenets of the communal-contextual paradigm, I ground this project in the lived experiences of two specific congregations. I do so through the inclusion of two congregational case studies, one based on my own experience with a particular faith community, and one based in the experience of another congregation. As I have noted, the case study method in pastoral theology was born of a desire to understand human persons and their struggles more fully. However, the approach I am using with these congregations differs somewhat from the traditional model pioneered by Boisen and subsequently developed by the discipline of pastoral theology. Instead of focusing on a single individual or on the pastoral relationship between a practitioner and a particular parishioner or client, I am instead trying to tell the stories of two faith communities and their struggles with theological conflict. While I want to depict the reality of these congregations as a whole, I am also determined not to lose the voices of individual persons and their experiences of the conflict

---

5. Early articulations of this awareness include Browning, "Pastoral Care and the Study of the Congregation" (1988); and Gill-Austern, "Rediscovering Hidden Treasures for Pastoral Care" (1995).

6. Patton, *Pastoral Care in Context*, 4–5, emphasis in original.

that occurred in their congregations. For this reason, I have adopted a *qualitative approach* to the case studies.

Social scientists Norman Denzin and Yvonna Lincoln describe qualitative approaches to research as placing "an emphasis on the qualities of entities and on processes and meanings that are not experimentally examined or measured (if measured at all) in terms of quantity, amount, intensity, or frequency."[7] In contrast to quantitative approaches, which tend to gather large amounts of numerical data and seek causal relationships between variables, qualitative research aims to discover "*how* social experience is created and given meaning."[8] Qualitative researchers thus study subjects "in their natural settings, attempting to make sense of, or to interpret, phenomena in terms of the meaning people bring to them."[9] Yet, such a focus on patterns and socially constructed meanings does not mean that qualitative research is unconcerned with empiricism. In fact, qualitative researchers rely heavily on empirical tools—including such diverse elements as interviews, participant observation, interpretation of cultural texts and productions, analysis of artifacts, participatory inquiry, and focus groups—in their quest to provide a rich description of the lives and practices of individuals and institutions.

From the vast array of available qualitative research approaches, I have chosen the case study as my primary means for investigating theological conflict within congregations. As I have already noted, case studies have been a mainstay of pastoral theology since its inception. My use of this methodology, however, moves beyond pastoral theology's traditional focus on the relationship between a single practitioner and care-receiver. Instead, I operate within a broader qualitative understanding that defines a case study as a "strategy of inquiry" relying on the specific methodological tools of interviewing, observing, and analyzing documents.[10] Such an approach enables me, as a researcher, to provide a richer description of the congregations I studied than would have been possible if I simply told their stories exclusively from my own perspective.

Of the three tools that most clearly characterize case study method—interviews, observation, and text analysis—I have relied most heavily on semistructured personal interviews because they provide me

---

7. Denzin and Lincoln, "Introduction," 8.
8. Ibid., emphasis in original.
9. Ibid., 3.
10. Ibid., 22.

with the most direct access to the voices of the people within the congregations I wished to explore.[11] In other words, I have chosen the case study approach because of the detail and particularity it allows me to see about each of the congregations I have studied. Indeed, as educational psychologist Robert E. Stake has asserted, "What all should be said about a single case is quite different from what should be said about all cases. Each case has important atypical features, happenings, relationships, and situations."[12] Thus, the key value of examining the individual case lies in its ability to communicate something unique about the issue under investigation. Stake also notes, however, that "Case researchers seek both what is common and what is particular about the case"; in any given case study, then, qualitative researchers are looking not only for what is unique, but also for those elements that may connect the case with other comparable situations.[13]

This is not to say that conclusions drawn from a particular case study may be generalized to all similar cases in all places and times. Even so, case studies—like other qualitative approaches—do have the potential, through their unique particularity, to reveal connections and meanings that might otherwise remain hidden. As practical theologians John Swinton and Harriet Mowat argue,

> While the findings of qualitative research studies may not be immediately transferable to other contexts, there is a sense in which qualitative research should resonate with the experiences of others in similar circumstances. . . . Qualitative research can therefore claim a degree of transferability insofar as it often raises issues and offers insights which reach beyond the particularity of the situation. It frequently (arguably always), creates a resonance with people outside of the immediate situation who are experiencing phenomena which are not identical, but hold enough similarity to create a potentially *transformative resonance*.[14]

11. In this sense, my approach demonstrates some important similarities with ethnography, which pastoral theologian Mary Clark Moschella defines as "a form of social research used . . . to study human beings in their social and cultural contexts" (*Ethnography as a Pastoral Practice*, 25). I should note, though, that while my project does try to include the richness of individuals' and congregations' experiences through description and qualitative interviews, it cannot be called a full-blown ethnography.

12. Stakes, "Case Studies," 439.

13. Ibid., 438.

14. Swinton and Mowat, *Practical Theology and Qualitative Research*, 47, emphasis in original.

The case study, then, functions both to reveal the distinctive features of a specific context and to point toward similarities with other contexts that may yield important insights for building new theory and developing more effective practices.

In fact, the desire to create more effective pastoral practices remains central to pastoral theology's use of the case study method. As pastoral theologian Emmanuel Lartey explains, the "learning cycle for liberative pastoral praxis" always begins with *concrete experience*, which is grounded in the "lived experience of living people."[15] This particular experience then provides the starting point for social and cultural analysis, theological analysis, critical analysis of the faith tradition itself, and generation of a pastoral response. The response, in turn, is taken back into the realm of experience and tested out in practice. In this way, pastoral practices are developed in a never-ending cycle of reflection and action. Although one concrete experience may form the starting point for reflection, it is assumed that such an experience has the potential—once it is engaged through a liberative learning cycle—to provide important insights that may be applicable in a variety of situations.

Despite the potential usefulness of the case study approach I have outlined, my research is also limited in particular ways that I must acknowledge. My choice to utilize case studies (rather than full ethnographies, for example) limits the breadth and depth of what I can know about these congregations. Instead, in this book I have chosen to focus on the particular issue of theological conflict within these communities of faith and have utilized the case studies to uncover some of the dynamics present within such conflicts. I argue that this approach provides a snapshot of what was happening within these congregations during a particular period of time. Examining the case studies of these two congregations side by side provides important insights about theological conflict that may prove useful to others in similar settings. Furthermore, these case studies, presented in chapter 2, form the basis for analysis from psychological, social psychological, and theological perspectives later in the book. It is important to note here that any conclusions drawn from these case studies are necessarily partial and heuristic—both because of the relatively small number of interviews I conducted and because a congregation is a living, changing organism that can never be fully captured in a few pages of text. Even with these limitations, I maintain that including

---

15. Lartey, *In Living Color*, 131–32.

the voices of congregation members in this study remains preferable to any approach that attempts to theorize about congregational conflict without hearing from persons who have experienced it.

Finally, like all social research, my findings are limited by my own social location and the ways in which my own perspective determined what I would discover. Postmodern approaches to research recognize that all inquiry is done from a particular vantage point; one simply cannot stand "outside" a culture or group in order to observe it objectively. As Moschella notes, all research "is influenced by the researcher's attitudes and inclinations and by his or her motivations for doing the research.... Ethnographic narratives depict the researcher's perceptions of the picture, and not merely the picture itself."[16] For this reason, qualitative accounts or explanations of phenomena "are better understood as narratives than as scientific treatises.... However rigorous, these accounts are neither definitive nor fixed; they are interpretations."[17] Because I am aware of the fact that my own perspective necessarily colors my interpretation of these case studies, I do my best throughout this book to maintain a stance of *reflexivity*, which is "the process of critical self-reflection carried out by the researcher throughout the research process that enables her to monitor and respond to her contributions to the proceedings."[18]

One unique aspect of my research that invites further reflection is the fact that I served as a pastor for one of the congregations featured in the case studies. In one sense, this gives me an advantage in my ability to describe that congregation in rich detail and to provide accounts of events that are supplemented by my own memory of them. At the same time, my personal involvement with Grace UCC necessarily colors the way I remember and depict what happened there, even though I have done my best to offer a fair representation of the community. One of the ways I tried to ensure that my own perspective did not dominate this case study was to conduct interviews with other members of the parish. In this way, I hoped to balance my account of events with the perceptions of others who were there. Yet, even this approach was complicated by the fact that the interviewees were also my former parishioners. That is, I recognize that in asking these individuals to share their reflections with me, I may have inadvertently influenced the ways in which they chose

16. Moschella, *Ethnography as a Pastoral Practice*, 28.
17. Ibid., 29.
18. Swinton and Mowat, *Practical Theology and Qualitative Research*, 59.

to respond. Again, I tried to address this issue by selecting interviewees that I believed would be candid and honest, but I fully acknowledge how difficult it could be to share "negative" perspectives with a leader with whom one has shared a respectful relationship.

At First UMC, my role as a researcher was quite different. Because I had no previous relationship with the congregation, the interviewees there would have felt little pressure to respond in any particular way to the questions I was asking them. However, these research subjects were originally recommended to me by the First UMC pastors as persons who had served on the worship committee and who would likely be willing to speak with me. The interviewees knew this, so it is possible that some of them may have perceived me as being allied with their pastors in a way that may have influenced how they responded to the interview questions. I attempted to mitigate any such influence by assuring each interviewee that his or her responses would be kept confidential and would be de-identified, and that no specific details of the interviews would be shared directly with the First UMC staff. Nevertheless, as I present my analysis of these case studies, I do so recognizing that any researcher—no matter her previous relationship or lack thereof with her subjects—will, in some way, influence the responses she receives. By taking this self-reflexive position in regards to my research and by noting the limitations of my conclusions, I hope to do justice to the stories of the congregations I have studied, while at the same time acknowledging the ways in which I have contributed to the ultimate shape the stories take in this book.

Gathering Data for the Case Studies

For the research I conducted in both congregations, I began by applying for official approval from Vanderbilt University's Institutional Review Board, which I received in May of 2010. Obtaining institutional approval for my research served two important purposes: first, it provided additional protection for all research participants to ensure that their confidentiality and other rights were respected throughout the process. Second, it created a relationship of accountability between me as a researcher and my sponsoring institution, so that ethical standards of research could be maintained at all times. Once I had received institutional approval, I set about requesting and receiving permission from each church's leaders to conduct focused interviews with individuals who indicated a willingness to talk with me about their experience of conflict in their congregations. When this step was completed, I was ready to contact the research participants to set up individual interviews.

At the time I conducted the primary research for this book, I was living in a different region of the country than where Grace UCC is located. Consequently, I took a ten-day trip in June 2010 for the sole purpose of interviewing research subjects there. During that time period I interviewed fourteen individuals about their experience of the conflict that took place in their congregation during 2005. The interview participants ranged in age from twenty-one to seventy-nine, and included eight women and six men, all Caucasian. At First UMC, which is located much closer to where I was living in 2010, I conducted interviews intermittently over a longer period, stretching from June through December of that year. This second group of research subjects ranged in age from forty-eight to seventy-nine, and included six women and six men, also all Caucasian. In both congregations, I conducted interviews in a semi-structured format; this means that I had several guiding questions that I had formulated prior to the interviews, but I did not necessarily ask them exactly the same way each time. Additionally, if the conversation went into areas that seemed useful for my research, I felt free to follow them even if they were not specifically geared toward answering a specific question I had posed.

All interviews were recorded with the express written permission of all twenty-six interviewees. The consent forms for this study assured participants that I would not use their real names in any publications related to this research, but would instead assign pseudonyms to individual interviewees, their congregations, and their geographic communities. The interviews were then transcribed without identifying markers so as to ensure the confidentiality of all research participants. Once I had completed all of the interviews, I set about writing the case studies themselves. I envision these case studies as "thick descriptions" of the conflicts that emerged in each faith community, constructed both from the interview data and from other information that I gleaned from various sources such as church documents[19], informal conversations, and my own knowledge about the congregations in question.

---

19. These documents include such items as minutes from church meetings, written communications (such as letters or newsletter articles) about what was occurring in the midst of the conflict, and church profiles that include reflection on the congregation's experience with the conflict in question.

Interview Questions Used with Research Study Participants

For Participants from Grace UCC

1. Please tell me about your experience of the discussions that took place here in 2005 surrounding decisions about denominational affiliation.
2. What was at stake for you in this process? What felt important or meaningful to you about staying in or leaving the denomination?
3. How did you understand the congregational decision-making process to work?
4. Looking back, what, if anything, would you like the church to have done differently as it approached this important decision?

For Participants from First UMC

1. Please tell me about your experience of the discussions that took place here in 2009 surrounding changes in worship.
2. What was at stake for you in this process? What felt important or meaningful to you about the worship service you were previously attending?
3. How would you define worship? What elements make a worship service meaningful?
4. How did you understand the congregational decision-making process to work?
5. What, in your view, were the key moments or events that helped the congregation move toward an agreed-upon solution?

Bibliography

Ackermann, Denise, and Riet Bons-Storm. "Introduction." In *Liberating Faith Practices: Feminist Practical Theologies in Context*, edited by Denise Ackermann and Riet Bons-Storm, 1–8. Leuven: Peeters, 1998.
Ali, Carroll A. Watkins. *Survival and Liberation: Pastoral Theology in African American Context*. St. Louis: Chalice, 1999.
Ammerman, Nancy T. *Pillars of Faith: American Congregations and Their Partners*. Berkeley: University of California Press, 2005.
Ammerman, Nancy T., et al., eds. *Studying Congregations: A New Handbook*. Nashville: Abingdon, 1998.
Asquith, Glenn H., Jr. "The Case Study Method of Anton T. Boisen." *The Journal of Pastoral Care* 34 (1980) 84–94.
Becker, Penny Edgell. "Congregational Models and Conflict: A Study of How Institutions Shape Organizational Process." In *Sacred Companies: Organizational Aspects of Religion and Religious Aspects of Organizations*, edited by N. J. Demerath III, 231–55. New York: Oxford University Press, 1998.
———. *Congregations in Conflict: Cultural Models of Local Religious Life*. Cambridge: Cambridge University Press, 1999.
Boisen, Anton T. *The Exploration of the Inner World*. Chicago: Willett, Clark, 1936.
Bretherton, Luke. *Hospitality as Holiness: Christian Witness amid Moral Diversity*. Aldershot, UK: Ashgate, 2006.
Brewer, Marilynn B. "Reducing Prejudice through Cross-Categorization: Effects of Multiple Social Identities." In *Reducing Prejudice and Discrimination*, edited by Stuart Oskamp, 165–83. Mahwah, NJ: Lawrence Erlbaum Associates, 2000.
Brock, Rita Nakashima. *Journeys by Heart: A Christology of Erotic Power*. New York: Crossroad, 1988.
———. "On Remembering What Is Impossible to Forget." In *Women and Church: The Challenge of Ecumenical Solidarity in an Age of Alienation*, edited by Melanie A. May, 8–12. Grand Rapids: Eerdmans, 1991.
Browning, Don S. *A Fundamental Practical Theology: Descriptive and Strategic Proposals*. Minneapolis: Fortress, 1991.
———. *The Moral Context of Pastoral Care*. Philadelphia: Westminster, 1976.
———. "Pastoral Care and the Study of the Congregation." In *Beyond Clericalism: The Congregation as a Focus for Theological Education*, edited by Joseph C. Hough Jr. and Barbara G. Wheeler, 103–18. Atlanta: Scholars, 1988.

———. *Religious Ethics and Pastoral Care*. Philadelphia: Fortress, 1983.

Browning, Don S., and Terry D. Cooper. *Religious Thought and the Modern Psychologies*. 2nd ed. Minneapolis: Fortress, 2004.

Brubaker, David R. *Promise and Peril: Understanding and Managing Change and Conflict in Congregations*. Herndon, VA: Alban Institute, 2009.

Burck, J. Russell, and Rodney J. Hunter. "Pastoral Theology, Protestant." In *Dictionary of Pastoral Care and Counseling*, edited by Rodney J. Hunter, 867–72. Nashville: Abingdon, 1990.

Calhoun, Craig, ed. "Object-Relations Theory." *Dictionary of the Social Sciences*, 342–43. Oxford: Oxford University Press, 2002.

Carroll, Jackson. *God's Potters: Pastoral Leadership and the Shaping of Congregations*. Grand Rapids: Eerdmans, 2006.

Chaves, Mark, and Shawna L. Anderson. "Continuity and Change in American Congregations: Introducing the Second Wave of the National Congregations Study." *Sociology of Religion* 69 (2008) 415–40.

Coffman, Elesha J. *"The Christian Century" and the Rise of the Protestant Mainline*. Oxford: Oxford University Press, 2013.

Couture, Pamela D. "Feminist, Wesleyan, Practical Theology and the Practice of Pastoral Care." In *Liberating Faith Practices: Feminist Practical Theologies in Context*, edited by Denise Ackermann and Riet Bons-Storm, 27–49. Leuven: Peeters, 1998.

———. "Introduction." In *Pastoral Care and Social Conflict*, edited by Pamela D. Couture and Rodney J. Hunter, 11–13. Nashville: Abingdon, 1995.

Couture, Pamela D., and Rodney J. Hunter, eds. *Pastoral Care and Social Conflict: Essays in Honor of Charles V. Gerkin*. Nashville: Abingdon, 1995.

Culp, Kristine A. *Vulnerability and Glory: A Theological Account*. Louisville: Westminster John Knox, 2010.

Denzin, Norman K., and Yvonna S. Lincoln. "Introduction: The Discipline and Practice of Qualitative Research." In *Handbook of Qualitative Research*, edited by Norman K. Denzin and Yvonna S. Lincoln, 1–28. Thousand Oaks, CA: Sage, 2000.

Dewan, Shaila. "United Church of Christ Backs Same-Sex Marriage." *NYTimes.com*. Last modified July 5, 2005. http://www.nytimes.com/2005/07/05/national/05church.html.

Deweese, Charles W. "Doing Freedom Baptist Style: Documents for Faith and Witness." Baptist History and Heritage Society and William H. Whitsitt Baptist Heritage Society. Last modified 2001. http://www.baptisthistory.org/pamphlets/freedom.htm.

Dunlap, Susan J. *Caring Cultures: How Congregations Respond to the Sick*. Waco, TX: Baylor University Press, 2009.

Edelson, Marshall. "Scapegoating." In *Rediscovering Groups: A Psychoanalyst's Journey beyond Individual Psychology*, edited by Marshall Edelson and David N. Berg, 248–64. London: Jessica Kingsley, 1999.

Farley, Edward. *Good and Evil: Interpreting a Human Condition*. Minneapolis: Fortress, 1990.

Franke, John R. *Manifold Witness: The Plurality of Truth*. Nashville: Abingdon, 2009.

Friedman, Edwin H. *Generation to Generation: Family Process in Church and Synagogue*. New York: Guilford, 1985.

Fulkerson, Mary McClintock. *Changing the Subject: Women's Discourses and Feminist Theology*. Minneapolis: Fortress, 1994.

———. *Places of Redemption: Theology for a Worldly Church*. Oxford: Oxford University Press, 2007.

Gandolfo, Elizabeth O'Donnell. *The Power and Vulnerability of Love: A Theological Anthropology*. Minneapolis: Fortress, 2015.

Gantt, Susan P., and Yvonne M. Agazarian. "Systems-Centered Emotional Intelligence: Beyond Individual Systems to Organizational Systems." *Organizational Analysis* 12 (2004) 147–69.

Gay, Volney P. "Glossary of Technical Terms and References." Glossary provided in the course "Post-Freudian Theories of Religion" at Vanderbilt University, Nashville, TN, Fall 2008.

Geertz, Clifford. *The Interpretation of Cultures: Selected Essays*. New York: Basic Books, 1973.

Gill-Austern, Brita L. "Rediscovering Hidden Treasures for Pastoral Care." *Pastoral Psychology* 43 (1995) 233–53.

Graham, Elaine L. *Transforming Practice: Pastoral Theology in an Age of Uncertainty*. London: Mowbray, 1996.

Grotstein, James S. *Splitting and Projective Identification*. Northvale, NJ: Jason Aronson, 1985.

Hiltner, Seward. "The American Association of Pastoral Counselors: A Critique." *Pastoral Psychology* 15 (1964) 8–16.

Hodgson, Peter C. *Winds of the Spirit: A Constructive Christian Theology*. Louisville: Westminster John Knox, 1994.

Hopewell, James F. *Congregation: Stories and Structures*. Philadelphia: Fortress, 1987.

Hunsinger, Deborah van Deusen, and Theresa F. Latini. *Transforming Church Conflict: Compassionate Leadership in Action*. Louisville: Westminster John Knox, 2013.

Hunter, Rodney J. "Religious Caregiving and Pedagogy in a Postmodern Context: Recovering Ecclesia." *The Journal of Pastoral Theology* 8 (1998) 15–27.

Hunter, Rodney J., and John Patton. "The Therapeutic Tradition's Theological and Ethical Commitments Viewed through Its Pedagogical Practices: A Tradition in Transition." In *Pastoral Care and Social Conflict: Essays in Honor of Charles V. Gerkin*, edited by Pamela D. Couture and Rodney J. Hunter, 32–43. Nashville: Abingdon, 1995.

Jennings, Theodore W. "Pastoral Theological Methodology." In *Dictionary of Pastoral Care and Counseling*, edited by Rodney J. Hunter, 862–64. Nashville: Abingdon, 1990.

Josselson, Ruthellen. *Playing Pygmalion: How People Create One Another*. Lanham, MD: Jason Aronson, 2007.

Kernberg, Otto. *Internal World and External Reality: Object Relations Theory Applied*. New York: Jason Aronson, 1980.

Klein, Melanie, and Joan Riviere. *Love, Hate and Reparation*. New York: Norton, 1964.

Kliewer, Stephen. *How to Live with Diversity in the Local Church*. Washington, DC: Alban Institute, 1987.

Kohut, Heinz. *How Does Analysis Cure?* Chicago: University of Chicago Press, 1984.

———. *The Restoration of the Self*. Madison, WI: International Universities Press, 1977.

———. *Self Psychology and the Humanities: Reflections on a New Psychoanalytic Approach*. New York: Norton, 1985.

Kornfeld, Margaret. *Cultivating Wholeness: A Guide to Care and Counseling in Faith Communities*. New York: Continuum, 2006.

Lartey, Emmanuel Y. *In Living Color: An Intercultural Approach to Pastoral Care and Counseling*. 2nd ed. London: Jessica Kingsley, 2003.

Leas, Speed B. *Moving Your Church through Conflict*. Washington, DC: Alban Institute, 1985.

Lyon, K. Brynolf. "Paranoid-Schizoid Phenomena in Congregational Conflict: Some Dilemmas of Reconciliation." *Pastoral Psychology* 47 (1999) 273–92.

———. "Scapegoating in Congregational and Group Life: Practical Theological Reflections on the Unbearable." In *Healing Wisdom: Depth Psychology and the Pastoral Ministry*, edited by Kathleen J. Greider et al., 141–56. Grand Rapids: Eerdmans, 2010.

Lyon, K. Brynolf, and Dan P. Moseley. *How to Lead in Church Conflict: Healing Ungrieved Loss*. Nashville: Abingdon, 2012.

Marshall, Joretta L. "Pastoral Care with Congregations in Social Stress." In *Pastoral Care and Social Conflict*, edited by Pamela D. Couture and Rodney J. Hunter, 167–79. Nashville: Abingdon, 1995.

McClure, Barbara J. *Moving beyond Individualism in Pastoral Care and Counseling: Reflections on Theory, Theology, and Practice*. Eugene, OR: Cascade Books, 2010.

McFague, Sallie. *The Body of God: An Ecological Theology*. London: SCM, 1993.

Mercer, Joyce Ann. "Drama, Trauma, and Comma: Researching Congregational Conflicts." Lecture, Vanderbilt Divinity School, Nashville, TN, April 23, 2012.

Miller-McLemore, Bonnie J. *Also a Mother: Work and Family as Theological Dilemma*. Nashville: Abingdon, 1994.

———. "Also a Pastoral Theologian: In Pursuit of Dynamic Theology (Or: Meditations from a Recalcitrant Heart)." *Pastoral Psychology* 59 (2010) 813–28.

———. "Feminist Theory in Pastoral Theology." In *Feminist and Womanist Pastoral Theology*, edited by Bonnie J. Miller-McLemore and Brita Gill-Austern, 77–94. Nashville: Abingdon, 1999.

———. "Introduction: The Contributions of Practical Theology." In *The Wiley-Blackwell Companion to Practical Theology*, edited by Bonnie J. Miller-McLemore, 1–20. Malden, MA: Wiley-Blackwell, 2012.

———. "The Subject and Practice of Pastoral Theology as a Practical Theological Discipline: Pushing Past the Nagging Identity Crisis to the Poetics of Resistance." In *Liberating Faith Practices: Feminist Practical Theologies in Context*, edited by Denise M. Ackermann and Riet Bons-Storm, 175–98. Leuven: Peeters, 1998.

Miller-McLemore, Bonnie J., and Melinda McGarrah Sharp. "Are There Limits to Multicultural Inclusion? Difficult Questions for Feminist Pastoral Theology." In *Women Out of Order: Risking Change and Creating Care in a Multicultural World*, edited by Jeanne Stevenson-Moessner and Teresa Snorton, 314–30. Minneapolis: Fortress, 2010.

Mirkinson, Judith. "Red Light, Green Light: The Global Trafficking of Women." Accessed April 28, 2015. http://feminism.eserver.org/gender/sex-work/trafficking-of-women.txt.

Moessner, Jeanne Stevenson, ed. *Through the Eyes of Women: Insights for Pastoral Care*. Minneapolis: Fortress, 1996.

Moschella, Mary Clark. *Ethnography as a Pastoral Practice: An Introduction*. Cleveland: Pilgrim, 2008.

Neale, Margaret, and Max Bazerman. *Cognition and Rationality in Negotiation*. New York: Free Press, 1991.

Neville, Robert C. *On the Scope and Truth of Theology: Theology as Symbolic Engagement.* New York: T. & T. Clark, 2006.

Nieman, James R. "Congregational Studies." In *The Wiley-Blackwell Companion to Practical Theology*, edited by Bonnie J. Miller-McLemore, 133–42. Wiley-Blackwell Companions to Religion. Malden, MA: Wiley-Blackwell, 2012.

Oakes, Penelope J., et al. *Stereotyping and Social Reality.* Oxford: Blackwell, 1994.

Oates, Wayne E. "Association of Pastoral Counselors—Its Values and Its Dangers." *Pastoral Psychology* 15 (1964) 5–7.

Pattison, Stephen, and James Woodward. "An Introduction to Pastoral and Practical Theology." In *The Blackwell Reader in Pastoral and Practical Theology*, edited by James Woodward and Stephen Pattison, 1–18. Oxford: Blackwell, 2000.

Patton, John. *Pastoral Care in Context: An Introduction to Pastoral Care.* Louisville: Westminster John Knox, 1993.

Pohl, Christine D. *Making Room: Recovering Hospitality as a Christian Tradition.* Grand Rapids: Eerdmans, 1999.

Poling, James Newton. *Rethinking Faith: A Constructive Practical Theology.* Minneapolis: Fortress, 2011.

Pruitt, Dean, and Sung Hee Kim. *Social Conflict: Escalation, Stalemate, and Settlement.* 3rd ed. New York: McGraw-Hill, 2004.

Ramsay, Nancy J. "A Time of Ferment and Redefinition." In *Pastoral Care and Counseling: Redefining the Paradigms*, edited by Nancy J. Ramsay, 1–43. Nashville: Abingdon, 2004.

———. "Contemporary Pastoral Theology: A Wider Vision for the Practice of Love." In *Pastoral Care and Counseling: Redefining the Paradigms*, edited by Nancy J. Ramsay, 155–76. Nashville: Abingdon, 2004.

Randall, Robert L. *Pastor and Parish: The Psychological Core of Ecclesiastical Conflicts.* New York: Human Sciences, 1988.

Reynolds, Thomas E. *The Broken Whole: Philosophical Steps toward a Theology of Global Solidarity.* Albany: State University of New York Press, 2006.

———. *Vulnerable Communion: A Theology of Disability and Hospitality.* Grand Rapids: Brazos, 2008.

Richardson, Ronald W. *Creating a Healthier Church: Family Systems Theory, Leadership, and Congregational Life.* Minneapolis: Fortress, 1996.

Roozen, David A. *American Congregations 2005.* Hartford, CT: Hartford Institute for Religion Research, 2007.

———. *American Congregations 2008.* Hartford, CT: Hartford Institute for Religion Research, 2009.

———. *American Congregations 2010: A Decade of Change in American Congregations, 2000–2010.* Hartford, CT: Hartford Institute for Religion Research, 2011.

———. "Peace, Peace!" *The Progressive Christian: Faith and the Common Good* 184 (2010) 29–30.

Saracino, Michele. *Being about Borders: A Christian Anthropology of Difference.* Collegeville, MN: Liturgical, 2011.

Sawyer, David R. *Hope in Conflict: Discovering Wisdom in Congregational Turmoil.* Cleveland: Pilgrim, 2007.

Schneider, Carl D. "'If One of Your Number Has a Dispute with Another': A New/Ancient Paradigm and Praxis for Dealing with Conflict." In *Pastoral Care and*

Social Conflict, edited by Pamela D. Couture and Rodney J. Hunter, 209–19. Nashville: Abingdon, 1995.

Sharp, Melinda A. McGarrah. *Misunderstanding Stories: Toward a Postcolonial Pastoral Theology*. Eugene, OR: Pickwick, 2013.

Southern Baptist Convention. "Basic Beliefs." Accessed April 12, 2015. http://www.sbc.net/aboutus/basicbeliefs.asp.

St. Clair, Michael. *Object Relations and Self Psychology: An Introduction*. 4th ed. Belmont, CA: Brooks/Cole, 2004.

Stakes, Robert E. "Case Studies." In *Handbook of Qualitative Research*, edited by Norman K. Denzin and Yvonna S. Lincoln, 435–54. Thousand Oaks, CA: Sage, 2000.

Steinke, Peter L. *Congregational Leadership in Anxious Times: Being Calm and Courageous No Matter What*. Herndon, VA: Alban Institute, 2006.

———. *Healthy Congregations: A Systems Approach*. Bethesda, MD: Alban Institute, 1996.

Stockton, Ronald R. *Decent and in Order: Conflict, Christianity, and Polity in a Presbyterian Congregation*. Westport, CT: Praeger, 2000.

Streufert, Mary J. "An Affinity for Difference: A Theology of Power." *Currents in Theology and Mission* 37 (2010) 28–39.

Suchocki, Marjorie Hewitt. *Divinity and Diversity: A Christian Affirmation of Religious Pluralism*. Nashville: Abingdon, 2003.

Swinton, John, and Harriet Mowat. *Practical Theology and Qualitative Research*. London: SCM, 2006.

Tajfel, Henri, and John C. Turner. "An Integrative Theory of Intergroup Conflict." In *The Social Psychology of Intergroup Relations*, edited by Stephen Worchel and William G. Austin, 33–47. Monterey, CA: Brooks/Cole, 1979.

———. "The Social Identity Theory of Intergroup Behavior." In *Psychology of Intergroup Relations*, edited by Stephen Worchel and William G. Austin, 276–93. Chicago: Nelson-Hall, 1986.

Tanner, Kathryn. *Theories of Culture: A New Agenda for Theology*. Minneapolis: Fortress, 1997.

Thatamanil, John J. *The Immanent Divine: God, Creation, and the Human Predicament*. Minneapolis: Fortress, 2006.

Turner, John C. *Social Influence*. Monterey, CA: Brooks/Cole, 1991.

Tyler, Tom R. *Why People Obey the Law*. Princeton: Princeton University Press, 2006.

United Church of Christ. "Testimonies, Not Tests of the Faith." Accessed April 12, 2015. http://www.ucc.org/beliefs/.

Volkan, Vamik D. *The Need to Have Enemies and Allies: From Clinical Practice to International Relationships*. Northvale, NJ: Jason Aronson, 1988.

Yong, Amos. *Hospitality and the Other: Pentecost, Christian Practices, and the Neighbor*. Maryknoll, NY: Orbis, 2008.

Yordy, Laura. "Biodiversity and the Kingdom of God." In *Diversity and Dominion: Dialogues in Ecology, Ethics, and Theology*, edited by Kyle S. Van Houtan and Michael S. Northcott, 166–97. Eugene, OR: Cascade, 2010.

Index

accessibility, in self-categorization theory, 111
Ackermann, Denise, 17
Agazarian, Yvonne, 175
alter ego need, 90–91, 93–102
American Association of Pastoral Counseling, 19
anxiety
    acknowledging difference, 169, 174, 176
    acute, 64–67, 97
    alter ego need, 95–97
    chronic, 26, 64–67, 97, 168
    and conflict, 48, 64, 168
    disintegration, 96
    group polarization, 119
    hybrid existence, 151
    in object relations theory (ORT), 77, 90
    polarization, 106, 130
    projection, 72
    as sense of threat, 12–13, 49
    sitting with, 179–81
    splitting, 72, 77, 82
    as threat to identity, 25–26, 30, 69–71, 77, 97, 127–28
    zero-sum thinking, 129
avoiding, 120

Becker, Penny Edgell, 5
bipolar self, 91, 93
Bons-Storm, Riet, 17
Bretherton, Luke, 164, 166

Breuer, Joseph, 72
bridging, 131–32
Brock, Rita Nakashima, 158
Browning, Don, 21, 28–29
Brubaker, David, 4
Burck, J. Russell, 14

Clinebell, Howard, 19
collective identity, 58, 106, 108–9, 111–15, 126
collective splitting, 79–82, 87–89
communal contextual paradigm, 21–22
comparative fit, 112
conflict strategies, 120
conflict
    anxiety, 48, 64, 168
    complexities of, 49
    cross-cutting relationships, 185–86
    and difference, 155
    effects of, 6, 15
    as gift, 146
    and identity, 58, 65
    individual suffering, 12
    pain of, 62–63
    pastoral theology, 9
    psychological aspects of, 71
    strategic choice, 119
    theological dimensions of, 5, 51–52, 54–57
    and "the tragic," 146

212 INDEX

congregational studies, 10–11, 13, 15, 17, 27
contending tactics, 120–23
Cooperative Congregations Studies Partnership, 3
Couture, Pamela, 17–19
cross-cutting relationships, 185–86
Culp, Kristine A., 158

defensive splitting, 75, 77–78, 80–81, 90
departures from rational choice, 128–29, 134
difference, 83, 139, 145, 147, 153
difference, acknowledging, 169–74, 176
difference, encounters with, 64–65, 71, 168
differentiation, 13, 162, 187–89
discernment, 156
disintegration anxiety, 96
diversity
    as gift, 140, 153
    as good, 145–46, 148, 154, 163
    limits of, 162
    reframing of, 185–86
    as theological norm, 146, 152, 162, 182
    in theology, 148–49, 152, 154–56, 163
    Trinitarian basis of, 147
double consciousness. *See* splitting
dual concern model, 125–28, 132–33
Dunlap, Susan, 23, 25

ecclesial hospitality, 140, 160–66
Edelson, Marshall, 78, 81
ego needs, 94–95, 99–100. *See also* alter ego need
escalation, 121, 124–25, 128
ethnography, 22–23

Fairbairn, Ronald, 73
Faith Communities Today (FACT), 3–4, 6, 15

family systems theory (FST), 12–13, 26, 48, 64, 138, 162, 187
Farley, Edward, 140–45, 158
feminism, 17
First United Methodist Church (First UMC), 38–46
    acknowledging difference, 171–72
    alter ego need, 101
    anxiety, 42, 48, 66–67, 102, 135
    bridging, 132
    collective identity, 58, 110, 114–15
    collective splitting, 87–89
    cross-cutting relationships in, 185
    fragmentation, 60–61
    functional subgrouping in, 175
    identity, 58, 65
    "intentional process" of discernment, 42–45
    interpersonal relationships, 184
    other-concern, 133
    polarization, 60–61, 117
    positive-sum thinking, 135–36
    problem solving, 121, 130, 132–33
    reframing diversity, 182
    self-categorization, 114
    sitting with anxiety, 179–81
    small group process, 175–77
    theological dimensions of conflict in, 53–57
    worship, 30, 40–41, 115
fit, in self-categorization theory, 111–12, 114
fixed pie myth. *See* zero-sum thinking
fragmentation, 59–61, 66–68
framing, 128–29, 134–35
Franke, John R., 153
Freud, Sigmund, 70–73, 91
Fulkerson, Mary McClintock, 191
functional subgrouping, 175–77

Gandolfo, Elizabeth O'Donnell, 158–59

Grace United Church of Christ
(Grace UCC), 30–38
  acknowledging difference, 169,
    171
  alter ego need, 99–100
  anxiety, 48, 67, 127, 134
  collective identity, 108, 112–13,
    126
  contending tactics in, 121–24
  desire for sameness, 98–100, 149
  fragmentation, 60
  homosexuality, 30, 34–38, 52,
    65, 85–86, 98–100, 150, 155
  identity, 57–58, 65
  interpersonal relationships, 184
  other-concern, 134
  pastors as focus of conflict,
    35–37
  polarization, 60, 116–17, 130
  projection, 72, 83
  reactive conflict, 66
  reframing diversity, 182
  scapegoating, 87
  sitting with anxiety, 180
  small group process, 174–75,
    178
  splitting, 72, 83–87
  theological dimensions of
    conflict in, 52–53
  zero-sum thinking, 129, 134
Graham, Elaine, 17
gray-making, 76
Grotstein, James S., 72, 75
group identity, 58, 107
group polarization, 116–19, 136,
    185

healthy conflict, 2, 26, 172
Hiltner, Seward, 19, 21
homosexuality, 30, 34–38, 52, 65,
    85–86, 98–100, 150, 155
hospitality. *See* ecclesial hospitality
human being, as "tragic," 139–41
Hunsinger, Deborah van Deusen,
    24–25
Hunter, Rodney J., 14, 19–22
hybrid existence, 150–52

idealizing need, 92–93
identity
  alter ego need, 94
  anxiety, 25, 30
  conflict, 58, 65
  congregational conflict, 57–58
  fragmentation, 61
  as hybrid, 150–52
  as pluralistic, 150–52
  polarization, 61
  and theological convictions, 6,
    57–58, 65
  threats to, 25–26, 30, 69–71, 77,
    97, 127–28
identity, group, 58, 107
individuation, 73
in-group bias, 107, 109
intercultural paradigm, 22
interhuman dimension of
    experience, 142–45

Jesus Christ, 6–7, 164–65
Josselson, Ruthellen, 78–79

Kernberg, Otto, 80
Klein, Melanie, 73, 75–76
Kohut, Heinz, 71–72, 91–97, 99

Latini, Theresa F., 24–25
leadership studies, 12–13, 15, 17, 27
liberating praxis, 17
Lyon, K. Brynolf, 24–25, 80

Marshall, Joretta, 24
McClure, Barbara J., 22, 29
McFague, Sallie, 153
mediation, 168, 189
Mercer, Joyce Ann, 168, 173
meta-contrast principle, 111–13
Miller-McLemore, Bonnie, 15–17
mirroring need, 92–95, 173
Moschella, Mary Clark, 22–25
Moseley, Dan P., 24–25

National Congregations Study, 3–4
negative framing, 134–35

Nieman, James R., 10
non-anxious facilitators, 176–77, 187–89
Nonviolent Communication (NVC), 24–25
normative fit, 112–13

Oates, Wayne, 19, 21
object relations theory (ORT), 71–77, 90–92
object relationship (O/R), 74–75
object-representation (OR), 74
other-concern, 125–26, 132–34

pastoral care, 9, 28, 196
pastoral practice, 13, 17–18, 23, 190
pastoral theology
　and congregational conflict, 9, 24–25
　as contextual theology, 14
　development of, 19, 23
　human condition, 15, 143
　interhuman dimension of experience, 143–44
　limits of, 18, 20–21, 23, 28
　lived experience, 14–15, 17, 23
　neglect of congregations, 18–21
　pastoral practice, 13, 17–18, 23, 190
　as resource for understanding conflict, 13–15, 17, 27
Pattison, Stephen, 14
Patton, John, 21
persuasive argumentation, 122–24
pluralism, internal, 152
poimenics. *See* pastoral care
polarization, 59–61, 66–67, 106, 116–17, 130, 185
polarization, group, 116–19, 136, 185
positive-sum thinking, 135–36
practices, congregational, 167–90
problem solving, 120–21, 130, 132–33, 135, 168
process theology, 147–48
professional support, 189–90
projection, 72, 77–78, 80–84, 90–91

promises, 122
psychodynamic psychology, 70–71, 104–5

Ramsay, Nancy J., 21–22
Randall, Robert, 94
reactivity, 64, 66
recognition, 173
reframing diversity, 182
repression, 70, 73
revised correlational method, 17
Reynolds, Thomas E., 158
risky shift, 116
Roozen, David, 4

salience, in self-categorization theory, 111–12
sameness, desire for, 72, 90, 97–100, 149, 186
same-sex marriage. *See* homosexuality
Saracino, Michele, 150
scapegoating, 80–82, 87
Schneider, Carl, 24
self psychology, 71–73, 93
self-categorization theory, 105, 110–12, 114, 118
self-concern, 125–26, 128, 130, 132–33
selfobjects, 92–94
self-representation (SR), 74, 77
Sharp, Melinda McGarrah, 159
small group process, 174–75
social comparison, 107–8
social identity theory, 105–8, 110
social identity, 128
social psychology, 105–6
splitting, 72–73, 77, 83–87, 91, 188–89
splitting, collective, 79–82, 87–89
splitting, defensive, 75, 77–78, 80–81, 90
Steinke, Peter, 66
Stoner, James, 116
strategic choice theory, 105, 119–20, 125
Suchocki, Marjorie, 147

suffering, human, 15, 141
systems-centered therapy (SCT), 175

Tajfel, Henri, 107
theological anthropology, 144, 146
theological identity, 6, 57–58, 65
theological plurality, 153
theological reframing, 182
theology
    and conflict, 30, 51–53, 139
    diversity in, 148–49, 152, 154–56, 163
    as reflection, 156–57
thick description, 10, 13
threats, 123–24
"tragic, the", 139–43, 146
trauma, 73
Trinity, 147
tripartite self, 91
Turner, John C., 107, 110–11, 117

United Church of Christ (UCC), 8, 33–34

Volkan, Vamik, 76
vulnerability to difference, 140, 142–44, 157–60, 165–66

warning, 123–24
Winnicott, D.W., 73
Wise, Carroll, 19
Woodward, James, 14
worship, 30, 40–41, 53–58, 115

yielding, 120

zero-sum thinking, 128–29, 134, 136